complete
dressmaking skills

complete
dressmaking skills

LORNA KNIGHT

BARRON'S

COMPLETE DRESSMAKING SKILLS
A QUARTO BOOK

First edition for North America
published in 2014 by Barron's
Educational Series, Inc.

All inquiries should be addressed to:
Barron's Educational Series, Inc.
250 Wireless Boulevard
Hauppauge, New York 11788
www.barronseduc.com

ISBN: 978-1-4380-0356-6

Library of Congress Control No.:
2013954395

QUAR.VGSS

Conceived, designed, and produced by
Quarto Publishing plc
6 Blundell Street
London N7 9BH

Project editor: Chelsea Edwards
Copy editor: Ruth Patrick
Art director: Caroline Guest
Art editor: Jackie Palmer
Designer: Karin Skånberg
Picture research: Sarah Bell
Proofreader: Julie Brooke
Indexer: Helen Snaith
Photographer: Simon Pask
Movies filmed by: Simon Pask
Movie "hands": Lorna Knight

Creative director: Moira Clinch
Publisher: Paul Carslake

Color separation in Singapore by
  PICA Digital Pte Ltd
Printed in China by 1010 Printing
  International Ltd

9 8 7 6 5 4 3 2 1

Contents

Foreword

All the students attending my sewing workshops tell me they love to be shown new skills and have difficult techniques demonstrated to them. So what better way to learn than with "Complete Dressmaking Skills" with its step-by-step photography showing the progressive stages of construction plus the added bonus of fifteen online video films? It is the perfect resource to keep by your side to help when making up garments at home.

This book takes the beginner through the basics, helping to establish a good grounding of skills while it also supports more experienced dressmakers, making them more confident and proficient. With clear photographs to show how to carry out all manner of sewing techniques and short films to follow, this book is truly the complete guide for the dressmaker.

Whether you want to discover how to sew in a zipper or find out how to get more from your serger or simply choose the most appropriate equipment for your project, "Complete Dressmaking Skills" is here to help. It will aid you in choosing the best methods to construct your garments and help you to learn new ways to achieve the results you want.

Lorna

Lorna Knight

About this book

Whether you are just starting to make your own clothes, or you're a more seasoned dressmaker looking to update your skills, there is a wealth of techniques to discover here. Follow the chapters for a logical progression, or skip around for specific details. However you use this book, don't forget to access the accompanying online movies.

The movies

Follow techniques on the move using your smartphone to view the online tutorials quickly via QR codes, or via the Internet on your laptop or netbook. It's like having your very own dressmaking tutor by your side!

The techniques that have an accompanying movie tutorial are marked in the Contents (pages 4–5) with a **V** symbol. Throughout the book you'll find the QR code for scanning with your smartphone on the opening page for the relevant technique. Simply download a free app to scan, if needed, or you may prefer to type the URL address into your web browser to link you to the relevant web page. All the movies come with expert commentary to guide you through the essential stages of the technique.

Browse all 15 movie clips

Want to see a complete list of all 15 movies, with live links to each one? Then scan the code, right.

No QR scanner? No problem!

Want to view all the movies in this book on your laptop or desktop? Then go to: http://barronsbooks.com/media/dressmaking/

Type the URL address into your web browser to be taken to the relevant web page.

Scan the QR code for instant playback on your smartphone.

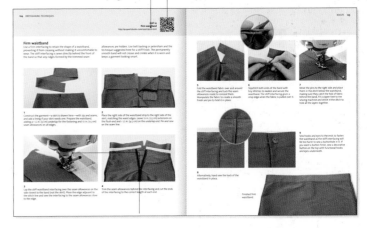

Sew as you watch, using the pause and rewind functions in your browser where needed.

A helpful zoom into the work at crucial stages makes sure that you can see exactly what's going on.

A worked example shows you the end result so you know what you're aiming for.

The book

Covering everything you'll need to get started, the different threads and fabrics plus their uses. This chapter provides the information required to select the most appropriate materials and notions for all types of sewing projects.

Succinct information on the materials available will help you select correctly for your given project.

Clear imagery shows the array of products available.

Whether you need to learn how to carry out a specific task or just need a reminder, here we provide comprehensive step-by-step instructions for a whole range of techniques, from inserting a zipper to lining a jacket.

Notes alongside the steps stress the most important details.

Different methods are shown in use, so you can compare how they work in practice.

Step-by-step images will show you the key stages in each technique.

CHAPTER 5: Working with patterns, pages 166–195

A complete guide to buying, using, and adapting commercial paper patterns, and what you need to consider when making your own.

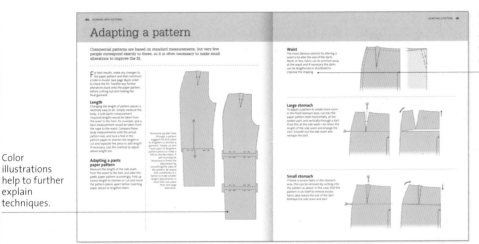

Clear written instructions are given that break down the technique into digestible segments.

Color illustrations help to further explain techniques.

CHAPTER 7: Couture techniques, pages 216–233

Do as the designers do and discover traditional finishing methods from the couture houses with these little-known techniques.

CHAPTER 6: Customizing clothes, pages 196–215

Adding that little extra something to make your clothes unique can be really rewarding. Here you'll learn how to use decorative stitching, appliqué, and smocking to set your garments apart.

CHAPTER 8: Troubleshooting, pages 234–245

An error in your sewing need not be a disaster. Learn how to avoid mishaps and how to fix common problems when they do arise with minimum fuss.

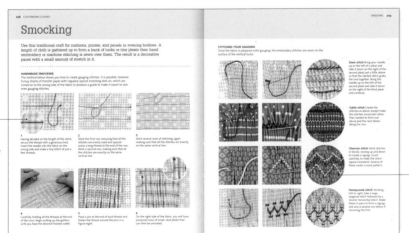

Zoomed-in step photography takes you through the main stages.

Close-up photography of the end product shows you what you should be aiming for.

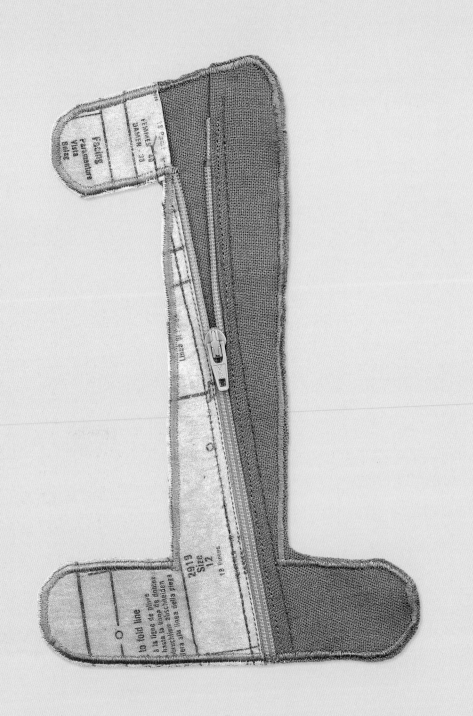

Tools and equipment

This chapter guides you through choosing the tools and equipment you need for sewing. Whether you are looking for the essentials for cutting and stitching, or gadgets for carrying out more specialized techniques, you will find the answers here.

Essential equipment

As with any craft, specialized tools help you achieve a good result. While a needle is the minimum requirement, there are numerous useful tools, gadgets, and materials that can make a sewer's life easier.

NEEDLES
Needles of various sizes are used for all sorts of tasks, from hand sewing and embroidery to basic machine stitching and decorative machine effects (see page 198).

PINS (1)
Pins hold fabric in place before basting and stitching. Craft pins are suitable for many projects, while longer, finer pins are better for delicate fabrics. Use safety pins for threading elastic and cords through channels, or for holding layers together when quilting. If you tend to lose or drop pins on the floor, buy ones with large pearl or beaded heads so you can find them more easily.

MEASURING TAPES (2)
These are necessary for accurate work and making sure that dresses and pants fit the wearer perfectly. Their pliability makes them ideal for measuring curves. When placed against an edge, a measuring tape can follow lines to give accurate sizing.

SCISSORS (3)
Scissors are essential for sewing (see page 18). Use long-bladed shears for cutting out fabric, and smaller, sharp-pointed needlework or embroidery scissors for snipping threads. A pair of paper scissors are also a must for cutting patterns and templates, as dressmaker's shears will blunt when used for paper or card.

RULER (4)
Use a 6 in. (15 cm) ruler for measuring shorter lengths like hem and seam allowances. It is easier to manipulate than a long tape measure or a 12 in. (30 cm) ruler.

IRON (5)
An iron is a vital piece of sewing room equipment. Use it to open seams, press hems, and create folds and creases. An iron can often reduce the amount of pinning or basting between steps. It also improves the finish of a piece of clothing, sharpening edges, smoothing creases, and reducing bulk.

SEAM RIPPER (6)
This small tool is shaped to make it easier to undo stitches sewn in the wrong place. They vary in size but choose one that fits comfortably in your hand.

WORK SURFACE
A flat surface at a workable height, such as a table or worktop, is a fundamental part of a sewing room. Although you can cover the floor with a sheet before laying fabric over it for cutting out, most work needs a surface at the correct height to prevent your knees and back from aching.

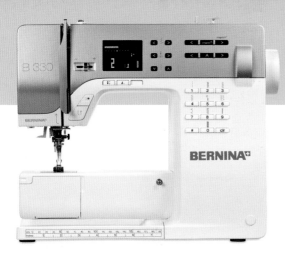

7

Pattern drafting tools

Choose good-quality tools and equipment that allow you to make or adapt accurate, well-fitting patterns. Take care of them and you will never need to replace them.

SEWING MACHINE (7)

Your machine need not be the latest in sewing machine technology, but it must be reliable and provide the functions you need. Look after it, keep it lint and dust free, and have it serviced regularly.

Marking

Transferring pattern markings from a pattern to fabric accurately is vital for a good fit. Choose a method that suits the fabric and your preference from the various options available.

CHALK (8)

Chalk is used to mark fabric because it is easily brushed away. It comes in different colors and forms, and providing the points or edges are kept sharp, it is an ideal way to transfer pattern markings to fabric.

FADE-AWAY PENS (9)

The ink in these pens marks the fabric as required, but fades within 48 hours. These are useful for marking important balance points, providing you plan to work on your project immediately, since they may fade before you need them. Always check on an extra piece of fabric that the ink is definitely temporary before using it in a prominent place.

WASH-AWAY MARKERS (10)

These pens use ink that will remain on the fabric until it is sponged or washed away. Again, this is a handy tool for transferring important pattern markings, but check that it does not stain your chosen fabric permanently before using it, especially if it is a delicate cloth.

FASHION RULE OR CURVE (11)

Also known as French curves, these are available in different sizes and help create smooth curves when making and adapting patterns. Use them for shaping hips and armholes to give a sharp, clear line. Choose the part of the curve best suited to the shape required.

PATTERN PAPER (12)

Available in large pieces or long rolls, pattern paper is marked with a grid for easier pattern making. The regular markings help to show grain lines. Tracing paper is also useful, as well as fine, plain cardstock for longer-life patterns.

MUSLIN (13)

Although not strictly a tool, this fabric is used as part of the construction process when creating garments. A plain, stable fabric in a natural color, muslin is perfect for making mock garments (toiles) to check fitting and style details while developing a design. It is easy to mark with lines and notes and will not stretch.

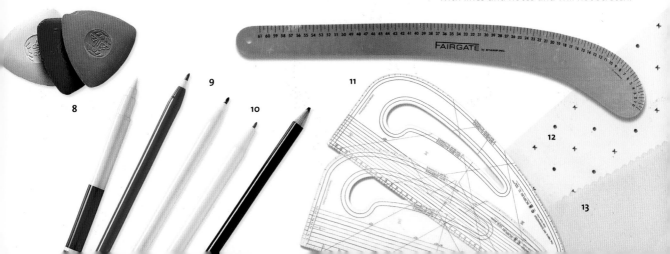

8

9

10

11

12

13

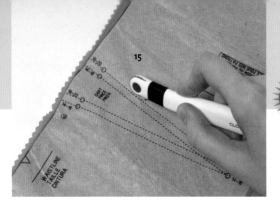

15

15

Useful extras

There are some tools that may seem like luxury items, but after you've used them you will wonder how you managed to sew without them.

17

DRESS FORM (14)

An adjustable dress form or stand is a useful piece of equipment to have when constructing garments. Without help, it is difficult to fit clothes on your own body, so having a mannequin in a similar shape and size to you can be useful. Adjust the dress form as required and check the fit of your garment as you sew.

PATTERN-TRACING WHEEL (15)

Used in conjunction with dressmaker's carbon paper, this tool marks a line of dots. It is more useful for heavier-weight materials.

MEASURING GAUGE (16)

This simple plastic tool is great for adding seam and hem allowances to patterns where there are none. Use it when working with patterns that do not include allowances, or when patterns are cut and manipulated and a seam allowance must be added.

TAPE AND GLUE

For joining and altering pattern pieces, use good-quality tape or glue.

TANK IRON (17)

A tank iron holds a large reservoir of water that is converted to boosts of steam when needed. The power of the steam is greater than that of an ordinary iron and it does not require refilling as frequently. It also provides horizontal steam so it can be used for drapes hung on rails and garments on a dress form.

SERGER

These useful machines (see page 22) are for neatening raw edges and giving clothes a professional finish. However, they also perform many other decorative functions and, although not essential, are a great asset.

CABINET STORAGE (18)

Storage is a problem for people who sew. Growing stashes of fabric, threads, and patterns, together with books and equipment, must be housed and retrieved when needed. Special cabinets holding sewing machines are very useful, as are drawers, shelves, and cupboards.

TAILOR'S HAM

A tightly stuffed, ham-shaped cushion used as a pressing aid. Place it under a shaped seam, like a bust or hip, while ironing to achieve a smooth finish.

This sewing workspace has lots of storage room, which can be neatly tucked away when not in use.

14

16

18

Needle know-how

The needle is the principal piece of sewing equipment—you must have one if you want to sew! Originally whittled from bone or wood, needles are now made from high quality steel in sizes for every application.

Choosing needles

It is important to select the correct needle for the task in hand, whether for hand or machine sewing. Neat hand sewing is easier to produce with the correct size and type of needle and, although machine needles may all look the same, subtle differences tailor them for particular threads or fabrics.

HAND NEEDLES

Hand needles come in a range of types and sizes to suit different tasks. Short, fine needles are ideal for sewing small functional stitches, whereas larger eyed varieties are needed to take thicker embroidery threads. Keep a range to hand, and select one most suited to your current project.

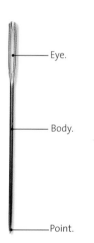

Eye.

Body.

Point.

MACHINE NEEDLES

Modern machine needles are adapted to suit particular fabrics and threads to give better results. The points vary, from sharp points that sew most fabrics without causing skipped stitches or damage to the fabric, to a rounded ball that slips between the yarns of knits without splitting them, and wedged points for cutting through vinyl or leather.

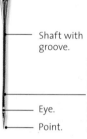

Groove: When the needle is in place, the groove faces forward. The thread lies within it. This enables the needle to slip through the fabric, carrying the thread in the groove so it causes less drag.

Shank.

Shoulder.

Shaft with groove.

Scarf: The scarf is a hollowed area at the back of the needle. It allows the bobbin hook to grab the needle thread more easily to form a stitch.

Eye.

Point.

CAN'T THREAD YOUR NEEDLE?
- Cut the thread at an angle. This makes it easier to fit through the eye.

- Place a piece of white paper behind the eye of the needle to make it easier to see the hole for the thread to go through.

- Use a needle threading wire or gadget. There are many of these on the market (see right), ranging from a simple diamond-shaped wire on a handle, to tiny hooks that pull a thread length through the eye.

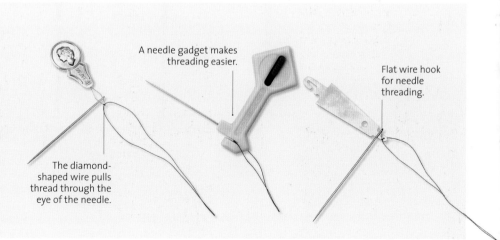

A needle gadget makes threading easier.

Flat wire hook for needle threading.

The diamond-shaped wire pulls thread through the eye of the needle.

HAND
Generally sizes range from 1 (largest) to 12 (finest).

Type	Embroidery (crewel)	Beading	Tapestry	Bodkin	Sharps
Description	Medium length with a long eye to take embroidery threads.	Long and very fine; thin enough to pass through the hole in a bead.	Blunt needle, shorter than a darner, with a large eye.	Long and broad with a rounded point and a large eye.	Medium length with a small round eye for general sewing.
Purpose	Embroidery.	Beading.	Tapestry, needlepoint, and silk ribbon embroidery.	Threading elastic, ribbon, or tapes through a casing.	General sewing projects.

MACHINE
Generally sizes range from 60 (smallest) to 120 (largest).

Type	Universal	Ballpoint	Stretch	Microtex	Denim
Description	Standard needle with a sharp point to penetrate most fabrics without causing damage.	Rounded point to slide between the fibers rather than split them.	Deep scarf to prevent skipped stitches.	Sharp point for fine fabrics.	Strong needle with a sharp point.
Purpose	Most weights of woven fabric.	Knitted fabrics.	Stretch fabrics, including knits, spandex, and synthetic suede.	Delicate silks and synthetic microfiber fabrics.	Denim and other strong fabrics with a dense texture.

Betweens	Darning	Milliner's (straw)	Leather (gls)	Chenille	Self-threading
Shorter needles with a round eye.	Long, with a large eye and a sharp point to take woolen yarn.	Longer length with a round eye.	A sharp, wedged, triangular point to pierce leather.	Longer in length with a sharp point and a large eye.	A sharp medium length with a slotted eye.
Detailed, precise work for tailoring and quilting.	Darning.	Basting, pleating, and hat making.	Leather, suede, vinyl, and other tough materials.	For sewing thicker fabrics with stranded threads, wool and ribbon.	Easier threading.

Metallic	Embroidery	Quilting	Topstitch	Wing (hem stitch)	Twin (triple) needle
Large polished eye holds thread and prevents it from shredding and skipping stitches.	Larger eye holds the embroidery thread, and scarf then allows dense stitching without shredding the thread.	Sharp point and narrow, tapered shaft.	Sharp with a large groove and eye to take thicker threads.	Wings on either side of the shaft push fabric threads apart; well-chosen stitches leave decorative holes in cloth.	Two or three needles fixed to a single body for parallel rows of stitching.
Metallic threads including monofilaments.	Rayon, polyester, and specialized embroidery threads.	Sewing through several thick layers without damaging them.	Topstitching.	Decorative heirloom stitching similar to hand-sewn thread work. (Iron fabric with spray starch for a stiffer finish before starting to sew.)	Heirloom stitching, pin tucks, and imitation cover stitch.

Cutting it

Blades of all shapes and sizes are available, and each has a task to perform in the sewing room. Get the best results by using the right tool for each job.

Type	Shears	Pinking shears
Description	Dressmaking shears or scissors have long sharp blades and shaped handles for comfortable handling.	Scissors with zigzag-shaped blades to make a notched cut.
Purpose	Cutting fabric.	Use these on fabric to prevent the edge from fraying.

Alternative Cutting Tools

As well as using scissors to cut fabrics and threads, there are other cutting gadgets in the sewing room. They are useful additions to your sewing box and will save both time and energy.

ROTARY CUTTER

This has a circular blade with a handle and is used with a self-healing cutting mat placed under the fabric. It cuts fabric accurately and several layers can be cut at once. This makes it ideal for patchwork and small garment pieces. It is a fast method of cutting out. Here are a few useful tips:
• Buy two blades so there is always a spare if one gets damaged.
• Buy the largest mat you have space for, especially if you are using it for clothes as well as patchwork.
• Keep the mat flat and away from heat, as it can bend and crack.

THREAD CUTTER

These handy little cutters hang around your neck so they can't get lost when you need them. The blade for cutting threads is concealed behind a disk with slots. The thread is cut by the blade when it is pulled into a slot.

CRAFT KNIFE

A knife is occasionally the best tool for a sewing task. Cut stiff vinyl or leather with a craft knife rather than scissors, as a much neater cut is achieved. Keep the knife sharp. A blunt knife is more likely to cut you because you'll be putting more pressure on the blade. A knife with a retractable blade will store it safely in your toolkit.

Rotary cutter

Craft knife

Thread cutter

Needlework/embroidery scissors	Serrated shears	Curved embroidery scissors	Paper scissors
Short-bladed scissors with sharp points.	The blades on serrated shears are textured not smooth.	Small, sharp, pointed scissors with short and curved blades.	Standard scissors with medium-length sharp blades.
For cutting threads and snipping notching seam allowances.	The ridges grip fabric to make cutting soft and light-weight fabrics easier.	Use these to snip thread ends close to your work.	Use these for paper projects only, and keep your fabric scissors sharp for cutting cloth.

THREAD SNIPS
Thread snips have no handles so they are easy to pick up quickly. Use them when sewing on the move and space for equipment is limited.

Thread snips

BUTTONHOLE CHISEL
Opening buttonholes neatly without snipping the threads can be difficult—but not with a buttonhole chisel. Place over the center of the buttonhole and tap the end to cut through the fabric.

SEAM RIPPER
A seam ripper cuts individual stitches when needed. The pointed end slips under the stitch and the sharp inside edge cuts the thread. They vary in size; choose a larger one for comfort, as it is easier to grip when undoing a long seam.

Buttonhole chisel

Seam ripper

TIPS
- If you attend a class or sewing group with friends, tie a length of ribbon to the handle of your fabric shears to make yours stand out.

- Blades become dull through use. Sharpen them when they need it.

- Dropping scissors on the floor can knock them out of alignment. Place them in the center of the table when not in use, not close to the edge.

- Keep scissors dry and out of damp conditions where they may rust.

Machine anatomy

With the help of a sewing machine and serger you can sew much more and much faster than you can by hand. Whatever machine you own or plan to buy, learn how to use it to appreciate its full potential.

Sewing machine

Although the most modern machines have needle threaders and cutters, multiple buttonhole options, dozens of pretty decorative stitches, and may even create intricate machine embroidery, some still just sew! When buying a sewing machine, select one that carries out the functions you need and consider the areas you want to progress into.

Thread guides
Guides are positioned to route the thread through the machine to create the stitches. Use the manual or the arrows provided to take the correct route.

Needle
The needle fits into the machine with a clamp or screw to hold it in place. On some machines it has a fixed position, but many offer a choice so that it can sew a straight stitch on the left, right, or center (and in between) and zigzag and decorative stitches too.

Presser foot
This foot places pressure on the fabric around the needle to support and encourage the layers to progress with the help of the feed dogs below. On some models the pressure or weight can be increased or decreased to suit the depth of the fabric.

Throat plate
This plate—normally made from metal—surrounds the feed dogs and has a hole through which the needle passes while it takes the thread down to meet the bobbin. There are generally guidelines etched into the metal throat plate to mark the most popular seam allowances. By feeding the fabric edge along under the presser foot and along one of these guides, the line of stitches will be parallel to the edge.

Feed dogs
The jagged teeth that sit under the needle within the throat plate move in a circular motion to steadily move the fabric. This means that as the needle rises the teeth move the fabric on, so when the needle lowers into the cloth it produces a stitch. The movement of the teeth can be adjusted to alter the stitch length and can also be dropped down out of the way for free-motion sewing (see page 202).

Thread spindle (hidden behind)
The reel of thread is placed on this before it is fed through the guides toward the needle. Additional spindles allow more reels to be used, for example, when sewing with a double or twin needle.

Bobbin winder
This winds thread quickly and evenly onto a bobbin.

Handle
The handle on the right of the machine rotates as the needle moves up and down through the fabric. Although the foot pedal or a stop/go button on the sewing machine controls the movement of the needle, sometimes it helps to be able to have fine control of the needle by using the handle.

HANDLING
Like any piece of equipment, it takes time to learn how to operate a sewing machine and get the best from it. Ideally, start sewing with stable, woven fabrics and simple shapes that are easy to feed through the machine. When you have mastered these, move toward fabrics that are more difficult to handle, like stretchy, lightweight, or thick ones. Through practice you will learn how to hold, support, ease, or pull, depending on the characteristics of the fabric you are sewing with.

Stitch selectors
Select and adjust the length and width of stitches with dials or buttons. A manual sewing machine normally has dials or knobs with symbols, while electronic machines often have a window showing the chosen stitch along with other information, for example, the presser foot to use with the selected stitch.

Bobbin/spool
The bobbin or spool sits under the throat plate in a race or holder where it freely spins. The bobbin/spool is either dropped in from above and covered with a plate, or pushed in at the front through a door.

Foot pedal
Most machines are powered by electricity, and this is generally by means of a cable and pedal that sits on the floor. However, some machines have a stop/go button on the front as an additional option. Use this for sewing automatic buttonholes or when creating a decorative stitch to ensure it is regular and consistent.

BERNINA✚

Sergers

A serger has become an essential piece of machinery for most serious sewers today. With its fast stitching and finishing of seams, it gives clothes a shop-bought look. It also creates some interesting and attractive stitches when used with decorative threads, and offers so much more than the chance to produce clothing with a manufactured finish.

ANATOMY OF A SERGER

A standard serger has two loopers and two needles through which the threads pass and form stitches to create and finish seams. A serger forms a sophisticated seam and joins layers of fabric together. A blade cuts a clean edge from the fabric, and two loopers and two needles carry threads that stitch the seam and cover the edges neatly. The two loopers sit below the fabric and wrap the cut edge with threads while the two needles pierce the fabric from above and produce the seam.

Needles

Most sergers have two needles, although you can use one or both depending on the stitch you need to create. These are held in place with a screw in the same way as in a sewing machine. Use the left or both needles for a wide serged seam and the right one only for a narrow serged seam.

Presser foot

As with a sewing machine, the presser foot sits on top of the fabric holding it against the feed dogs, and this allows the fabric to progress under the needle. On some models it can be adjusted to suit thicker or thinner fabrics.

Foot pedal

Sergers are powered by electricity by means of a cable and pedal that sits on the floor.

Thread guide bar

This keeps the threads untangled as they travel from the spool to the needles or loopers. This bar can be extended and should be raised up to its highest position to allow the threads to travel smoothly.

Tension adjustments

The thread tension is normally adjusted with dials on the front of the serger, although some brands use an alternative operating system where it is automatically controlled. Generally, the tension is increased by turning the dial to a larger number and reduced with a lower number.

Feed dogs

On a serger there are two sets of feed dogs; the front set pushes the fabric under the needle and the second set pulls it away from behind the needle. These can be adjusted to work in conjunction with each other, and work in the best possible way with different types of fabric (see differential feed, opposite).

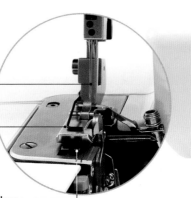

JANOME

Thread guides
The thread guides are normally color coded with diagrams printed on the serger casing to make threading up easier. There are often additional buttons or sliders to help reach difficult-to-access parts in the body of the machine.

Thread spindles
Four threads or cones are placed on the spindles; the two on the right are for the loopers housed below the needle, and the two on the left are for the needles.

Stitch length dial
This dial controls the length of the stitch by moving more or less fabric past the needle between needle revolutions.

Differential feed
This controls how the feed dogs work. For stable fabric, the two sets work at the same rate to feed the fabric under the foot and needle. It can also be adjusted to feed stretch knit fabrics evenly or to encourage a fabric to gather into tiny tucks or to stretch a fabric to form a wavy edge.

Handle
Rotates to move needles up and down.

Loopers
These are the final levers of the threading route under the needle plate. These control the threads that enclose the raw edges.

Blades
The upper and lower blades sit to the right of the needles and these cut the fabric edges cleanly before they reach the needles and loopers for stitching. The lower blade is fixed in position and the upper blade moves to produce the cut. The blade can be locked or removed so that stitches can be made without cutting the fabric.

Stitch finger (slider)
This small bar lies next to the needles and forms a support when the stitches are formed for balanced stitching. It is removed for rolled hemming to allow the fabric edge to curl when stitched.

Thread guides

Handling
If you have mastered the handling of a sewing machine, the only significant difference with a serger is the introduction of the blade. As the fabric edge is cut off while you serge, it is important to keep a check on the seam to ensure only the edge to be stitched is fed under the presser foot; a nasty slice can be created if folds of fabric sneak through with the fabric edge. The blade can be removed or locked out of use for some tasks.

Sergers are particularly good at producing seams in stretchy fabric, since the dual set of feed dogs allow consistent progression of the fabric. This prevents wavy, permanently stretched edges that can occur if sewn with a sewing machine.

Sergers sew faster than sewing machines and create finished seams very quickly. This extra speed is an obvious advantage but can cause problems for an over-confident beginner!

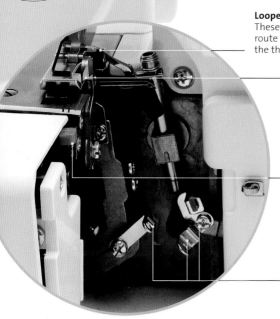

9300DX

Sewing machine feet

When you buy a sewing machine, it comes with a standard presser foot and a small number of additional feet for specific tasks such as inserting zippers and sewing buttonholes. However, there are many more specialized feet and attachments that may be fitted to your sewing machine to make tricky techniques much easier.

Some sewing machine brands offer a large number of specialized feet and attachments, while others have only a limited range. There are some universal feet available that may fit your machine if you are short of choice, but always choose those designed for your brand first before seeking an alternative. The most common feet are listed here, and are generally included when you buy a sewing machine.

STANDARD FOOT
For straight and zigzag stitching, this foot has a smooth base and it clips or screws in place. It is designed for everyday tasks like sewing seams and topstitching hems.

Tip: Although great for general sewing, this foot does not always work for decorative stitching where the stitch is bulky and the flat base may be hindered by the buildup of stitching. Swap it for a foot with a channel in the base like the open-toe foot.

ZIPPER FOOT
These vary in design from brand to brand, but generally consist of a single prong with an indent at either side so that the foot can stitch close to the zipper teeth.

Tip: Zipper feet are very versatile and are great for sewing piping too, since the needle can get close to the edge of the thick cord.

BUTTONHOLE FOOT
These come in many different styles, but they all allow the stitches to be formed as two straight parallel rows of satin stitch with a narrow gap between.

Tip: If you have an automatic buttonhole attachment on your machine, do not forget to lower the sensor as this ensures that all the buttonholes you make are identical.

BLIND-HEM FOOT
A blind-hem foot has a vertical guide in the center to help when feeding the hem under the foot so that the stitches are placed in the correct position. The guide may be set or adjustable depending on the brand.

Tip: Experiment with your fabric before sewing the hem to get the perfect stitch position and adjust the stitch length so that the stitches are farther apart for a less visible finish on the right side.

OVERCASTING FOOT
This foot has a prong or finger that sits over the cut edge of the fabric while you sew. The stitches are formed over this guide before sliding off and onto the raw edge without pulling and distorting it. The foot allows you to create a simple serger-style stitch using your sewing machine and only two threads.

Tip: Trim the cut edge so that it is smooth before stitching, otherwise ragged edges may show through the stitches.

Other useful feet

Once you have mastered using the basic sewing machine feet you may want to go on to using some of the many specialized feet available, in order to take your sewing to the next level.

CONCEALED ZIPPER FOOT

An invisible zipper cannot be inserted with a standard zipper foot as it does not get close enough to the teeth. A concealed zipper foot has grooves in the underside that twist the teeth out of the way for stitching.

Tip: Sew the zipper tape with a standard zipper foot to hold it in place first and then use the concealed foot to stitch in the correct place. Insert the concealed zipper then sew the seam afterward for a neat join at the base of the zipper.

OPEN-TOE/CLEAR-VIEW FOOT

This foot is open in the center, giving an unhindered view of the stitching while you sew. It also has a channel in the underside to sit over bulky decorative stitching.

Tip: Use it for appliqué, machine smocking, attaching ribbon, and decorative sewing where you need to see the point of the needle as it enters the fabric.

WALKING FOOT

This chunky attachment is screwed to the sewing machine with its lever placed over or around the needle bar. This allows the feet on the underside to raise and lower with the needle bar to "walk" over the fabric. This provides even feeding when sewing thick layers of cloth or stretch fabric. The angled bar slots into the walking foot and can be adjusted to suit the distance required between quilt lines. Once set in position all rows of quilting will be equally spaced.

Tip: Use this foot when sewing a bold printed or striped fabric so that the pattern matches along the full length.

FREE-MOTION FOOT

The free-motion or darning foot sits around the needle but does not apply pressure to the fabric below. It is long and slim, often with a spring, and is clipped to the ankle of the sewing machine. It circles the needle with a ring, horseshoe, or saucerlike guard. Use it with the feed dogs lowered for free-motion machine embroidery or quilting.

Tip: For machine embroidery, stabilize your fabric and place it in a hoop for easier handling.

Fabrics and notions

With beautiful textiles and notions just waiting to be purchased, an understanding and knowledge of their construction and handling will help you to make wise decisions. Here you will find the information required to make the best choices when selecting fabrics and notions for your dressmaking projects.

Choosing your thread

All kinds of threads are available for sewing, and choosing the best one for each project is easy with a little help. Here we identify the various types, their characteristics, and the purposes to which they are best suited.

GENERAL-PURPOSE THREAD (1)

Standard sewing thread is made from highly spun fibers. It may be polyester, mercerized cotton, or be produced as a polyester core covered in cotton to combine the best properties of both. It is ideal for general sewing projects, e.g. making clothes, curtains, or soft toys.

COTTON THREAD (2)

One-hundred percent mercerized cotton thread is perfect for projects using cotton fabric. The completed garment can be boil washed without fear of the thread deteriorating, and the thread and fabric will share the same properties. Cotton thread does not stretch like polyester does, so use it for decorative drawn thread work as well as for sewing functional seams.

SILK THREAD (3)

Use silk thread when sewing silk and woolen fabrics, since they are natural animal fibers and their properties are alike. It is ideal for machine sewing, although silk thread is also great for knot-free hand sewing too. Silk thread is expensive, but for many projects polyester thread can be used as a cheaper alternative.

HAND EMBROIDERY THREAD (4)

Skeins of stranded embroidery thread or floss are wound into bundles. They are generally produced from cotton, silk, or rayon. Use them in their grouped strands or split them for finer stitching. Perlé cotton is twisted thread for hand embroidery. Hand embroidery thread is ideal for embroidery, embellishment, and couching (see page 200).

MACHINE EMBROIDERY THREAD (5)

These threads are normally made from rayon or polyester as they have a high luster. The thread is very fine and can be used to fill blocks of color with machine embroidery. Use with a machine embroidery needle and specialist bobbin thread (see opposite). Variegated threads are available to give shading effects.

METALLIC THREAD (6)

These threads are fine metallic filaments, or can be spun around a core thread for strength. They add a sparkle to your projects. Use with a metallic needle and bobbin thread to avoid shredding.

BASTING THREAD (7)

Basting or tacking thread is loosely spun with less strength than standard thread. This makes it ideal for temporary stitching as it can be removed when it is no longer needed without damaging the fabric.

TOPSTITCH THREAD (8)

Topstitch, button twist, or upholstery threads are thicker than standard sew-all thread. This makes the thread stronger and more prominent, so it is perfect for decorative topstitching, sewing on buttons securely, and when sewing upholstery fabrics. Sew with a topstitch needle with a large eye.

BOBBIN FILL THREAD (9)

A very fine white or black thread is available for winding onto your bobbin for machine embroidery. Since it is very thin you can wind far more than usual onto the bobbin, so reducing the number of refills you need to make. It does not affect the color you are using on the surface. This thread is also available on pre-wound bobbins.

SERGER THREAD (10)

Sergers use a lot of thread to sew and neaten seams so threads are available on large reels or cones in lengths of 3,000–17,000 ft (1,000–5,000 m) for this purpose. The range of colors is normally limited, but adequate for serging seams.

INVISIBLE THREAD (11)

Invisible thread is a clear, fine filament that is soft and flexible enough to work like thread. Its lack of color allows it to blend with the fabric.

SPECIAL-PURPOSE THREADS

Specialized threads are available for a variety of purposes. A few are mentioned here, but check out your local store or next large exhibition for new novelty and specialized threads coming on the market.

Smocking thread: When used in the bobbin, this thread shrinks with the heat of the iron to give a crinkle effect to fabric.

Thread fuse thread: Used in the bobbin and perfect for a facing. Once heated with an iron, the thread will melt and fuse with the layer of fabric below.

Glow-in-the-dark thread: As the name suggests, when stitched, this thread is luminous in the dark and is great for embroidering novelty shapes and outlines.

Wash-away thread: This is ideal thread for basting to hold pieces in place while stitching.

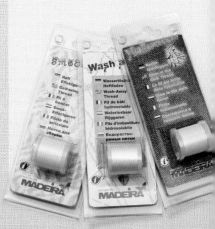

TIPS

- Choose good-quality thread for every project and keep vintage reels, passed on to you by elderly relatives and friends, as nostalgic mementos! Old thread will disintegrate or wear out long before the modern fabrics it is holding together, resulting in seams coming apart and pockets falling off.

- Choose appropriate needles (hand and machine) for your choice of thread. For example, a machine needle designed to sew metallic thread has an eye that will not shred it, and a crewel needle has a longer eye, making it easier to use with embroidery thread.

- Match the fiber content of the thread and fabric where you can. Use cotton with cotton, polyester with synthetic fabrics, and silk for silk and wool. If this is not possible, a good sew-all thread is a wise choice.

Dressmaking notions

Notions are those extra little items you need to finish your sewing projects, such as zippers, ribbons, tapes, and fastenings—they are sometimes overlooked but are essential.

If you are following a paper pattern, check the materials list on the back of the envelope. But if you are designing your own garment consider what you will need and how much—for example, the number of buttons and their size, or the length of ribbon needed to decorate an edge. Select these when you are buying your fabric in order to get a good color match and to save return trips to the store.

ZIPPERS
Zippers are available in many forms and for all kinds of garments and projects (see page 74).
Uses: There is a zipper for every purpose from strong, blue in color, and metal-toothed for jeans, to lightweight and open-ended for evening bodices.
Tip: Use the appropriate presser foot to make it easier to insert different zippers, e.g. concealed zipper foot or adjustable zipper foot (see pages 24 and 25).

BUTTONS
Buttons of all sizes, shapes, and styles can be sewn on to fasten and embellish garments (see page 86).
Uses: Fastening garments and bags of all styles.
Tip: Choose buttons wisely and sew an appropriately sized buttonhole to fit the button (see page 88).

SATIN RIBBON (1)
Ribbons come in a range of widths and are available in many colors to suit every purpose. Polyester ribbons have a high

sheen and are fairly stiff, while those made from rayon are slightly softer.
Uses: Decorate collars, cuffs, and hems, or use narrow ribbons for hanging loops (see page 134).
Tip: Sew in place by hand with tiny stitches, catching each edge, or use a sewing machine with a straight stitch or preprogrammed blanket-style stitch. Use a Microtex machine needle to avoid damaging the satin.

PETERSHAM RIBBON
This stiff, closely woven tape is available as straight or curved and has a ridged edge. It looks like grosgrain ribbon but is more rigid and firm, and provides a stronger finish.
Uses: For waists and belts to create a strong, supportive band. Sew a length around the inside rim of the crown of a hat to help it keep its shape.
Tip: Some people prefer the curved Petersham to grosgrain ribbon because it gives a closer fit since the waist band tilts toward the upper body.

GROSGRAIN RIBBON (2)
This ribbed ribbon is stiff and strong and available in a range of widths for a variety of uses. Novelty designs are popular, with hearts or flowers, but it comes in plain shades too.
Uses: To protect the fabric on the inside edge of pant cuffs, or as a waist stay. Decorate edges on the outside of jackets or skirts.
Tip: Machine stitch on the edges or hand-sew in place to hold it flat. Pre-press grosgrain ribbon to shape it if it is to be used as a decorative finish on a curved edge.

RICKRACK BRAID (3)
Decorative braid and rickrack may be added to embellish the surface of a garment. Many styles and designs are available to suit a whole range of projects.
Uses: Choose luxury braids to embellish jacket edges and cuffs. Rickrack is available in many colors for all kinds of projects.
Tip: Choose braid appropriately and hand sew in place with tiny, invisible stitches. Use silk thread and a small needle. Sew rickrack by machine with a good color-matching thread.

CORDS (4)
Decorative and functional cords are available under different names for a variety of purposes. Piping cord (in a range of diameters) can be covered with bias strips to insert into edges. Rattail is tubular with a satin finish, while mousetail is a slimmer version.
Uses: Covered piping defines an edge when sewn into a seam and adds a decorative detail to all sorts of projects. The satin finish of rattail and mousetail makes it suitable for embellishment for couching (see page 200), although it can also be used under the surface for textured channel stitching.
Tip: Use a zipper or piping foot to stitch close to the cord.

HEAT-FUSIBLE ADHESIVE (5)
This is a dry film of glue that melts when heated with an iron to stick two layers together. It comes as a ¾-in. (1.5-cm) strip on a roll, or as a sheet with a paper backing, for easier application. The backed variety may be bought in pieces or on a roll by the yard.
Uses: Use the strip adhesive for hemming pants and the paper-backed adhesive for appliqué (see page 204).
Tip: For appliqué, cut a piece and iron to the back on the additional fabric then cut out a precise shape to achieve a clean edge.

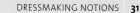

BIAS BINDING (6)

Bias binding is precut strips of fabric cut on the cross and folded ready for stitching. It comes in a good range of shades and also in pretty prints, stripes, and novelty versions.

Uses: To cover and neaten raw edges.

Tip: Sew bias binding with good color-matching thread. An adjustable binding foot is a useful tool for sewing on binding.

TWILL TAPE (7)

This narrow tape with a diagonal grain is available in black or white to suit your purpose. Traditionally made from cotton, today it is sometimes made from polyester.

Uses: For stabilizing edges and waists to prevent them from stretching.

Tip: Choose 100 percent cotton tape as there is no give in this tape and it can be preshrunk before being sewn in.

Selecting fabric

There are some beautiful fabrics available from which to make clothes in a wide range of colors and textures. Learning how to handle and work with different fabrics can take years, so use the guide on the following pages to help develop your knowledge so you can choose wisely.

The outside of a pattern envelope gives valuable information about the fabrics suitable for the design within. There is usually a range of appropriate materials to choose from, allowing everyone the opportunity to find something to suit their individual taste. In addition, it will also advise on the amount of material you need to buy, depending on the width of the roll.

FIBER AND FABRIC FACTS

There are two key pieces of information you need to know when choosing fabric: The fiber that it is made from and the way the material is constructed.

FIBERS

Natural fibers are individual filaments found in plants and animal hair that are gathered together and used to form yarns and fabrics. The most common plant fibers used for fabric are cotton (from the boll of the cotton plant) and linen (from the stem of the flax plant).

Animal fibers include wool (from sheep, goats, and llamas for example) and silk (from the cocoon of the silk moth). In recent years, man-made and synthetic resources have been produced to broaden the range of fabrics available. These have been developed in search of particular characteristics, such as their handling and laundering properties, or to recreate expensive natural fabrics more cheaply.

The original man-made fibers were viscose or rayon, which come from regenerated cellulose using wood pulp or short cotton fibers, and acetate that is derived from acetic acid.

The true synthetic fibers—nylon, polyester, and acrylic—are petroleum-based and were invented during the middle of the twentieth century.

The most recent addition to the garment fiber industry is spandex, and with its incredible stretch and recovery properties, it is often used with other fibers to produce stretchy fabric.

Blending fabrics is very common and allows different fiber features to be combined; for example, polyester and cotton is a quick-drying and absorbent fabric often used for shirts or bed linen; when knitted, cotton and spandex produce a stretchy, absorbent fabric that is ideal for sportswear.

FABRIC

The yarn or thread formed by spinning the fiber filaments is woven or knitted to produce cloth ready for garment making. The only exception to this is where the fibers are matted together to form a bonded fabric, or felt. This method is often used for crafts, disposable overalls, or interfacings, and less often for fashion clothing due to its lack of strength.

Fashion fabric is generally dyed and the surface is often printed. Alternatively, the detail in the fabric may be created by weaving or knitting different-colored threads to form a pattern.

Fabric may be finished with a treatment to improve its handle or properties. Find out as much information as possible about the cloth you choose for a specific project and experiment with small pieces before starting to cut and sew.

WOVEN FABRICS

Generally, medium-weight, woven fabrics are easy to handle and are the best choice for beginners. Stiff and bulky fabrics, or those that are fine with little body, are more difficult to sew with.

Type	Structure	Description	Uses	Tips
Denim	Plain, woven cotton.	Originally designed for workwear, this blue cotton fabric is absorbent, strong, and hardwearing. Available in medium- and heavyweight, and popular as a fashion fabric for casual wear.	Choose lightweight denim for shirts or dresses and heavier examples for jeans, skirts, and casual jackets.	Use a strong jeans needle and lengthen the sewing machine stitch to 8 spi (3 mm). Plain and flat-fell seams work well and topstitching in a contrasting thread is a popular finish.
Cotton lawn	Cotton, plain weave.	A smooth, fine, and lightweight fabric sometimes plain and often printed.	Ideal for dresses, shirts, blouses, and lingerie. Can be used on the inside as an underlining to add body or depth to a fashion fabric.	Use long-bladed sharp shears for a clean-cut edge, and sew with a standard size 9 sewing-machine needle and a stitch length of 12–10 spi (2–2.5 mm). Plain and French seams work well and decorative stitching, with twin or wing needles, creates an attractive decorative finish.
Muslin	Closely woven cotton.	This plain-finished, stable, unbleached cotton fabric is available in various weights.	Use this for test garments, or toiles, when developing a design to check the fit and style. Muslin is also popular for craft projects and bag making.	Use a standard needle in a size to suit the weight of the cloth, and choose a 10 spi (2.5 mm) stitch length. Use plain seams to join fabric pieces.
Linen	Plain-weave natural cloth.	Linen has an obvious plain weave and a tendency to wrinkle unless treated.	It is a classic choice for jackets, pants, skirts, and suits, while lighter weights make good shirts and dresses.	Cut with sharp scissors to give a good clean edge. Work quickly, since linen has a tendency to unravel. Consider neatening raw edges before construction. Sew with a standard needle, and use a medium stitch length of 10 spi (2.5 mm). Choose plain and flat-fell seams.
Chiffon	Plain weave in silk or synthetic fiber.	This transparent cloth is soft and sheer. It was traditionally made from silk, but polyester is commonly used today.	Popular for skirts, blouses, and scarves, and often used in multiple layers or with a lining below.	Cut chiffon with long-bladed, sharp scissors, and sew with a new size 9 standard sewing-machine needle to avoid snags. Shorten the stitch to 12 spi (2 mm) and use French seams for a tidy finish.
Shirting	Woven cotton, silk, linen, or polyester-and-cotton mix.	A fine-weight cloth, generally with a smooth finish, either plain, printed, or with a woven stripe or check.	Shirts, blouses, and dresses.	Use a standard needle in a fine or medium size (9–11), depending on the weight of the cloth, with a medium stitch length of 10 spi (2.5 mm). Choose plain, flat-fell, and French seams for construction.

SILKS

This natural fiber is made by unraveling and spinning the cocoon of the silkworm into silk threads, which are then woven into fabric.

Type	Structure	Description	Uses	Tips
Silk dupioni	Plain-weave silk.	This is a crisp fabric with an uneven texture because of the slubs in the threads it is woven from. It has a dull sheen.	Jackets, suits, dresses, and pants, generally for evening or occasion wear.	As it unravels badly, consider neatening the raw edges before construction. Use a standard size 11 sewing-machine needle to sew with, and choose silk or polyester thread. Use plain seams to join panels.
Silk organza	Plain-weave silk.	This transparent fabric is woven from highly spun threads, making it fine, strong, and crisp.	Use it for evening wear backed with lining. One-hundred percent silk organza is a useful underlining providing support without adding depth or weight.	Sew with a fine size 9 sewing-machine needle, and use French or hairline seams for a delicate join. Sew with silk or polyester thread.
Silk satin	Silk woven into satin (polyester and acetate fibers are also popular).	A satin fabric reflects light because of the many flat threads that lie on the surface, so it has a shiny finish.	The surface threads are easily damaged, so this makes it a delicate fabric more suited to special occasion and evening wear.	Use a new, sharp, Microtex needle to prevent damaging the threads in the weave, and sew with a 10 spi (2.5 mm) stitch length. Plain and French seams work well. Sew with silk or polyester thread.
Habotai	Plain-weave silk (polyester fiber may also be used).	This fine and plain fabric is very soft and lightweight.	Use habotai silk for lingerie items and blouses. It is also ideal as a lining fabric for coats, jackets, and skirts.	Cut with long, sharp blades or use a rotary cutter with a self-healing mat (see page 18). Choose a fine (size 9) Microtex needle and small stitch length, 12 spi (2 mm), for seaming. French seams are a good choice. Change the needle frequently to avoid damage to the silk. Use silk or polyester thread.

WOOLS AND WOOL MIXES

Wool fabrics vary enormously, depending on the breed from which the fibers come, whether they are used alone or mixed with other fibers, and how the fabric is constructed. Woolen fabric can be used for making pants and coats.

Type	Structure	Description	Uses	Tips
Worsted wool	Plain- or twill-weave wool.	A worsted-wool yarn is produced from long, combed fibers that are highly twisted. It is smooth, strong, and fine.	Use worsted wool for suits, jackets, skirts, and pants.	Cut with sharp shears and sew with a standard size 11 needle with good-quality polyester thread. Use a medium stitch length of 10 spi (2.5 mm) and join panels with plain seams pressed open. Take care when pressing, and use a pressing cloth to protect the surface and prevent a shine.
Wool crepe	Twisted weave.	Crepe fabric can be made from wool but also silk, synthetic fibers, or a mix. Crepe has a pebbly surface and tends not to wrinkle. Although woven, the fabric may have a slight stretch to it.	Crepe is suitable for dresses, pants, and skirts and works best for soft, draping styles.	Preshrink crepe before cutting out, and sew with a standard size 11 needle with a 10 spi (2.5 mm) stitch length. Construct garments with plain seams pressed open, or use a serger.
Bouclé	Woven or knitted with a textured yarn.	Generally made from wool or a wool-and-synthetic mix of fibers, bouclé has a thick surface textured with curly, twisted loops.	Bouclé fabric is popular for coats, jackets, and cardigans.	Cut fabric pieces with sharp shears, and sew with a stretch needle in a size 12. Choose a longer stitch length of 10–8 spi (2.5–3 mm) and opt for a stretch stitch or narrow zigzag if the fabric is very stretchy.
Loose-weave tweed	Loosely woven yarns of wool, silk, or synthetic fibers, or a blend.	Loosely woven tweed is generally made from thicker yarns for a luxurious look. Although woven, it may not be stable, and the yarns unravel easily from its cut edges.	Use any tweed fabric for jackets and coats.	Consider neatening the edges immediately after cutting and before sewing. Alternatively, cut a lightweight, fusible interfacing, and back all pieces to reduce fraying and stabilize panels. Use a size 11 or 12 needle and a 10–8 spi (2.5–3 mm) stitch length. Finish garments with a lining or bind raw edges.
Tartan and checks	Twill-weave wool or wool-mix fibers.	The pattern within the fabric is created by different-colored yarns woven in a sequence through the cloth. The weave may be tight or loose.	Tartan is more popular during some seasons than others, and is used for kilts, skirts, pants, jackets, and coats.	Take care when placing pattern pieces on fabric to account for matching at the seams. Sew with a standard size 11 or 12 needle and use a 10–8 spi (2.5–3 mm) stitch length. Fit a walking foot to the sewing machine to help feed the fabric evenly and make matching seams easier.
Wool coating	Woven wool or mixed fibers.	A coating is a thick and warm cloth.	As implied by the name, this fabric is used for coats and winter jackets.	The problems when sewing this cloth occur because of its thickness. When seaming, the upper layer tends to slide over the lower layer, so fit a walking foot to help encourage an even feed. Cut with long-bladed scissors and sew with a large size 14 machine needle. Extend the stitch length to 8 spi (3 mm) because this will work better with the thick fabric.

KNITTED FABRIC

Knitted fabrics are constructed from loops rather than warp and weft threads that are woven together. The fibers used to make the threads/yarns may be natural wool, cotton, or synthetic, or various blends of these, creating a multitude of knitted fabrics.

Type	Structure	Description	Uses	Tips
Cotton knit	Knit.	Light- to medium-weight stretchy cotton. It is very absorbent. When mixed with spandex, the stretch-and-recovery properties are even better. The fabric may be dyed a solid color, or can be surface-printed.	Most commonly used for T-shirts, but also for dresses, skirts, and underwear.	Use a stretch needle, and choose a stretch stitch if one is available on the sewing machine. If not, set a zigzag to a standard length and narrow width so the seam line will move if the fabric is pulled. A serger is a good tool to use for cotton knit fabric.
Slinky knit	Knitted viscose/rayon.	Viscose/rayon is a heavy yarn that has a slinky handle, and when knitted, it stretches and drapes beautifully.	As it is available in different weights, use this for dresses, skirts, cardigans, and unstructured jackets intended to drape.	Place the fabric on a work surface covered with a cotton sheet to prevent it from moving or slipping when cutting. Fit a stretch needle and set to stretch stitch when using a sewing machine. A walking foot helps to feed the fabric more evenly, too. Sew with a serger if one is available.
Sweatshirt fabric	Knit.	Although more stable than many other knitted fabrics, cotton sweatshirting does stretch and pull. It has a knitted surface with a soft backing.	Sports clothing and leisure wear. This is a comfortable and warm cloth. Use sweatshirt fabric for loose-fitting pants, sweatshirts, and casual zippered jackets.	Choose a stretch or ball-point needle in a size 12 or 14, and sew with a serger or, if using a sewing machine, a stretch stitch and walking foot. Hem with a twin needle to imitate a manufactured stitch.

BONDED FABRICS

A bonded or felted fabric is produced direct from fibers which are matted together, rather than spun then woven or knitted together.

Type	Structure	Description	Uses	Tips
Felt	Matted fibers.	A material produced from bonded fibers. It is available in a large range of colors.	Mainly for crafts, appliqué, and plush toys.	As felt does not fray, there is no need to neaten the edges when cut. Use sharp scissors or a rotary cutter for a clean edg

SPECIAL-OCCASION FABRICS

Occasion wear makes use of the most luxurious fabrics. Fibers from all sources are constructed in a variety of ways to create special fabrics and garments.

Type	Structure	Description	Uses	Tips
Velvet	Woven (sometimes knitted) backing with dense pile on surface.	Made from silk, cotton, viscose/rayon, or polyester fibers, velvet varies and this affects its handling. It is a thick material with a luxurious pile held in place by its backing. Velvets on a knitted base drape well.	Suitable for jackets, skirts, bodices, and special-occasion wear. Velvets that drape well are ideal for skirts and dresses.	Cut all pieces in the same direction to avoid differences in the way the light catches the panels. Iron with care, using a piece of the same velvet and very delicate pressure. Use a size 12 standard needle and a 8 spi (3 mm) stitch length. Use plain seams and finger press. If fitting a zipper, insert a concealed version so there will be no topstitching.
Lace	Sewn on net, or a knitted or crochet construction. It may be stable or stretchy.	Lace is a delicate transparent fabric with an intricate pattern incorporated into it. It varies a great deal in quality and price, and is available as all-over lace on the roll or as edging in various widths.	Use edging lace for trimming skirts, dresses, blouses, and lingerie. All-over lace is perfect for wedding dresses and nightgowns.	Pin with long, large-headed pins, and sew with a fine size 9 machine needle. Lap the seams to retain the pattern and sew with a zigzag, then cut away the excess.

IMITATION FABRICS

The advent of these fabrics has allowed the look of animal fur and skin to be used without having to harm any animals in the process.

Type	Structure	Description	Uses	Tips
Faux fur	A knitted base with a dense pile.	Faux fur imitates animal fur of all types and is dyed accordingly. The length of the dense pile and quality of the finish varies.	Generally, as a fashion fabric, faux fur is used for coats, waistcoats, hats, and trims.	Cut through the backing fabric with needlework or embroidery scissors, then tease the pile fibers apart to avoid spreading them all over the room. Sew with a stretch needle and use a short, narrow zigzag stitch to sew the backing together when joining panels.
Faux suede	Knit or woven.	Most modern examples look very realistic, but are much easier to launder and keep clean than real suede.	Use faux suede for coats, jackets, pants, and bags.	Place all pattern pieces in the same direction for cutting. Use a Microtex needle to sew with a 10 spi (2.5 mm) straight stitch. Sew with a good-quality polyester thread. Flat-fell seams make a good finish.

Fabric preparation

With the pattern cut and ready to use, it is time to consider your fabric.

The information on the outside of the pattern envelope will have informed you of the material suitable for your garment and how much of it to buy, but now you need to check for flaws and preshrink it in preparation for cutting. Many factors influence how to prepare the fabric, such as fiber content, construction, and the type of outfit being made.

Fabric construction

Most of the fabrics that we use for clothes are either woven or knitted. These handle differently and so are used for different purposes. A woven fabric is fairly stable and will only stretch if pulled diagonally along the cross or bias grain, while a knitted fabric will stretch in at least one direction when pulled because of its loopy structure. This is why it is important to follow the guidelines given for fabric choice, since the drape or fit will depend on the fabric formation.

Checking for flaws

It is unlikely that the fabric you buy will have anything wrong with it, but check it first, just in case. A good way to check for pulled threads or print mistakes is to iron the entire length of cloth before laying it out for cutting. This allows you to check the surface of the cloth, and in addition, ironing it with a steam iron will help to preshrink the fabric. If you do find any problems with the material, you can either take this up with the retailer or work around any minor imperfections.

Preshrinking

Most fabric is sold with a small shrinkage allowance, and for peace of mind you should preshrink the length of fabric before cutting out your garment. Use the steam-ironing method, mentioned above, for woolens and materials that require dry cleaning when constructed. Where you will be combining different fabrics, for example, one with a lining or those embellished with laces or trims, preshrinking is recommended. To preshrink the fabric, just launder it as directed by the fabric manufacturer. If

this information is not available, treat it as you intend to wash the finished garment.

Squaring up skewed fabric

Sometimes you will find your fabric length has been pulled off-grain, giving a slight diamond shape rather than a regular rectangle. If this is the case, ease the fabric back into shape by pulling diagonally in the opposite direction to rectify the problem. Finish by pressing with an iron and lying flat to cool.

Laying out fabric

Fabrics are usually laid out with the selvage edges placed together so that two fronts, backs, or sleeves can be cut out together and will therefore be identical. However, sometimes it is better to lay the fabric in a single layer, turning and reusing the pattern templates to cut more than one panel. Use a single layer when cutting a bold pattern or checks to make matching easier, or if the fabric is particularly slinky or slippery. Cut the latter on a cotton sheet to prevent the fabric from sliding off the table.

Woven fabric

Knitted fabric

Pulling the fabric diagonally will square up your skewed fabric.

Printed directional fabric
Cut all pieces in the same direction.

Pile fabric
When cut in opposite directions, shading differences are obvious.

The layout options given in the pattern envelope will include suggestions of how to place the pattern pieces according to the width of the fabric and whether the material has a nap or direction. Follow the directions given until you have sufficient experience to be able to create your own best layouts.

Fabric direction

Some fabrics will have "direction." This may be due to a design or print with an obvious top and bottom, or a surface nap or pile that is brushed in a particular direction, such as flannel or velvet. When laying out the fabric, it is important to place all the pattern pieces in the same direction, otherwise shade differences may be apparent, or flowers may be upside down.

PILE FABRIC: FINDING THE RIGHT SIDE

The surface of a fabric is sometimes obvious, but the right and reverse sides may appear very similar. To work out which side is intended to be the right side, look for tiny holes running along the selvages of the fabric. This is where the fabric was supported during processing with "tentering" hooks. If you run your finger over the holes, one side will be smooth and the other rough. The rough side is the right side, as the hooks are placed through the material from the wrong side so the edge of the hole is pushed to the surface.

USEFUL FABRIC TERMS

Selvage This is the narrow, heavier band that runs down both sides of a length of fabric. It is where the weft (filling) threads have wrapped around the edge of the warp (lengthwise) threads and returned to be woven in the opposite direction.

Warp These are the lengthwise threads that are placed on the loom first to form the basis of the fabric.

Weft These are the filling threads that weave up and down through the warp threads to create the cloth.

Grain The grain of a fabric follows the length and is parallel to the selvage edges. When placing pattern pieces on fabric, the grain arrows must lie parallel to the selvage for the garment to hang properly.

Bias The true bias or true cross lies at 45 degrees to the warp and weft. The fabric is unstable when pulled in this direction, as it does not follow the grain. However, this can be an advantage if a draping effect is required, because clothes hang softly when cut this way. Bias binding is cut on the bias to prevent crinkles and unsightly tucks when covering a shaped edge.

CUTTING A STRAIGHT END ON WOVEN CLOTH

To cut a length of fabric across the grain and achieve a perfectly straight line, pull out one thread from the weft, i.e. the threads across the length and not parallel to the selvage. As you pull out a single thread, the fabric will crinkle and, if it pulls free without breaking, a line will be obvious through the fabric. Cut along this line.

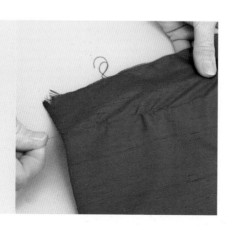

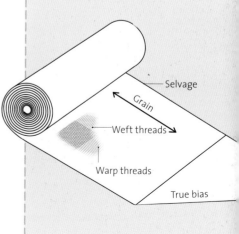

Selvage

Grain

Weft threads

Warp threads

True bias

Basic sewing

In this section we cover the essential information needed by even the most novice sewer, providing the perfect foundation to build on. Cutting, joining, and shaping, and choosing the most appropriate techniques, are laid out in a progressive order.

Hand stitching

Everyone should know how to sew by hand for those emergency situations when buttons fall off or hems come down. Of course, as well as being practical it can be a pleasure too.

Finished tailor's tacks.

E ven if you use a sewing machine for most of your projects, hand sewing is an essential skill when dressmaking. It can be functional as well as decorative, but often the same stitches are used for both purposes. A little practice with a needle can improve the finish of a garment, by producing hand-sewn invisible hems, or keeping facings in check so that they do not roll to the right side. Hand embroidery, even if based on a small number of simple stitches, can be a beautiful addition to decorate clothing, bags, or home furnishings. It is worth investing a little time in learning the basics.

In this section we take you through the process of creating the most useful stitches in easy steps.

TIPS
- Cut short lengths of thread to sew with. Elbow to thumb to wrist is a good length guide—anything longer is likely to tangle and knot.
- Sew with 100 percent silk thread when you can. Although it is more expensive it slides easily through the fabric and is less likely to become knotted.
- Choose a suitable needle with an eye just large enough to hold the thread snugly.
- Sewing with a small needle encourages small, neat stitches.
- Wash your hands frequently when hand sewing to keep the fabric and thread clean.

Tailor's tacks

Tailor's tacks are loose loops of thread sewn into fabric to mark important positions when transferring information from a pattern to fabric. These temporary tacks are made with a relatively weak thread so that when removed they will not damage the fabric.

1
Thread your needle with a double length of tacking thread, or a weak thread, in a contrasting color to your fabric so it will stand out and be seen.

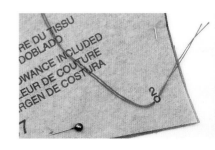

2
Take the needle through the dot on the paper pattern and through the layers of fabric below it, then back up to the surface. Leave a tail approximately 1 ½ in. (4 cm) long on the surface.

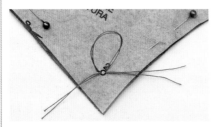

3
Take the needle back down very close to the point where the needle exited and up again, leaving a loop next to the tail on the surface. Cut the thread from the needle leaving a tail a similar length to the first.

4
Ease the paper away from the fabric, trying not to rip it too much, and separate the layers of fabric. Snip the threads between the fabric layers to leave short threads marking the position on the material.

Running stitch

Running stitch is the simplest of stitches to sew and has numerous applications. Use it to join fabrics, make a seam, gather a length of fabric, or ease in a sleeve head. You could also stitch with embroidery thread for decoration.

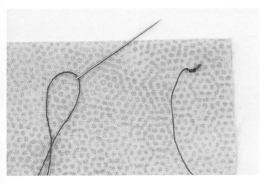

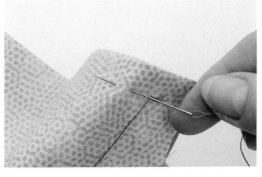

> **TIP**
> **BASTING**
> Use running stitch for temporary basting. Start with a knot and make your stitches and gaps approximately ½ in. (1 cm) long.

1
Anchor your thread according to your preferred method, by either tying a knot in the end of your thread or sewing two stitches on top of each other.

2
Take the needle down through the fabric and bring it up beyond it on the sewing line, keeping the stitch and space the same length (approx ¼ in. [6 mm]). Pull the thread taut but not tight.

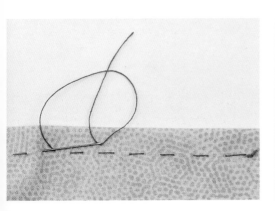

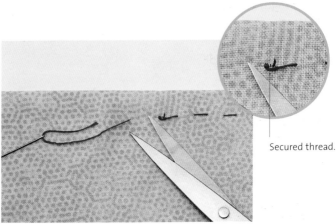

Secured thread.

3
Continue making stitches along the sewing line, making sure they are even and consistent for the length required. Keep the tension regular so that the stitches sit in the fabric but do not crinkle or gather it.

4
When your thread is too short to continue, finish with two stitches on top of one another to secure it, and snip off the excess before continuing with a new length.

Simple flower made with embroidery thread and back stitches.

Backstitch

Backstitch is a strong hand stitch and is the best substitute for machine-sewn seams if a sewing machine is not available. A row of backstitches has an element of stretch in it because of its construction, so it works well for stretchy fabrics. Use it with embroidery thread for decorative work too.

TIP
If you have trouble threading your needle, cut the end with sharp scissors at an angle. This helps to ease it through the eye. Do not moisten the end of your thread—this only works with cotton thread but not with the general polyester thread we tend to use for dressmaking today.

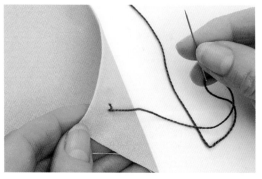

1
Anchor your thread in the wrong side of the fabric at the start of your work. Use your preferred method, by either tying a knot in the end of your thread or sewing two stitches on top of each other.

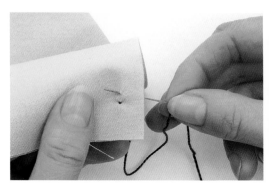

2
Bring the needle from the wrong side to the surface of the fabric at the end position of your first stitch. Your stitch length will be determined by the purpose of your work, but generally the smaller the stitch the stronger the seam will be.

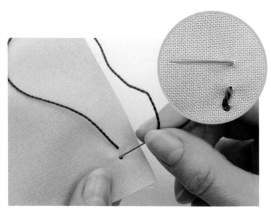

3
Take the needle to the starting position of your first stitch and take it to the wrong side, under the fabric, and back up at the end of your second stitch. Ease the thread through so that the stitch sits securely in the fabric and does not pull the cloth too tight.

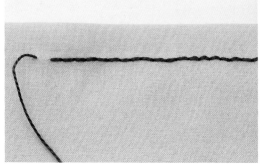

4
Complete the second stitch by taking the needle down through the fabric at the start of the second stitch filling the gap between this and the first stitch. Continue creating backstitches along the sewing line, forming a solid row of stitches with no spaces left between them.

Blanket stitch

Blanket stitch is traditionally used to neaten edges. The regularly spaced stitches cover the edge of a fabric, leaving a twist to strengthen and protect the edge. When sewn very close together it becomes buttonhole stitch.

BUTTONHOLE STITCH

Buttonhole stitch is very similar to blanket stitch, but the stitches touch each other with no space left between. This forms a very strong edge.

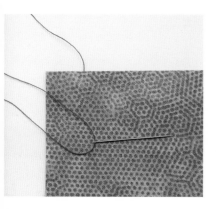

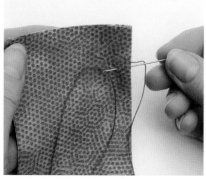

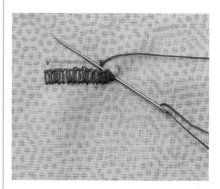

1
Secure the thread end in the fabric as discreetly as possible, with a knot or two stitches on top of each other, and bring the needle out on the edge of the fabric to start.

2
Imagine the position of your first stitch and take the needle down through this point to the wrong side. Do not pull the thread tight; instead, leave it loose on the front and top edge.

TIP
Run your thread through beeswax and iron it in a fold of paper to set the wax and prevent it from staining the fabric. This strengthens the thread and helps it to slide through your fabric. This is especially useful for sewing buttons and buttonholes.

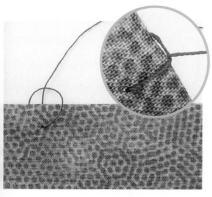

4
Repeat steps 2 and 3, creating stitches along the edge of the cloth. Keep the tension, stitch length, and distance between each stitch consistent. To finish, take the needle over the last stitch to hold it in place, and anchor it securely with two tiny stitches.

3
Take the needle fully through the fabric and bring it up at the edge and over the length of thread. Pull the thread and use your fingers to manipulate the stitch into place so that it sits across the edge and over the surface in a right angle.

Ladder stitch

Ladder stitch is sewn from the right side to close up a gap. It is similar to a slip stitch (see page 58) and is almost invisible. Use it as an invisible repair when a seam opens up, or to attach a patch pocket on a hand-tailored jacket. For a strong finish, keep the stitches small and close together.

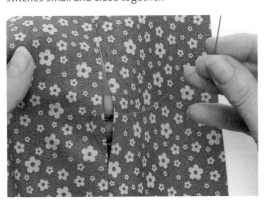

1
Secure the end of the thread in the fabric at the start of your work as discreetly as possible. Use a knot or two stitches together for a secure start. Bring your needle through the folded edge on one side.

2
Take a small stitch on the fold directly opposite and slide the needle through the fold, bringing it out ¼ in. (6 mm) further on. Pull the thread through without making it tight.

4
After making a few stitches, pull on the thread so that the folded edges ease together and close up the opening. Continue creating these stitches, pulling them tight every so often, until you reach the end. Finally, pull the thread tight to close it completely and secure the tail.

3
Cross back to the first edge, taking the needle into the fold at the same level and slide through ¼ in. (6 mm) as before. Pull the thread and continue to form a series of tiny, straight stitches that look like a ladder.

Herringbone stitch

Herringbone stitch looks like an offset cross stitch, and it is useful for creating couture and hand-tailored garments. It is often hidden away on the inside and used to hold layers and tapes in place, although it can be used decoratively with embroidery thread. Use for stretch fabric where the stitches need to move with the cloth.

Use herringbone stitch to attach a ribbon or tape. This holds it flat and prevents it from twisting.

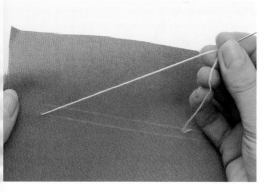

1
Imagine two horizontal and parallel lines on your fabric where your stitches will be formed. Starting on the left (right for left-handed sewers), secure the thread end on the wrong side, and bring your needle to the surface on the lower line.

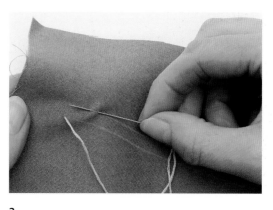

2
Move a stitch length to the right and make a short horizontal stitch on the upper line. Before pulling the needle through entirely, make sure the thread tail lies below your needle.

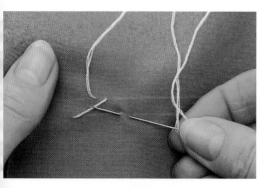

3
Pull the needle out and move a stitch length to the right making a short stitch, as before, on the lower line. This time keep the thread tail above the needle.

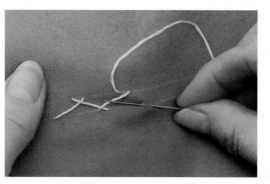

4
Continue making stitches in this way, working to the right and taking short horizontal stitches on the upper and lower imaginary guide lines, until the row is complete. As always, finish the thread end securely so that the row of stitches will not unravel.

TIP
Use tailor's chalk (see page 13) to draw guidelines on fabric when hand sewing. This will encourage consistent stitching, and the lines can be brushed off when they are no longer needed.

Pad stitch

Pad stitch is used in tailoring, and helps to form shape and structure in particular areas of garments, such as lapels and collars, by permanently attaching the interfacing to form rolled and curved edges. This stitch looks like a chevron, but is practically invisible on the right side as only a few threads are taken from the fashion fabric in each stitch.

Pad stitching joins the interfacing and fashion fabric layers together, shaping them at the same time.

1
Hold the fabric and interfacing over your hand to create a roll, interfacing uppermost. Using a knotted thread, make a very small stitch through the interfacing, just catching a couple of threads of the fashion fabric.

2
Moving down the line of the roll, make another tiny stitch. The threads on the interfacing will be angled slightly to the left.

3
Repeat the last step until you have completed a row. Fasten the thread off at the end of the row, then stitch a second row.

4
Continue to roll the interfacing and the fashion fabric, and make lines of stitching, until the area is complete.

Stab stitch

Stab stitches are tiny stitches made vertically through the fabric, and used to hold fabric firmly in place. Bound pockets and buttonholes use stab stitches between the main fabric and the binding. You can also use stab stitches to apply a hand-sewn zipper.

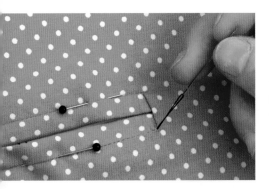

1
Secure the thread at the back of the work, and bring the needle through to the front. If working on a bound edge, bring the needle through right on the stitching line.

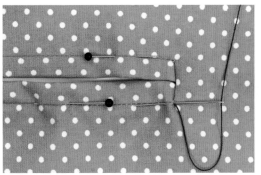

2
Insert the needle into the stitching line very close to where it emerged from the seam, and make a stitch about 1/4 in. (6 mm) long.

Stab stitches hold the layers together neatly and securely.

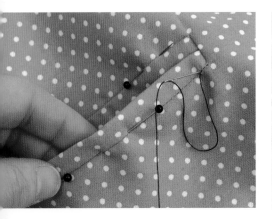

3
If you are sewing a few layers at once, or the fabric is thick, make vertical stitches down through the fabric and straight back out 1/4 in. (6 mm) along. Repeat this, placing the needle in the right side a thread away from where it emerges, and making stitches 1/4 in. (6 mm) apart, pulling the thread taut after each one.

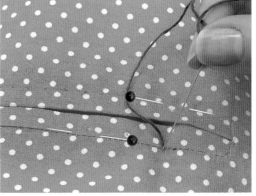

4
Complete the line of stitching and fasten off on the reverse side.

Seams

Seams join fabric pieces together and it is important to select a seam type to suit the garment or project you are sewing. You also need to consider the location of the seam, whether it is straight or curved, and the material you are working with. Use these step-by-step guides to help you choose appropriate seams for each situation.

Plain seam

A plain seam is the simplest method of joining two pieces of fabric. Use it for flat and shaped seams, and on all types of material. This versatile seam can be finished in many different ways, and snipped and trimmed for a smooth, flat finish.

Finished seam

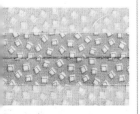

Right (above) and wrong (top) sides of a plain seam.

TIP
Start and finish by reversing over one or two stitches to secure both ends of the seam so that it will not come undone.

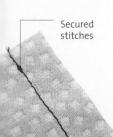

Secured stitches

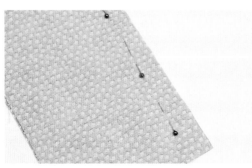

1
Place the right sides of the fabric together with the edges level. The seam line is normally ⅝ in. (1.5 cm) parallel to and inside the cut edge, but may vary depending on the project and its purpose. Pin along the seam line.

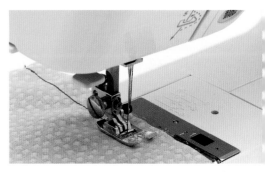

2
Set the sewing machine to straight stitch and sew along the seam line, removing the pins as you go. Use a reverse stitch at the start and end to secure the seam.

3
For a really smooth seam, press it flat to set the stitches before opening it up. This reduces any crinkles in the seam and gives a better finish.

4
Press from the wrong side with the iron, then turn over and iron lightly from the right side. If the fabric is delicate, remember to use a pressing cloth to protect the surface of the cloth.

Flat-fell seam

A flat-fell seam is traditionally, but not exclusively, used for the decorative seams on denim wear. It is strong with an uncluttered finish as the raw edges are encased within the join. It may be finished with a contrast topstitch thread for a casual style often associated with denim.

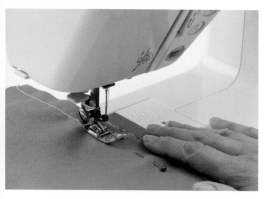

1
Place fabric with wrong sides together. Set your machine for straight stitch with standard thread in the bobbin and topstitch thread in the needle. Fit a topstitch needle to take the thicker thread, and sew a seam ⅝ in. (1.5 cm) from the edge.

2
Press the raw edges to one side with the topstitch thread on top and the bobbin thread hidden. Lift up the upper seam allowance and trim the lower one to ⅛ in. (3 mm).

Finished seam

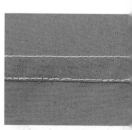

The finished seam has the topstitch thread on the surface and the bobbin thread on the back.

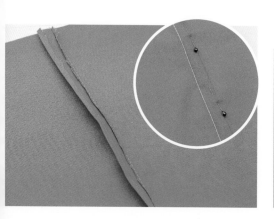

3
Fold over a ⅛ in. (3 mm) edge on the upper seam allowance and press carefully with an iron. Place this over the lower cut edge and pin in place.

4
Edge stitch the upper seam allowance over the seam to hide the raw edges beneath and to create a strong seam.

Mock jeans seam

Mimic a flat-fell seam (see page 51) with this simple method if you are a beginner or you are short of time. From the outside the seam looks very similar to a traditional flat-fell seam, but this has neatened raw edges on the inside rather than a smooth join.

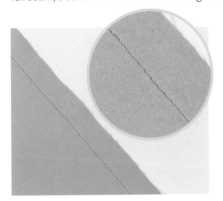

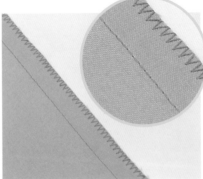

1
Set the sewing machine to straight stitch with standard thread in the bobbin and above (through the guides and needle). Set the stitch length to 10 spi (2.5 mm) unless using very thick or ultra-thin fabric (see page 32). Sew with right sides together.

2
Neaten the raw edges with a zigzag stitch or a serger three-thread balanced stitch (see page 55).Press the seam flat (see page 50, step 3) for a crease-free finish then press the neatened seam allowances to one side.

TIP
If you cannot find an appropriate color of topstitch thread, wind some standard thread onto a bobbin and place the bobbin on the spare spindle.

Run both threads (from reel and bobbin) through the same guides and through the eye of the needle.

3
Fit a topstitch needle to the sewing machine and increase the stitch length to 8 spi (3 mm) then sew a line of straight stitching approximately ½ in. (1 cm) from the seam, catching the allowances below. Here are the right (above left) and wrong (above right) sides of the finished seam.

The resulting seam has a bolder finish and looks almost like a topstitched seam.

French seam

A French seam has a lovely neat finish with all the raw edges concealed. It was a popular seam construction before sergers became readily available for the home sewer, so quick and easy serged seams have tended to replace it. For those who don't own a serger it is still a great way to make a tidy seam, and works best on lightweight fabrics such as lawn and silk.

1
Unlike a standard plain seam, place your fabric with the wrong sides together and the edges level. Pin and sew ¼ in. (6 mm) from the edge with a straight stitch.

2
Trim the raw edges to approximately half and press open. It is important to cut the edges short and clean to avoid any tiny fibers from being visible on the outside when the seam is finished. Fold the seam so that the right sides are now facing and press flat so that the stitched seam is right on the edge.

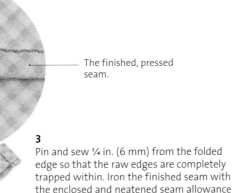

The finished, pressed seam.

3
Pin and sew ¼ in. (6 mm) from the folded edge so that the raw edges are completely trapped within. Iron the finished seam with the enclosed and neatened seam allowance pressed to one side.

Finished seam

The wrong side of the finished seam.

TIP
Although you are working with a very narrow seam, by pressing it open at step 2, step 3 becomes much easier as the ironed edges lie flat against one other and the seam sits on the outer edge. This makes pinning and sewing the second line of stitching much easier.

The right side of the finished seam.

Hairline seam

A hairline seam is made in the same way as a French seam, but it is much narrower and produces a more delicate effect. It is ideal for joining pieces of fine, translucent fabric like chiffon or organza as it is hardly noticeable, but it does lack the durability of a plain or French seam. Use it for overskirts and dresses in chiffon or lace that are constructed with a separate lining.

Finished seam

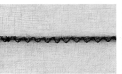

When finished, the narrow seam appears like a fine line.

If you have a serger, set it to sew a rolled hem and use this to join fine, sheer fabrics. It looks similar to a hairline seam and is much quicker to produce.

1
As with the French seam method (see page 53), first place the wrong sides together and pin then sew a row of straight stitching 12 spi (2 mm) from the cut edge. As you are likely to be using a fine fabric, reduce the stitch length to 12 spi (2 mm).

2
Sew a second line of stitching adjacent to the first, keeping as close to it as possible. Trim away the raw edges as close to the stitching as possible.

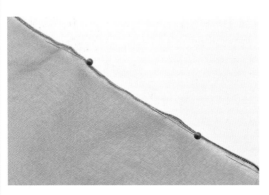

3
Fold the seam so that the right sides are now facing and press it flat so that the stitched seam is right on the edge. Pin the seam, making sure the two lines of stitching are trapped at the outer edge.

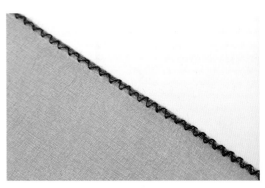

4
Set the sewing machine to a narrow zigzag approximately 12 spi (2 mm) wide and 12 spi (2 mm) long. Stitch over the edge with the zigzag to catch the rows of stitching inside. Adjust the zigzag width so that it covers the internal stitching.

Balanced serging seam

A four-thread, two-needle serger, produces a seam plus a back-up line of security stitching with threads wound over the raw edges. When the tensions are balanced, this seam is ideal for making strong, neat seams. Use it on almost all types of fabric, woven and stretchy. It is versatile and quick.

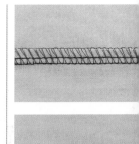

Right (above) and wrong (top) sides of a balanced seam.

1
Prepare your serger: choose appropriate needles (both the same); thread up with suitable thread; and check the tensions are balanced by running a test piece of fabric through the machine.

2
Pin on the seam line with the right sides together. Line up the pins with the left needle to ensure the correct seam allowance. Remove the pins while you sew and before they reach the presser foot to avoid accidents or damage to the machine.

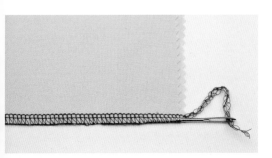

3
When the seam is completed, thread the chain into the eye of a blunt needle and take it back through the last few stitches. Cut off the excess. This will neaten and secure the seam ends.

4
Alternatively, use a tiny drop of fray-stopping glue on the thread chain where it leaves the fabric. When it dries, cut through the glue and chain for a neat, secure seam.

TIP
Sew a test sample first and adjust stitching to check that the tensions are balanced and perfect before starting to sew. The looper stitches should cross on the cut edge with no pulling or overlap and the stitches created by the needles should sit flat in the fabric without looping or tugging.

Flatlocked seam

A serged flatlock seam is sewn in a traditional way along the edge of two layers of fabric, but pulled flat when finished to create a flat join with loops on the surface and a ladder-type stitch on the reverse. It normally uses both loopers and one needle of the serger, but some models also produce a two thread flatlock stitch, in which case check your manual for specific instructions. Use for decorative seams on knit fabrics.

TIP
Do not forget to tighten up the screw when you remove a needle. If it is not tightened up the vibration of the machine will cause it to rattle and fall out.

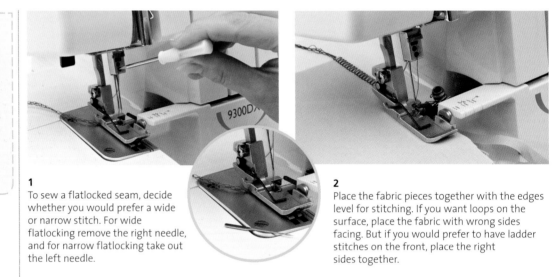

1
To sew a flatlocked seam, decide whether you would prefer a wide or narrow stitch. For wide flatlocking remove the right needle, and for narrow flatlocking take out the left needle.

2
Place the fabric pieces together with the edges level for stitching. If you want loops on the surface, place the fabric with wrong sides facing. But if you would prefer to have ladder stitches on the front, place the right sides together.

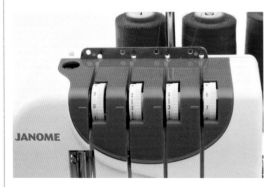

3
Set the serger for flatlocking by reducing the needle tension to "o" and increasing the tension of the lower looper. Run a test piece of fabric to check the stitch before sewing your seam.

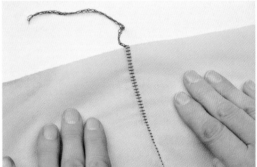

4
Separate the two layers of fabric and gently pull them apart. The stitches will open up flat, revealing ladder stitches on one side and loops on the other.

Hems

Choosing a hem type depends on where it is on a garment (e.g., sleeve or bottom edge), the type of garment, and the material it is to be made from. Consider the finish you need too—should it be invisible with an expensive, couture appearance, or would you prefer it to have a sharp and factory-made look?

Simplest hem

Neatening an edge can be carried out in different ways: with a deep or narrow hem; single or double-folded finish; a decorative frill; or by hand or machine. The simplest hem is created by folding the fabric and sewing by machine or hand.

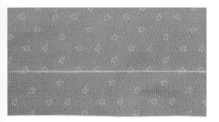 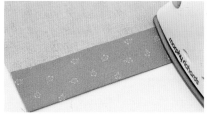 

1
Decide where the finished hem should be and mark it with pins or chalk.

2
Press this hem to the wrong side and create a crease. Remove the pins if you used them.

3
Open up the hem and fold the cut edge up to the crease then refold, trapping the raw edge inside. Press, pin, and baste to hold it in place.

4
Choose a slip stitch (see page 58) or hemming stitch (see page 59) and sew the hem in place, or alternatively set up the sewing machine with straight stitch and sew through all layers to hold up the hem with a topstitch.

Slip stitch	**Hemming stitch**	**Topstitch**

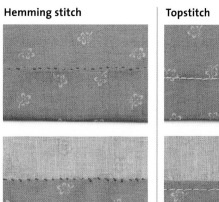 

Hand slip-stitched hem

Using a slip stitch to sew a hem by hand makes a very discreet finish. Providing the thread is a good color match and tiny, regularly spaced stitches are taken in the fabric, it will be hardly visible. We have used a contrasting thread in this example for demonstration purposes.

Finished hem

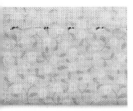

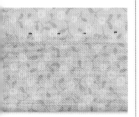

Right (above) and wrong (top) sides of a hand slip-stitched hem.

TIP
Keep a regular tension and do not pull the stitches too tight. Keep checking that the stitches are hardly seen on the right side as you sew.

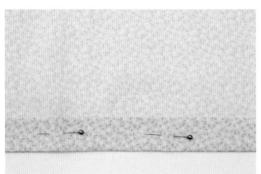

1
Having established the finished length required, press the hem allowance to the wrong side creating a crease at the hemline. Open this up and place the raw edge a little away from the crease then fold back up to conceal the cut edge. Pin the hem in place.

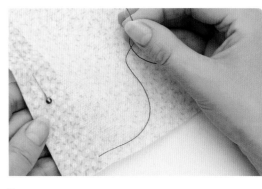

2
Thread up a needle with a length of fiber-matching thread (polyester, cotton, or silk). Secure the thread end in the hem with a knot or two or three stitches on top of one another.

3
Working from the right to the left (left to right for left-handed sewers), take a tiny stitch on the wrong side of the garment, level with the folded hem, catching one or two strands of fabric.

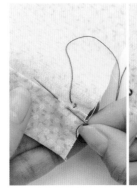
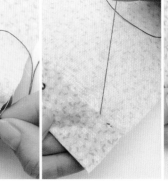

4
Take the needle back to the folded hem and slide it through the fold to the next stitch position. Continue in this way taking little upside down V-stitches until it is all held in place.

Hand hemming

This stitch is stronger and more functional than a slip stitch but is normally visible on the right side, unless a thicker fabric is used, so a good color-matching thread is essential. The small diagonal stitches are made close together along the fold of the hem on the inside. It forms a very secure hem.

1
Fold a double hem to the wrong side of the garment at the appropriate level. Pin or baste the hem in place to hold it while you sew.

2
With the hem in your left hand (right for left handed sewers) work from right to left or bottom upward. Thread up a sharps or betweens needle (see pages 16 and 17) and secure the end in the folded hem with a knot, or by sewing two or three stitches on top of one another.

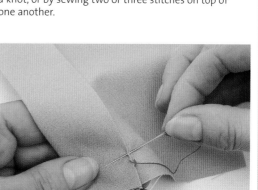
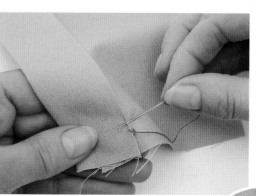

3
Take a tiny stitch in the wrong side of the fabric of the garment a little ahead of where the thread tail leaves the folded hem, then take the needle through the folded hem opposite.

4
Take the next stitch in the garment above the hem, slightly ahead as before and continue. Form even-sized and regularly spaced stitches along the hem to hold it in place.

Finished hem

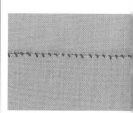

The finished hem is a strong one but it is not necessarily invisible from the right side. It will be less noticeable when a thicker fabric is used. The right side is shown above and the wrong side is shown top.

Topstitched hem

A topstitched hem finish is frequently used for manufactured clothing, so choose this method if you would like your friends to think you have bought your outfit and have not made it yourself. The topstitch can be sewn with either a thread that blends in, or a contrasting color as a decorative feature.

TIP
It is possible to sew the hem with the wrong side of the garment facing upward. This makes it easier to follow a fold but the quality of the stitch may not be quite as good, since sewing machines are generally set up with a better-looking tension on the surface.

1
Fold up an appropriate double folded hem to the wrong side concealing the raw edges within and press to give a flat finish. Place pins along the hem.

2
Baste through the middle of the hem to hold it in place. Stitching here will mean that it will not interfere with the topstitching at the folded edge. Thread up the sewing machine with standard thread in the bobbin and needle, or choose a topstitch thread in the needle for a bolder finish if this is required. (Don't forget to use a topstitch needle for thicker thread.)

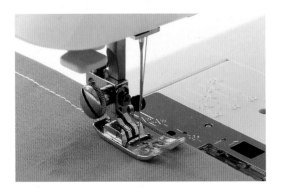

3
With the right side of the garment uppermost, place the hem under the presser foot. Check that the needle will sew through all three layers of fabric and note the position of the lower edge in relation to the guide lines etched on the throat plate. Sew.

4
Sew around the hem, keeping the folded edge level with the guide on the throat plate. This will keep the stitching parallel to the lower edge. Do not start and end with reverse stitches; instead, sew the last few stitches over the first few to trap them in place and snip off the thread tails.

Machine blind stitch hem

Use a machine blind stitch hem for a quick, almost invisible hem on curtains as well as pants, skirts, and dresses. With the appropriate preprogrammed machine stitch selected, and a blind stitch presser foot fitted to the sewing machine, this is an easy technique to carry out. It works best with medium and heavyweight fabrics as the stitches disappear into the depth of the cloth.

1
Prepare your hem with a single or double fold. Pin and baste through the center of the hem allowance. If choosing a single folded hem neaten the raw edge with serging (see page 55), zigzag stitch, or with a bound edge (see page 66).

2
Set up the sewing machine with color-matching thread and replace the standard presser foot with a blind hemming foot. Select the blind hem stitch from the preprogrammed options.

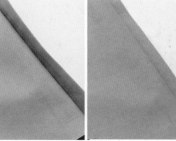

3
Place the hem on the work surface, and with wrong side facing up, twist the hem under.

Finished hem

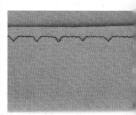

Right (above) and wrong (top) sides of a machine blind stitch hem.

4
Take the upper hem edge and place it under the presser foot. With the fold placed to the vertical guide on the presser foot, sew through the hem catching the fold as the needle swings over the guide to form small V-shaped stitches. Catch the fold so that it holds the hem but the stitches do not show on the right side.

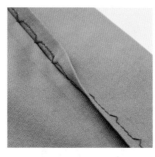

5
To finish, fold the lower edge down to reveal your blind hem.

BLIND HEMMING FEET

These vary in appearance and some are adjustable to make sewing a blind hem even easier. Some feet are fixed but allow the stitch to move left or right in order to catch more or less fabric. Whatever the method, watch the fold on the left as the needle catches it and makes a stitch in the hem.

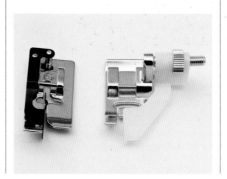

TIP
Increase the stitch length so that the stitches are further apart and not so obvious.

Scalloped hem
This type of finish works well with a scalloped hem. Controlling the tiny tucks and closely trimmed fabric without a facing would create a bulky and even untidy edge.

Faced hem

The addition of a facing is the best way to finish a deep, curved hem. This gives a flat hem as the excess fabric is removed and replaced with hem facing pieces that match the shape of the lower edge, and so do away with any bulky tucks and folds. Use it on evening wear and wedding gowns where the added weight at the hem gives a luxurious and expensive appearance.

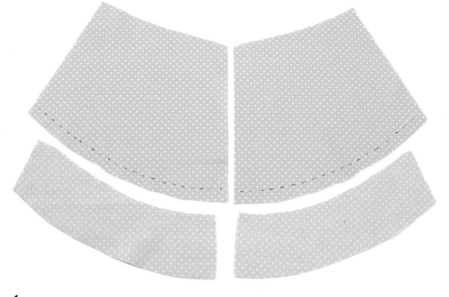

1
Establish the finished hem position and add a 5/8 in. (1.5 cm) hem allowance. Cut away all the excess hem allowance and cut facing pieces matching the shape of the lower edge panels.

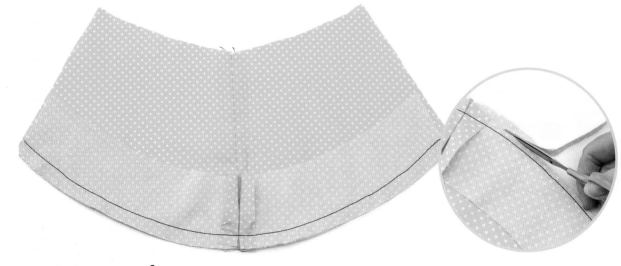

2
Join the skirt pieces at the seams and press open. Place the separate facing pieces to the hem of the skirt with lower edges level and pin on the sewing line. Press the seam allowances back and sew the facings to the lower edge of the hem. Trim.

CLIP 1
Faced hem
http://qr.quartobooks.com/vgss/clip1.html

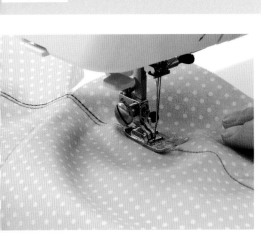

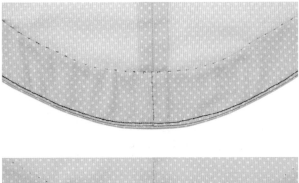

3
With the trimmed allowances of the hem and facings placed to the hem, understitch these layers together. Stitching through these layers and not the garment improves the line of the hem and prevents the facing rolling to the right side.

4
Turn the faced hem to the inside and ladder stitch (see page 46) the facings together at the seams.

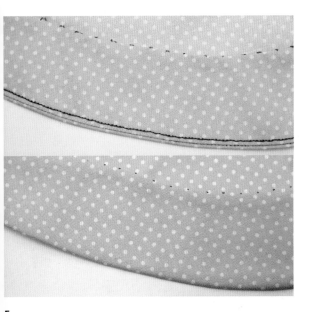

Finished hem

5
Turn under the top edge of the hem and hand sew in place with slip stitching.

Right (above) and wrong (top)sides of a faced hem.

Rolled edge

A rolled edge can be sewn by hand, sewing machine, or with a serger. A serged rolled hem is particularly quick to produce, while a hand-sewn rolled hem is slower to create. A special foot can be fitted to the sewing machine to make a rolled hem. Use either method for a delicate hem on light-weight silk, chiffon, and lawn.

Rolled hem (serger).

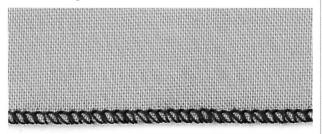

Rolled hem (sewing machine).

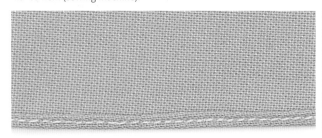

Rolled hem (hand).

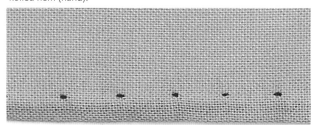

ROLLED HEMMING (SERGER)

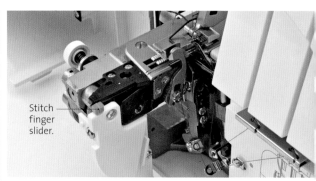

Stitch finger slider.

1
Set the serger for rolled hemming by following the guidelines in the manual. If these are not available, remove the left needle, tighten the lower looper, shorten the stitch, and remove the stitch finger. (For decorative rolled hemming see page 211.)

2
Feed the fabric edge under the presser foot with the right side uppermost, and the hemline level with the needle. Stitch all around the hem and sew the last few stitches over the starting chain. Neaten the remaining chain with a fray-stopping glue (see page 55.)

Finished hem (right side).

Finished hem (wrong side).

ROLLED HEM (SEWING MACHINE)

1
Sew a row of straight stitches ¼ in. (6 mm) below the hemline and trim close, removing any excess fabric.

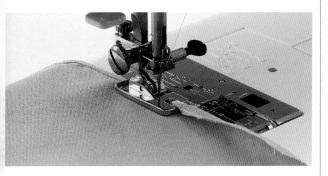

2
Fit the rolled hem foot to the sewing machine and feed the stitched edge into the guide at the front of the foot. Lower the foot and stitch (with straight or narrow zigzag stitch), guiding the fabric as you sew.

Finished hem (right side).

Finished hem (wrong side).

ROLLED HEM (HAND SEWN)

1
Sew a row of straight stitches ¼ in. (6 mm) below the hemline and trim close.

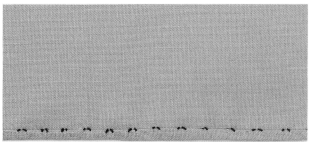

2
Roll the edge toward the inside, concealing the row of stitching, then pin and/or baste in place. Sew with slip stitch, catching the hem in place.

Finished hem (right side).

Finished hem (wrong side).

Edges

Question: What can you do to neaten a fabric raw edge on a seam allowance or a hem? Answer: There are various methods to choose from and their selection will depend on the tools you have available, as well as the position on the garment and the type of fabric that you are using.

NONE
Some fabrics do not need neatening as they will not ravel or fray—for example, polar fleece or leather.

Cut the fabric with sharp shears in order to produce a smooth edge.

Use our guide to help you choose the most appropriate edge for each project you make. Take time to examine the material you are working with. Consider the thickness or density of the fabric because folding layers or covering edges with stitches may prevent raveling, but will make them bulky and obvious. Some fabric frays badly while others stay intact unless agitated, and this will influence your selection. Fabrics with a knitted construction may not fray too badly, but may have a tendency to curl and neatening the edge will help control this. You do not need to neaten the raw edges of garments with linings as this will conceal the seam allowances and protect them from abrasion during wear. For a Hong Kong finish, see page 218.

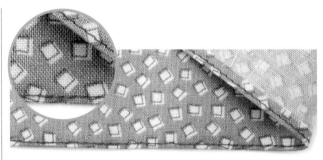

STRAIGHT STITCH
This traditional form of finish was very popular before swing-needle sewing machines became widely available and a straight stitch was all that could be made. Hence, this method is now seldom used. If you do decide this method suits your needs, fold over 1/8 in. (3 mm) to the underside, press, and edge stitch in place.

PINKING SHEARS
The simplest method of tidying up a raw edge and preventing it from fraying is to trim it with pinking shears. This produces a zigzag cut on the fabric so that the woven threads cannot work themselves loose from the weave.

With sharp pinking shears, cut along the raw edge to make a neat zigzag.

BOUND EDGING
Bind the raw edge with bias tape for a tidy and secure edge. Buy a bias-cut tape or make your own and sew this over the edge.

The easiest way to attach a binding is to press the folded tape in half and slide it over the raw edge. Pin and baste it if you prefer, then stitch with a straight stitch, catching all layers together. Accurate pressing means that the fold underneath gets caught as you sew. Alternatively, stitch the tape to the right side, fold it over the edge, and hand hem the binding to the wrong side.

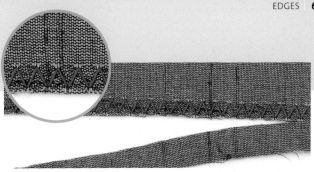

ZIGZAG STITCH (WITH A SERGER PRESSER FOOT)

If zigzag stitch is sewn right on the edge of a single layer of fabric, the edge will curl in and create a ridge. With a specialist foot fitted to the sewing machine, the finger or pin fixed to the foot sits over the edge of the fabric so that each zigzag stitch is supported before it slides off onto the fabric edge, without pulling it.

Cut a clean, jagged-free edge and fit the presser foot. Feed the smooth fabric edge under the pin on the foot.

ZIGZAG STITCH (WITHOUT A SERGER PRESSER FOOT)

When you sew a zigzag stitch directly on the fabric edge, the stitches pull the fabric causing a ridge to form. To overcome this problem and create a flat finish, sew inside the edge.

Place the edge of the foot to the cut edge and zigzag parallel along its length. Finish by trimming close to the stitches to remove the excess allowance.

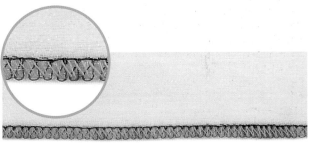

SERGING (WIDE)

For thicker or more loosely woven fabrics, remove the right needle and leave the left to produce a wider stitch for a more secure finish.

Remove the right needle and set the machine according to the manual, then skim the edge from the cloth to cut and cover with threads.

Note: Skim the edges of your fabric pieces with the serger to neaten the fabric before the panels are sewn together or serge them after the seams are sewn. You can also choose whether you serge the seam allowances together or separately according to the seam type.

SERGING (NARROW)

Although a serger can be used to produce and finish seams all in one, you can use it to neaten the edges after the seams have been sewn with a standard sewing machine.

Use three threads, not four (four adds unnecessary bulk), and remove the left needle of the serger to produce a narrow finish. Use this for lightweight materials for a delicate finish.

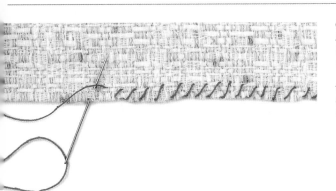

OVERCASTING

A hand-sewn overstitch covers the fabric edge to prevent fraying. Use this traditional method when you do not have a sewing machine available.

Simply thread up a needle and sew over the cut edge to prevent the weave from raveling. Choose a good color-matching thread (a contrast color is shown here for clarity), and keep your stitches regular and consistent.

Darts

Use darts to shape a garment by pinching out segments of flat cloth to make it three-dimensional. Darts help to fine-tune the shape of a piece of clothing so that it fits the figure well, and follows the body's silhouette.

U se single-pointed darts for waist, hip, and bust shaping, and darts with double-pointed ends to follow the shape of a waist in a dress or jacket. Choose the balanced dart method on page 220 as an alternative if you wish to use a true couture method. This technique has a smooth, ridge-free finish on the surface and is perfect for tailored jackets and coats.

Single-ended dart
These are generally marked on a pattern as a simple triangle with dots that must be transferred to the fabric, but a little bit of shaping helps to improve their function when they are made up.

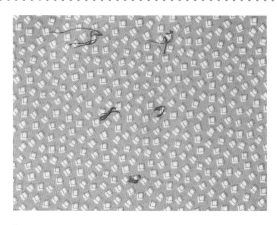

1
Transfer the pattern markings from the paper pattern to the fabric with tailor's tacks (see page 42), chalk, or temporary marker pen. Remove the pattern carefully to prevent it from tearing yet still leaving the marks or threads clearly on the fabric.

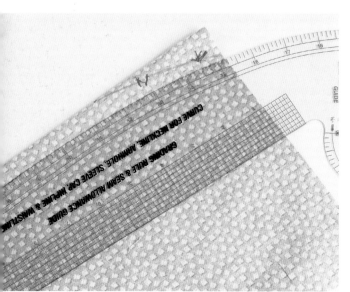

2
Fold the dart in half with right sides together, matching the chalk marks or tailor's tacks and pin to hold it in place. With a temporary marker or chalk, draw in a natural curved guideline to follow. Do not use a ruler—a French curve gives a good shape.

3
Sew from the wide end toward the point, starting with reverse stitching but leaving thread tails at the point. A reverse stitch at the point would be bulky and prevent a smooth, flat finish.

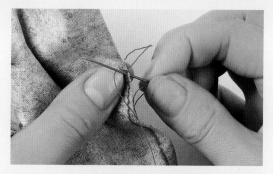

If you prefer not to tie off the ends (see step 5), put the threads into a needle and work them into the body of the dart where they will be secure but not visible.

4
Remove the tailor's tacks if you used them, and tie off the tails securely, either with a knot or by threading them on a needle and working them in.

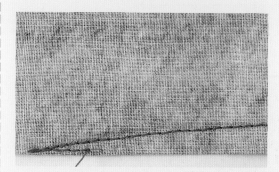

Another thread finishing technique is to pivot at the point and sew into the body of the seam where you can reverse over the last few stitches to secure them. This works well with a bit of practice, but can be a little bulky and distort the ends of the dart.

5
Press the dart to one side. Use a tailor's ham to make pressing easier and create a natural smooth line with no bump or dimple at the point.

Slip a piece of thin card beneath a dart when pressing it to prevent a shiny ridge from forming on the right side.

Double-ended darts

This type of dart shaping has a point at each end and tends to be used to contour the waist of a dress, jacket, or coat where there is no horizontal waist seam.

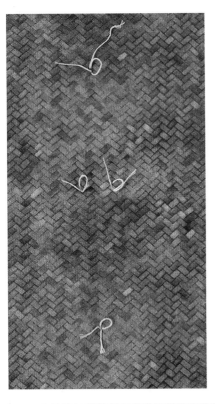

1
Transfer the important markings from the pattern to the fabric pieces with tailor's tacks, chalk, or temporary marker pen (see pages 13 and 42). This will ensure that the darts are placed correctly—this is especially important for symmetry.

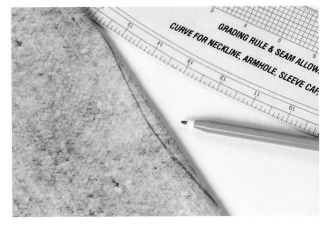

2
With the right sides together, fold the dart in half from point to point and pin, matching the pattern markings. Draw a guideline through the markings but create a natural curve (using a French curve) between the points to produce a smooth shape when sewn.

3
Start sewing from the center at the widest part of the dart and stitch toward one point. Do not start with a reverse stitch, instead leave a short length of thread at the end to tie off later.

TIP
Darts make a huge impact on the fit of a garment. A dart may be the correct width to match the figure, but if it is too long it will cause a garment to appear too tight or to sit unnaturally. A good example, is a waist dart in a straight skirt—if the dart is too long the skirt will ride up, causing the waist to sit above waist level. If you pull it down so that the waist is at the correct level, the skirt will be tight on the hip. Simply shorten the dart.

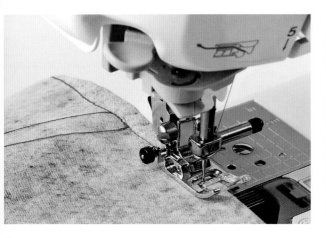

4
Sew from the center again to the opposite point of the dart, overlapping the first few stitches to secure the thread ends. At the point, leave a tail of threads to tie off later. To make handling easier, you will need to turn your work over to sew the second half of the dart.

5
Cut away the thread ends where they overlap in the center and tie off the thread tails securely at each end.

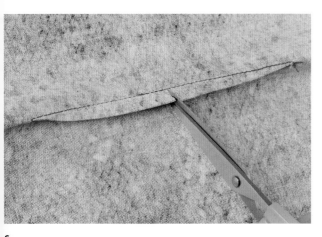

6
Press the dart to one side—towards the side seam is usual. It may be necessary to snip into the center of the dart to allow it to lie flat. Make a small horizontal cut at the widest point but keep away from the stitching.

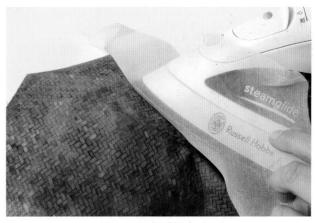

7
Use a tailor's ham to provide a shape to iron over and use a pressing cloth to protect the surface of the fabric if necessary.

Dressmaking techniques

Whether you want to learn how to carry out a specific technique or just need a reminder, in this section you will find comprehensive step-by-step instructions for a range of techniques. Each process, from inserting a zipper to lining a jacket is illustrated with clear photographs.

Zippers

Zippers come in a variety of types and weights making them a great practical choice of fastening for many kinds of garments and accessories. Select the most appropriate style of zipper and method of insertion.

Whether you need a zipper with metal or plastic teeth, in fine or chunky gauge, closed or open ended, they are available in lengths and colors to suit all circumstances. This makes it possible to find the perfect zipper for a thick winter fleece, a delicate boned evening bodice, a child's party dress, casual jeans, or smart men's pants. Once you've chosen the perfect zipper you can select the most appropriate method of sewing it in.

Basic methods include centered and lapped, where the teeth sit behind double or single flaps of fabric. A concealed or invisible zipper requires a specialized presser foot to allow the stitches to be sewn under the curled teeth to give a neat and smooth finish. Pants generally have a fly front zipper, and some contemporary dresses use a very obvious style where much of the tape surrounding the teeth is left on view. More traditional dresses may have a hand-inserted zipper for a couture finish.

Types of zippers

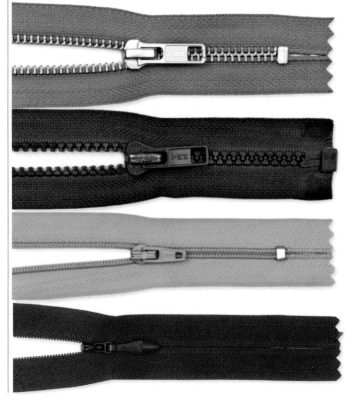

PANTS ZIPPER
Generally short in length with metal teeth and a catch at the top to prevent the zipper from opening unexpectedly. Choose a fly zipper insertion.

CHUNKY AND FINE OPEN-ENDED OR SEPARATING ZIPPER
Open-ended zippers are ideal for jackets because the two sides can be completely separated. They are normally available in longer lengths, but are now available in shorter lengths and lighter weights for close fitting evening and bridal bodices or corsets. Choose the centered or lapped method of insertion.

FINE NYLON ZIPPER
This fine-toothed zipper is available in all lengths and sometimes as a continuous piece to be cut as required for soft furnishings. The fine nylon teeth make it soft and flexible so it is more suited to light-weight garments.

CONCEALED/INVISIBLE ZIPPER
An invisible zipper lies hidden in the seam when inserted and has no topstitching on the surface. An invisible zipper foot is essential for sewing it in place and the order of working is altered to achieve a good finish.

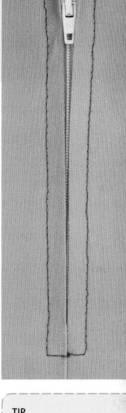

Finished centered zipper.

Centered method

This simple method for inserting a zipper places the teeth directly behind the opening as part of a seam. It is an ideal method for beginners, and may be used in a variety of circumstances for both garment making and soft furnishings. Note: A contrasting thread has been used in this sequence for clear demonstration.

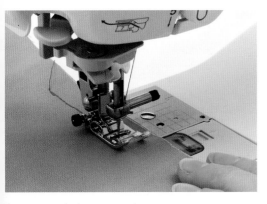

1
Sew the seam between the hem to the base of the zipper leaving a gap where the zipper will be placed. Make sure the ends of the seam are secured with reverse stitching.

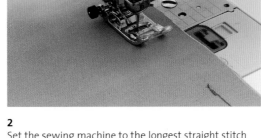

2
Set the sewing machine to the longest straight stitch and return to sew up the gap left where the zipper will be inserted. Do not secure the ends of this seam as this is a temporary row of stitching.

TIP
When sewing the zipper in place, you will need to move the zipper tab out of the way of the machine foot. To do this, unpick the basting stitches to access the zipper tab (see below), pull it out of the way past the needle, and sew neatly around it.

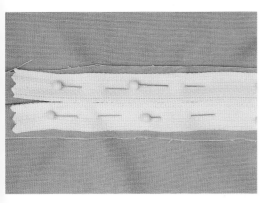

3
Press the seam open and place the seam with right side facing down on the work surface. Place the zipper face down and centered over the temporary seam. Pin, then hand baste in place.

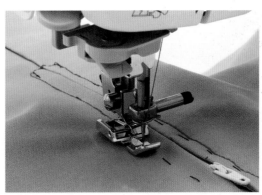

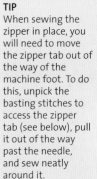

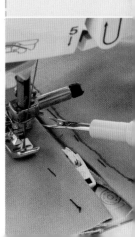

4
Using a zipper foot and working from the right side, choose a 8 spi (3 mm) stitch length and topstitch the zipper in place, following the basting stitches as a guide. Sew from the base of the zipper to the top on both sides. Remove basting. Take the thread tails to the wrong side to finish them off securely.

Lapped method

A lapped or offset zipper is edge stitched close to one side of the seam with the opposite edge lying over it and concealing the teeth. This method is ideal for dresses and skirts, and is a fairly straightforward technique to master. Use a 1 in. (2.5 cm) seam allowance in a lapped zipper seam.

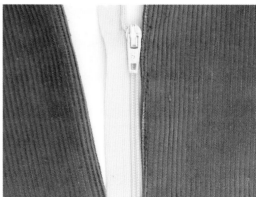

Finished lapped zipper

1
With a standard length 10 spi (2.5 mm) straight stitch sew a plain seam from the base of the zipper position to the hem. Secure the ends of the thread with reverse stitching to ensure a strong finish. Press the seam open.

2
Place the open part of the seam over the zipper and pin the folded edge on the right hand side to the tape close to the teeth. Fit a zipper foot and edge stitch from the base of the zipper to the top.

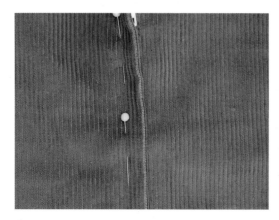

3
With the zipper closed, place the left folded edge to the edge stitching on the right, concealing the teeth below. Pin the fabric to the zipper tape below it to the left of the teeth. Baste, if you prefer, to hold the layers together.

4
With a zipper foot fitted appropriately, select straight stitch with a length of 8 spi (3 mm). Topstitch the zipper in place sewing from the base to the top. Start below the teeth so that the needle does not hit the teeth and break.

Fly front zipper

A fly front or pants zipper technique completely hides the teeth of the zipper. It has a guard on the inside for added comfort. Use it for skirts, shorts, and pants. For men the zipper is sewn with the left flap placed over the right, while women's garments are sewn with the flap right over left.

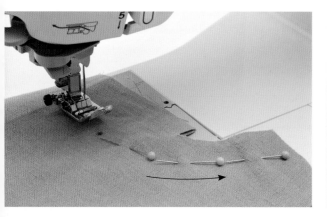

1
Mark where the base of the zipper will sit on the fabric and sew the seam from this point toward the inside leg seam.

2
Stop sewing 1 ¼ in. (3 cm) from the end of the seam to make it easier when you sew the inside leg and crotch seams later.

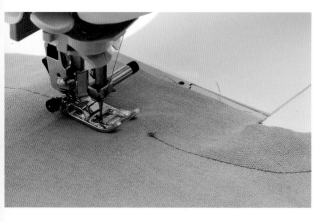

3
Sew the remainder of the seam as a temporary seam using machine basting. Use the longest straight stitch for this temporary seam and do not fasten the thread ends. Finger press the seam open.

4
With the right side of the pants face down on your work surface, place the zipper face down and centered over the temporary seam. Pin the left side of the zipper to the seam allowance below it.

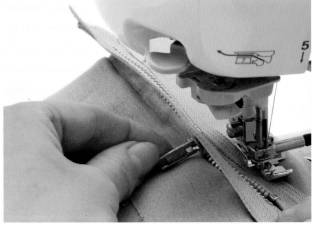

5
Fit a zipper foot to the sewing machine. Starting at the bottom of the zipper, sew through the zipper tape and seam allowance approximately $1/4$ in. (6 mm) from the outer edge of the tape. Do not sew through the pants layer at this time—only the zipper and seam allowance.

6
To sew past the zipper pull, leave the needle down and raise the presser foot then maneuver the pull past the needle and out of the way.

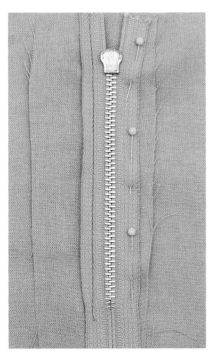

7
Working with the inside of the pants uppermost, pull the zipper to the right —the seam allowance on the left will also shift and this is correct. Pin the right side of the zipper to the pants, through the tape and all the layers below.

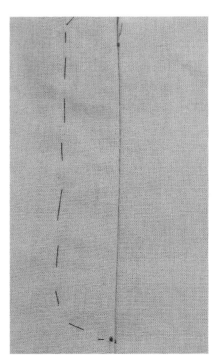

8
Turn the pants over so you are now working from the right side. Hand-baste the zipper in place from the base to the top, feeling for the teeth and using the pins as a guide. Remove the pins.

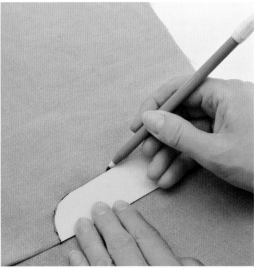

9
Using a card template, draw a guide line on the front of the pants with tailor's chalk or temporary marking pen to show the topstitching line.

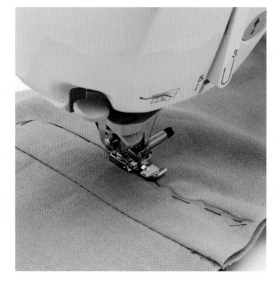

10
Follow this guide line with topstitching, sewing from the base of the zipper to the upper edge. Then remove the basting stitches.

11
Remove the temporary seam on the right of the zipper and pull the zipper down and up to test it. You will notice that the teeth are offset behind the fly to give a neat finish where the front flap completely covers the teeth.

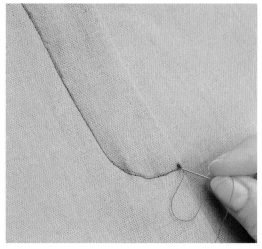

12
Insert the thread ends through the eye of a needle and take these thread tails through to the wrong side at the base of the zip. Sew the tails into the fabric and secure the end of the stitching.

13
Make a zipper guard for the inside of the pants with one layer of fabric and one of lining. Cut rectangles in each, measuring 2 in. (5 cm) wide and 1 in. (2.5 cm) longer than the zipper. Trim the lower corner to form a smooth curve.

14
Place the right sides of the guard together and pin. Using the edge of the sewing machine foot as your guide, sew a narrow seam along the outside edge, removing the pins as you go.

TIPS
- Place the lining side of the guard next to the body for comfort.
- Use a good quality, strong, metal-toothed zipper.
- Take care when topstitching and sew around the teeth so that the needle does not break.

15
Trim the guard, turn through, and press flat.

16
Place the guard under the zipper with approximately 1 ¼ in. (3 cm) showing beyond the teeth. Pin through the zipper tape and the guard to hold in place.

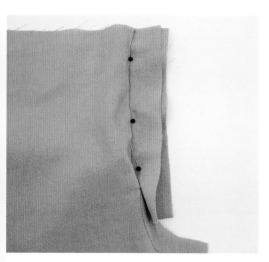

17
When happy with the position, turn the fabric over and repin along the right of the seam (within the seam allowance).

18
Turn the fabric back over and remove the pins at the front on the zipper tape.

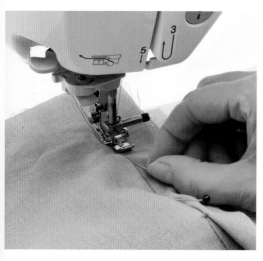

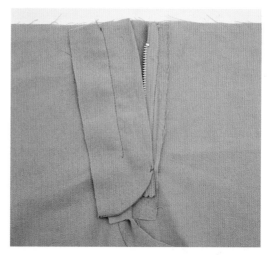

19
Using a zipper foot, stitch the zipper guard in place. Use the pins as a guide and remove them as you go.

20
To prevent the guard from flapping open, pinch the guard and right hand seam allowance together and sew two or three stitches backward and forward to secure in place.

Finished fly front zipper.

CLIP 3
Concealed zipper
http://qr.quartobooks.com/vgss/clip3.html

Concealed zipper

A concealed or invisible zipper provides a very clean finish as it is stitched directly into a seam. When the zipper is closed, the tab or pull is the only part visible.

Many factory-made garments include concealed zippers, and sewing them at home is easy with the correct tools. A concealed zipper has its teeth set under the zipper tape so that they are hidden when the zipper is closed. A specialist zipper foot has deep grooves in the underside to tilt these zipper teeth out of the way so that the stitches can be sewn very close to the teeth, allowing the tape to be sewn on the seam line.

The most important factor to remember for a neat finish is to insert the zipper before sewing the seam.

1
Place one side of the zipper face down over the right side of the fabric at the zipper opening. Pin the tape to the fabric and stitch in place with a standard zipper foot. This line of stitching will hold the layers in position for stitching later and is not intended to secure the zipper in position. Use a long stitch if you intend to remove this row of stitching later.

2
Repeat Step 1 with the opposite side of the zipper, sewing the tape to the seam allowance of the other half of the opening. Make sure both sides of the zipper sit at the same distance from the top edge.

Visible zipper

Some designers like to insert a prominently positioned zipper with much of the tape on show. A contrasting tape makes this a feature of the design.

There are various methods of inserting a zipper with the tape showing, but this is a simple-to-sew approach that gives a flat, tuck-free finish.

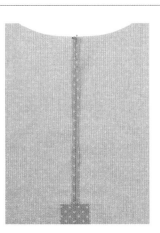

1
Pin and sew the seam where the zipper will be inserted and press the seam open. Place the zipper in position over the seam and mark the base of the zipper teeth with a pin. Trim the seam allowance of the seam where the zipper will be sewn to a minimum. Leave the rest of the seam allowance as it is.

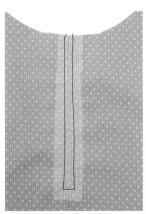

2
Cut a rectangle of lining fabric or silk organza 2 in. (5 cm) wide and 1 in. (2.5 cm) longer than the zipper. With the seam right side up, center the strip of lining over the seam where the zipper will be placed. Stitch the long sides and the base of the zipper position ¼ in. (6 mm) from the center seam.

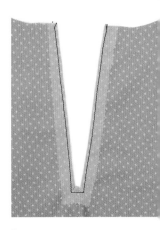

3
Snip through the center of the seam and lining, cutting into the corners at the base of the zipper position. Cut as close as you dare to the stitches to allow the opening to lie flat when turned through without snipping them. Trim the seam allowance to a minimum.

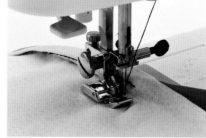

3
Attach the concealed zipper foot to the sewing machine and, with the zipper open, feed the teeth under the foot and into the grooves underneath. As you sew, ease the teeth open so that the groove holds them out of the way and stitches directly at the base of the line of teeth. Repeat for the other half of the zipper.

4
Find the point at which the stitching stops at the base of the teeth. The seam will be sewn from this point to the hem. Fit a standard zipper foot or an adjustable zipper foot to the sewing machine and lower the needle at the start of the seam. Secure the end with neat, reverse stitching and complete the seam.

The zipper tail is hidden beneath here.

Completed concealed zip.

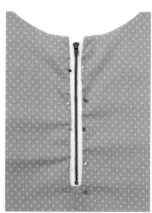

4
Turn through and press flat or pin to hold the edges. Make sure the lining or silk organza is tucked very slightly to the inside so that it is not seen when the zipper is inserted.

5
Place the zipper right side up on the work surface with the prepared seam opening over it. Pin, or baste if you prefer, the zipper tape to the edge of the opening before edge stitching the layers together.

6
Complete the garment with facings to neaten the neck edge if inserting a center-back zipper.

Fastenings

Fasteners or closures, such as buttons and buttonholes, hooks and eyes, or snaps allow a garment to be put on and taken off easily, and keep it closely fitted when it is being worn.

Hooks and eyes or bars are generally placed at the top of a zipper to keep it securely closed and prevent it from unzipping, while tiny snaps are used to keep a lapped edge in place. These are purely functional closures that are hidden and not intended to be seen. Buttons, on the other hand, might be practical but they may also be decorative and form part of a design, rather than just blend into a garment. Most fasteners are sewn in place, but snaps, whether small and functional or large and more decorative, can be clamped into position without any sewing at all. These no-sew snaps are normally used in manufactured garments, so use these when you want to recreate this effect.

Snaps

Snaps come in all sizes in brass, nickel, painted metal, or clear plastic. They are simply sewn through their holes to fabric where required and are intended to hold layers together rather than take much strain.

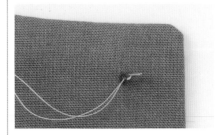

1
Snaps should be sewn to two layers of fabric for greater anchorage. Mark the position on both edges to be joined, lining them up carefully to make sure they will meet precisely. Use a double length of thread in your needle and secure the thread end on the marked position.

2
Bring the needle up and through one of the holes in the snap. Take the needle over the edge of the hole and into the fabric before bringing it up through the snap again. Pull the thread taut and repeat three or four times, depending on the size of the snap and hole.

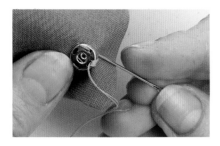

3
Take the needle under the snap to the next, and subsequent, holes and repeat. When the snap is securely in place, neaten the thread end in the back of the work.

4
Sew the opposite snap to the other side of the garment in the same way so that they will close together.

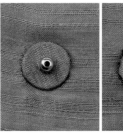

For a delicate finish on bridal and evening wear, or on couture tailored garments, cover the snaps before stitching them to the garment.

No-sew snaps

Manufactured garments such as jeans or casual waterproof jackets often have snaps, rivets, buttons, and eyelets clamped into position. These closures are available in small kits, perfect for the home sewer to use to fix them securely in place.

These closure kits contain various tools for the job and generally give good instructions for attaching the studs, snaps, rivets, or clasps to the fabric. If no instructions are provided, follow the general guidelines below.

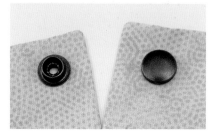

1
Mark the positions where the snaps will be placed on the fabric and use the piercing tool with the disk below. Pierce the fabric to form a neat hole in the correct size. Use a punch with a hammer or spin the punch on the fabric over a hard metal surface.

2
Place the appropriate snap through the hole and attach the backing part to it. Use the clamping tool provided to support the pieces and hammer them together.

3
Fit the linking part of the snap to the other marked point and clamp in place in a similar way to the first. Make sure all parts are securely locked before testing the fastening.

Eyelets and grommets

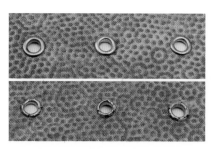

1
Make a clean hole in the fabric in a size slightly smaller than required. Use a punch post with a hard metal surface beneath with the right side of the fabric uppermost. Alternatively use a belt hole punch.

2
Push the shank of the eyelet through the hole from the right side and fit into the clamping tool. Clamp or hammer in place depending on the tool type provided until the eyelet is secure in the fabric.

3
Arrange and fit the eyelets as required on the piece of clothing with the smooth side on the right side (top).

Buttons

Everyone has to sew buttons on from time to time, and although it is an easy task, there are a few pointers to make them stay on securely and work well.

Buttons either have a stand underneath with a hole to sew through, or they have two or four holes. You need to create a stand for those with two or four holes as you sew them in place to take up the depth of the cloth in the buttonhole. So, this means a button with holes on a light cotton blouse needs a smaller stand than one on a tweed jacket, as the fabric in the jacket is much thicker.

Sew buttons, and buttonholes, to two layers of interfaced or stabilized fabric for a strong hold. Buttons are normally used on a lapped opening—for example, the front edge of a jacket or on the cuff of a shirt. Both of these areas are interfaced to provide added support, and an additional stabilizer is not usually required.

BUTTONS WITH HOLES

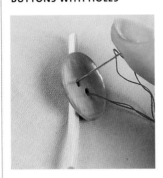

1
Use a double thread length, with equal tails, and secure the ends in the fabric to the button position. Place a darning needle or matchstick next to the button position. Bring the needle up through one of the holes in the button, across the top and down through the other, over the darning needle or matchstick, and into the fabric below.

2
Repeat this process six or seven times to hold the button in place. The number of times will depend on the size of the button and number of holes in it. Bring the needle out between the button and fabric.

Four-hole buttons are attached in the same way as two-hole buttons and can be sewn as two parallel bars or as a cross. If you want to recreate a manufactured finish, sew the bars parallel as this is the way they are often sewn on factory machines. You can sew on buttons using your sewing machine at home too—look at the manual and check the presser feet supplied with it, as there is often a special foot provided that holds the button steady while you stitch it. For a couture, or hand finish, cross the threads in the center.

3
Remove the darning needle or matchstick and wind the tail around the strands of thread between the fabric and the button to pull them together and form a stand, so that the button sits away from the fabric and not tight to it.

4
Take the needle to the wrong side and loop through the threads to gather them together before securing the thread end.

TIP
Draw your thread tails through beeswax and iron between a folded piece of paper (see page 45). This improves handling and makes a stronger hold.

COVERED BUTTONS

If you cannot find the perfect button to match a piece of clothing, choose a covered button. These can be covered in the same fabric as the garment for a perfect match, and are available in plastic and metal in a range of sizes.

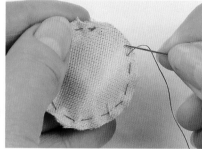

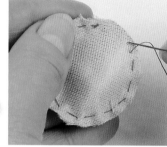

1
Iron a lightweight fusible interfacing to the wrong side of the covering fabric—just enough for the number of buttons to be covered. Measure the diameter of the button and make a template, in paper or card, twice this size. Draw around the template and cut out the fabric for each button.

2
Run a gathering stitch around the outer edge of the fabric circle and pull up around the button. Make sure it is anchored tightly so that you do not pull the stitches out.

BUTTONS WITH A STAND OR SHANK

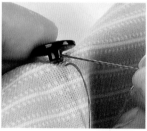

1
As for any type of button, secure the two thread tails in position and take the thread through the single hole in the stand.

2
Take the needle through the fabric and the button several times to hold it in place before taking the needle to the wrong side and looping through the threads and finishing securely.

3
Pull the stitches tight around the shank of the button, ensuring that the gathers are evenly spread around the button leaving no tucks or creases, and secure the thread end. Push the fabric into the cavity around the button stand.

4
Place the back of the covered button over the shank, trapping the raw edges of the cloth as you do so. Check that the fabric lies over the button smoothly then push the back into place.

5
Sew the button into position as you would a standard button with a shank (see right).

Buttonholes

Most modern sewing machines include a range of automatic buttonhole options, making it easy to find and stitch the best buttonhole for every project.

A plain buttonhole with a bar at each end is the minimum on offer, with many machines providing keyhole and stretch alternatives too. While you can still sew a buttonhole by hand if you wish, the pre-programmed machine varieties are quick and easy to make, giving consistently good results. The only task for you is to mark the buttonhole positions on a piece of clothing—the machine will do the rest.

MANUAL SEWING-MACHINE BUTTONHOLE

If you have an older machine that does not offer pre-programmed buttonholes, set your machine to narrow satin stitch to produce the edges of your buttonhole. This requires more measuring and accuracy but is just as effective for a plain finished buttonhole.

1
Mark the position and length of each buttonhole on your fabric.

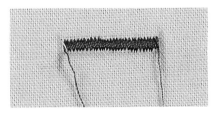

2
Set your sewing machine to zigzag stitch and shorten the length so that the stitches touch each other. Adjust the width to suit. Use a manufactured garment with buttonholes already made in it as a guide. Stitch one side of the buttonhole carefully, following the guide marks.

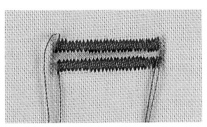

3
Sew a second line of satin stitches close and parallel to the first. Leave the thread tails long when you remove it from the machine and do not cut them yet.

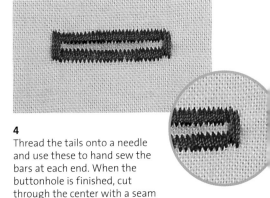

4
Thread the tails onto a needle and use these to hand sew the bars at each end. When the buttonhole is finished, cut through the center with a seam ripper or a buttonhole chisel.

AUTOMATIC BUTTONHOLES

Some sewing machines include a buttonhole foot that has a sliding case at the back to hold your button. This, in conjunction with a sensor, allows a perfectly sized buttonhole to be sewn every time for the button selected.

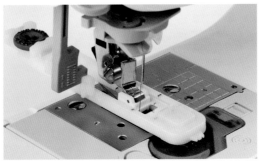

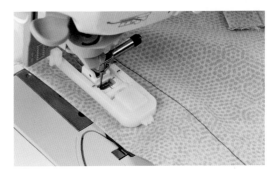

1
Mark the start position of each buttonhole on your garment with pins, chalk, temporary pen, or tailor's tacks.

2
Fit the buttonhole presser foot to the machine and lower the sensor. Select the buttonhole required and thread with appropriately colored thread. Insert your button.

3
Lower the needle into the fabric at the start of the buttonhole by turning the wheel. Make sure the foot is sitting straight and level before lowering it to hold the fabric in place.

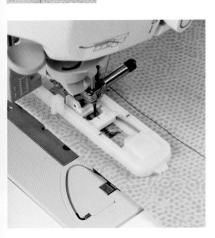

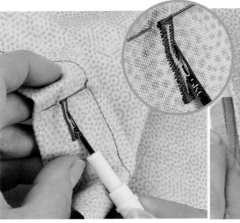

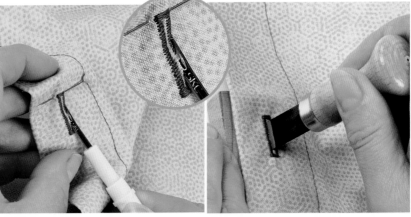

4
Start stitching and, in most cases, the sewing machine will create the complete buttonhole by stitching each side and the ends before stopping. It uses the sensor lever to judge the length, and providing this is not altered, all subsequent buttonholes will be the same length.

5
When all the buttonholes are sewn, cut through the center of each using a seam ripper or a buttonhole chisel. If using a seam ripper, place a pin across the end to prevent cutting through the thread bars.

BUTTONHOLES ON SHEER FABRIC

When sewing buttonholes on sheer fabric, it is important to provide stability to cope with the point of stretch, yet if the fabric is translucent, most interfacings and stabilizers will be visible. The perfect solution is to use silk organza because it is sheer but strong and fine too.

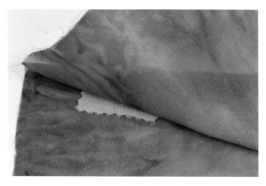

1
Place one or two layers of neutral-colored silk organza between the layers of fabric and baste in place. They must be a little larger than the finished buttonhole but not too large. Mark the position of the buttonhole.

2
Select the lightweight buttonhole option and fit the presser foot. Lower the needle at the end of the buttonhole position before lowering the presser foot. Stitch the buttonhole.

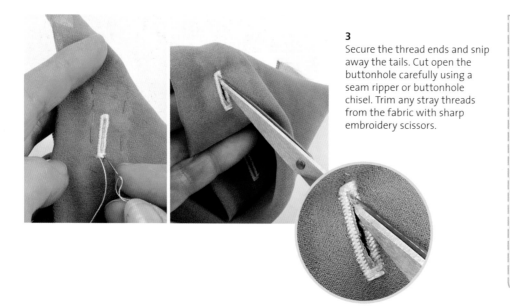

3
Secure the thread ends and snip away the tails. Cut open the buttonhole carefully using a seam ripper or buttonhole chisel. Trim any stray threads from the fabric with sharp embroidery scissors.

TIP
Use a layer of "wash-away" or "iron-away" stabilizer under the fabric when sewing a buttonhole on sheer or fine fabric to give extra support and prevent it from puckering. Cut away excess stabilizer then remove the remainder with a damp cloth or an iron.

BOUND BUTTONHOLES

A bound buttonhole with a contrasting edge is a good choice for jackets and coats, although it is just as acceptable on lighter-weight dresses and blouses. Separate material is used to cover the edges of the buttonhole, giving a strong finish.

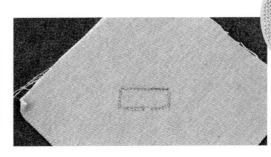

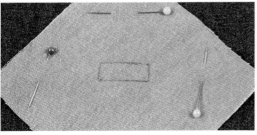

1
Place a bias-cut piece of fabric on the surface of the jacket with right sides facing. Pin or baste around the outside to hold the layers together.

2
Mark the outline of the buttonhole in the correct position. Shorten the stitch length, to give a stronger finish, and sew on the line. Start on the straight edge and overlap the first few stitches with the last few stitches.

4
Pull the bias piece through the center and pull neatly over the two "lips" of the buttonhole. Manipulate the corners for a tidy, crease-free finish and hold in place with small stab stitches sewn in the ditch.

3
Cut through the center of the buttonhole and close to the corners, taking care not to snip the stitching. Remove your basting.

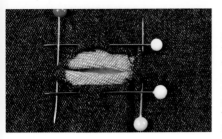

5
To complete, fold back the facing over the wrong side of the buttonhole and mark the position of the buttonhole corners with pins. Snip through the center and into the corners, then press the edges back to reveal the inside of the buttonhole. Pin and slip stitch into place.

Hooks and eyes, bars, toggles, buckles, and eyelets

Hooks and eyes are used where edges meet, at the top of a zipper, or at the center back of a neckline, for example, while hooks and bars are used for edges that overlap, as on a waistband. They range in size and weight and are available in black or silver.

SEWING HOOKS AND EYES IN PLACE

Use thread that matches the color of the fabric and choose a fine needle. Silk thread is great and easy to use as it does not tend to tangle.

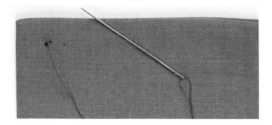

1
Find the best position for the hook and eye to give a flat finish and mark the position before securing the thread end in the fabric.

2
Place the hook or eye—both are attached in the same way—over the thread in the fabric and sew with blanket stitch (see page 45) over the metal wire and through to the fabric below. Work from one side to the other for a neat finish. Secure the thread with two backstitches on the wrong side.

MAKING BARS

Use a thread bar for a softer finish or for a better color match (metal is more noticeable). Choose a good-quality matching thread and a small needle. Run your thread through beeswax for a stronger finish. Make a looser version of a thread bar as a button loop—ideal for pearl buttons.

Finished thread bar.

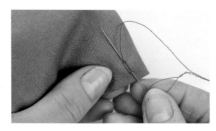

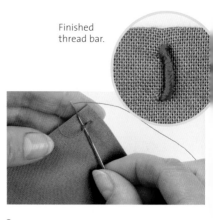

1
Decide where the bar will sit and mark both ends of it with temporary marking pen. Secure your thread end to one side.

2
Make two or three straight stitches in the bar position, taking the needle though the layers of fabric each time to form a base for the thread bar. Do not leave these strands loose or pull them too tight. Note: If making a button loop, make four or five strands to create a thicker cord.

3
Cover the strands with buttonhole stitches (see page 45) from one side to the other, then finish the thread end on the inside, out of sight.

HAND-SEWN EYELETS

Metal eyelets (see page 85) are often used in manufactured clothing, but sometimes a hand-sewn eyelet is required, for example, when attaching a buckle.

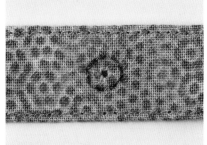

1
Mark the eyelet position and punch a hole through the fabric layers.

2
With a temporary marking pen, mark a ring around the punched hole approximately 1/16 in. (2 mm) away from it to use as a guide for regular stitch length.

3
Use a button twist thread and sew buttonhole stitches around the hole to strengthen it.

BUCKLES

Buckles are available in many styles, materials, and sizes, but are generally used with a strap or belt to make an adjustable fastening. They may be chosen as a purely functional closure, but are often a major design feature of an outfit. Hold buckles in place with a strap of fabric and create a small hole or hand-sewn eyelet through which the prong will protrude. Opposite the buckle, fit a strap with eyelets so that the buckle fastening can be adjusted.

HOOK AND LOOP (VELCRO)

Hook and loop comes in lengths of tape or spots, and is made up of two sides of nylon hooks and loops that stick together when they touch. Although not a primary fastening in clothing, this type is used for outdoor jackets. Attach to fabric with machine edge-stitching.

FROGS AND TOGGLES

Frogs and toggles are decorative fastenings. Buy these in a style to suit the garment and sew them in place by hand, or you could always try making your own by knotting and weaving cord. Wooden toggles were traditionally used on woolen duffle coats and are paired with a cord loop. Toggles have a hole drilled through the center so that they can be stitched to a garment.

Collars and necklines

The neckline edge must be neatened, and there are various ways to do this. A facing or band may be used as a simple finish, or a collar added to act as a frame at the neck of a garment.

· ·

Collars are generally grouped into three styles: flat, rolled, and standing. A flat collar lies over the garment around the neck edge (Peter Pan or sailor style); a rolled collar sits up around the neck and falls down onto the garment (shirt style); and a standing collar sits up as a band around the neck (turtle or mandarin/grandad style). Whatever the style chosen for finishing a neck edge, it must be neat, tidy, and symmetrical as it is such a prominent part of a garment.

TIP
When fusing interfacing to fabric, trim the interfacing pieces slightly smaller than the fabric so that they do not stick to the ironing board cover or iron.

Peter Pan collar

This curved collar is made in two halves and sewn to the neck edge. It lies flat on the upper chest and is usually finished on the inside with a facing (see page 101). The collar pieces are made up of two collar halves, two facing halves, and two pieces of interfacing in a suitable weight to support the fabric.

1
Choose a soft, fine interfacing for light support and iron it to the wrong side of the two upper collar pieces to fuse it in place. Trim the interfacing before ironing it to the collar so that it does not stick to the iron or ironing board.

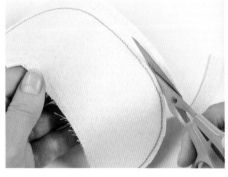

2
Pin the interfaced upper collars to the collar facings with right sides together. Sew the curved outer seams, then trim.

3
Turn through to the right sides, and press flat. Make sure both collars are exactly the same size and shape.

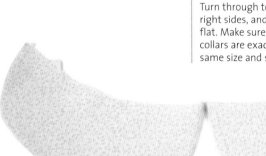

4
Place the raw collar edges to the neck edge, making sure the interfaced collars are uppermost and the faced side underneath. Pin and baste the layers together at the neckline.

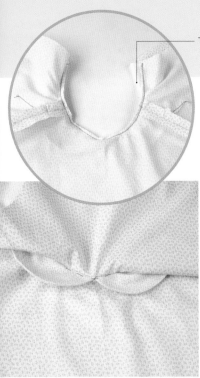

Trim the neckline edge.

Collar stand

The collar "stand" on its own—without the collar "fall"—is variously called a mandarin, grandad, or stand-up collar. It is an interfaced band that sits over, and conceals, the raw edges of the neck. Once the shirt has been constructed, make up the stand and sew it to the neck edge.

1
Choose an interfacing to suit the fabric and style of the garment so that a stiff, crisp finish or a softer, more casual collar can be made. Attach the interfacing to the wrong side of the outer collar band. Leave the collar facing without interfacing support. The interfaced piece will sit on the outside, providing a smoother finish.

2
Pin and sew the interfaced collar to its facing with right sides together. Trim and layer the seam allowances and notch any curves to reduce bulk and to allow the collar to lie flat when turned through.

3
Place the outer collar to the right side of the shirt yoke and pin on the neck edge. Sew on the seam line.

4
Turn the collar over and into position then pin the neck edge. Stitch in the ditch or edge stitch (see page 199) from the outside.

5
Place the neck facing or yoke over the collars with right side down, then pin and sew on the seam line. Trim and snip the seam allowances, then turn the neck facing to the inside.

Finished collar.

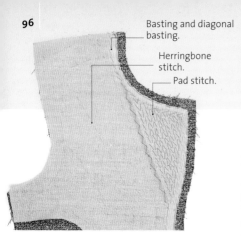

Basting and diagonal basting.

Herringbone stitch.

Pad stitch.

a. Coat-weight fusible.   b. Fine and sheer fusible.   c. Bonded fusible interfacing

Jacket collar

Traditionally, a collar on a tailored jacket or coat was sewn with the internal layers and held in place with countless hand stitches to create a sculptured, three-dimensional shape that would stand up to years of wear. Today, specially designed, fusible interfacings are applied to the inside to form the shape of, and to support, manufactured collars and lapels. Make your own jackets with these same specialist interfacings, or choose to use more traditional techniques if you prefer.

Traditional techniques

PAD STITCHING

Layers of interfacing and underlining are attached to the wrong side of a tailored garment with tiny diagonal stitches called pad stitches (see page 48). These hold the layers together and control the shape of the lapels and the under collar. Smaller pad stitches are sewn at the tip to control this point.

HERRINGBONE STITCHES

Herringbone stitch (see page 47) is used to secure linen stay tape to the fold line of the lapel to stabilize the crease. When positioned carefully, this ensures both lapels fold back at the same place and so are symmetrical.

BASTING AND DIAGONAL BASTING

Basting is used to hold a tape to the outer seam line of the jacket, and control the edges so that they keep their shape. Thin ribbon or organza selvage may be used as the materials are thin yet strong. Use basting on the seam line edge and diagonal basting on the other edge. Temporary basting is also used to hold the interfacing to the fabric during construction.

Modern interfacings

If you search hard you will be able to find some excellent fusible interfacings in various weights and degrees of stretch to suit the nature of the tailoring fabrics you are sewing with. When applied, these hold fast to the wrong side of your fabric and enhance the structure of your

finished garment to the extent that they can act as an internal coat hanger. These interfacings reduce the need for painstaking hand stitching, and cut down the time involved in making a jacket or coat. However, making a jacket using fusible interfacings still takes time to achieve a good finish you will be proud of.

FUSIBLE INTERFACINGS

These range in weight and stretch and should be chosen to create the effect required of the finished garment. A thick, coat-weight fabric will need a stronger interfacing (a), while a silk jacket will require something softer and thinner (b). Modern interfacings are knitted or woven so they move in a similar manner to the fabric they are adhered to. Older-style interfacings, made up of bonded fibers like paper, are stiffer and harsher, and control the garment rather than letting it flow or drape (c).

POSITIONING INTERFACING TO A JACKET

As well as deciding the type of interfacings to use to support the inside of a tailored collar, it is important to cut and place them appropriately. This extends into the body of the jacket so that the entire garment looks good across the shoulders and front. Instructions are not generally included for these interfacings in most commercial sewing patterns but the basic techniques can be applied to any jacket or coat pattern.

For full interfacing details, see page 97.

Medium-weight woven interfacing applied to front, extending into the shoulder to support the body of the jacket (1); ⅝-in. (1.5-cm) wide off-grain tape fused into seam allowance to control front lapel edge (2); ⅝-in. (1.5-cm) wide straight-grain tape fused to lapel fold line (3).

1. Medium-weight interfacing
2. Off-grain tape
3. Straight-grain tape

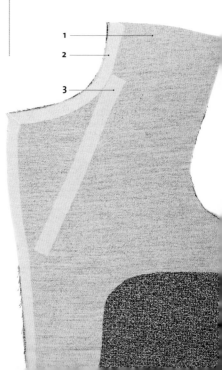

CLIP 4
Jacket collar part 1
http://qr.quartobooks.com/vgss/clip4.html

CLIP 5
Jacket collar part 2
http://qr.quartobooks.com/vgss/clip5.html

JACKET COLLAR

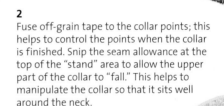

1

Cut interfacing for the under-collar pieces (on the bias) and fuse them to the wrong side of the under-collar pieces (also cut on the bias). Join them together at the center with a plain seam and press open. Cut a collar stand piece from interfacing (on the bias) and fuse to the lower edge of the under collar between the pattern marks. The stand interfacing supports this area and the bias cut of the two under-collar pieces allows the collar to be molded into shape.

2

Fuse off-grain tape to the collar points; this helps to control the points when the collar is finished. Snip the seam allowance at the top of the "stand" area to allow the upper part of the collar to "fall." This helps to manipulate the collar so that it sits well around the neck.

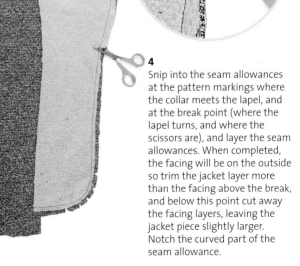

Break point.

3

Prepare the jacket front with interfacings and tapes as shown left, and fuse lightweight woven interfacing to the wrong side of the front facing. Place the facing on the jacket front and pin along the seam allowance from the pattern marking dot, where the collar and lapel meet, to the hem. Sew both front pieces.

4

Snip into the seam allowances at the pattern markings where the collar meets the lapel, and at the break point (where the lapel turns, and where the scissors are), and layer the seam allowances. When completed, the facing will be on the outside so trim the jacket layer more than the facing above the break, and below this point cut away the facing layers, leaving the jacket piece slightly larger. Notch the curved part of the seam allowance.

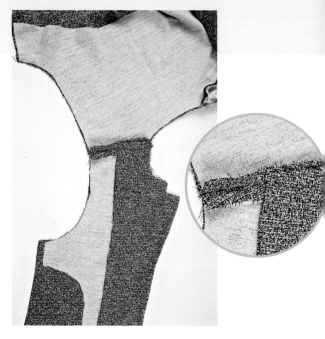

5
Turn through and press the front edges and lapels flat and with a crisp edge. Press the edge so that the seam is turned slightly to the underside to hide it. Make sure the seam allowance extends at the collar position where you snipped it so that the collar can be attached.

6
Iron an interfacing to the upper back of the jacket and join the front and back pieces together at the shoulder seams. Press these seams open.

7
Pin the under collar to the neck edge with the right sides together. (Snip the neck edge seam allowance to allow the two pieces to fit together easily.) Sew these together, starting and finishing at the facings.

8
Fuse a lightweight interfacing to the wrong side of the top collar piece. Place the upper collar to the under collar with right sides facing and pin. Sew the two collar layers together starting and finishing at the facings.

TIP
Make sure the pattern markings are made accurately and sew the collar and lapels exactly to the dots. It may be necessary to count the stitches so that both left and right sides match and will be symmetrical. Symmetry is essential for a professional-looking collar.

9
Layer the seam allowances, turn through, and press the collar flat. Place the collar over a tailor's ham or dress form and manipulate the collar into shape. Fold under the seam allowances of the top collar and facing, and slip baste where they meet.

10
Turn the slip-basted seam to the outside and machine stitch to produce a secure seam. Alternatively, sew the seam from the outside with tiny, strong ladder stitches.

11
Press the collar and lapels to form a crisp edge using a pressing cloth (not shown) to protect the surface of the fabric. Finish with edge and topstitching (see page 60) or choose stab stitching (see page 49) for a more traditional couture effect.

Finished collar.

Neck band

Adding a band is a good way to neaten the neckline of a casual garment like a T-shirt or sweatshirt, as it is a particularly useful way of finishing stretch knit fabrics.

Sew a folded band or rib to the neck edge of a stretch garment to neaten it without having to add an opening or a fastening as the band stretches so it can be pulled on or off. The depth of the band may be narrow—approximately ½ in. (1 cm)—or deep—2 in. (5 cm)—and folded down to form a turtle-style neck.

1
Sew the shoulder seams of the T-shirt and measure the neckline. Place your tape measure on its side for an accurate measurement of the seam line.

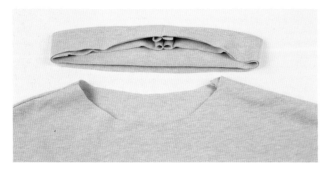

2
Cut a rectangle of the same fabric or of a ribbed fabric in the same or a contrasting color. It should be 80 percent or four-fifths of the neck measurement, and twice the depth plus seam allowances. Stitch the neck band into a circle and fold it in half with the wrong sides on the inside.

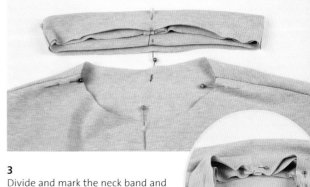

3
Divide and mark the neck band and the neck edge into quarters and match them with pins. Place the three raw edges level with the band on the right side of the garment. If you do not "quarter pin," the band will not be evenly sewn to the neck and there may be tucks at one side and a smooth finish at the other.

Pin the band to the neck edge in quarters.

5
When the band is sewn in place turn the seam allowances to the inside so that the band sits up at the neck.

A deep, folded-down neck band is attached by the same method.

4
Stitch the band to the neck edge, pulling to extend the band to the length of the neckline as you sew. Set the sewing machine to stretch stitch to sew on the neck band, or use a serger to stitch and neaten at the same time.

TIP
For an alternative finish, sew the facing to the inside of the neck edge and bring it to the outside as a feature. The faced edge is turned under and edge-stitched down to the garment. This is most effective when a contrasting color is chosen.

Faced neckline

A facing is the simplest way to neaten a neckline. Use it for all shapes of neckline: round, v-neck, sweetheart-shaped, or square.

A facing is a piece of fabric cut to the same shape as the neckline, sewn to the right side then turned through to the inside to hide all the raw edges. It provides a flat and fuss-free finish, but it must be cut and sewn accurately since it forms such a prominent part of a garment—symmetry is key. The facing is supported with interfacing to hold the shape of the neckline.

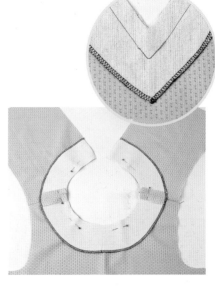

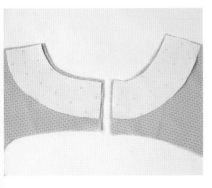

1
Cut the facing pattern shapes from fabric and interfacing. If a facing pattern is not supplied, make one following the shape of the neckline and approximately 2 ½ in. (6 cm) deep.

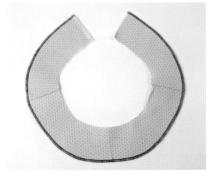

2
Fuse the interfacing to the wrong side of the pieces of the neck facing. Sew the shoulder seams together and press open. Neaten the outer edge with serging, zigzag stitching, or by tucking under a narrow edge and edge stitch in place.

3
Place the facing to the neckline with right sides together, matching the shoulder seams and pattern markings. Pin and sew on the seam line. Reduce the stitch length to ¹/₁₆ in. (2 mm) for a strong seam and reinforce the point if creating a v-neck.

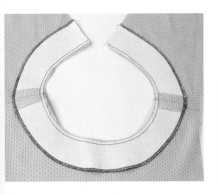

4
Trim and snip the seam allowances to allow the facing to turn through and produce a flat and smooth finish. For a flat finish, layer the seams so that the edge farthest from the front is shorter and the snips are alternated to reduce the chance of weakening the join. Hold the facing in place with under stitching or edge and topstitching (see page 60).

Finished faced neckline.

Plackets and cuffs

Cuffs finish the lower end of a sleeve. They generally have an outer layer (cuff) and an inner layer (facing) with interfacing sandwiched in between. They are normally sewn in place with a placket, which neatens the opening above the cuff so that you can slide your hand through.

Traditional tailored cuffs on a jacket or coat finish with a simple hem and a placket opening that is often buttoned down. A man's shirt is interfaced with a stiff interfacing to make it crisp, while casual shirts or blouses have a softer cuff, but both are constructed in a similar way. Other cuff styles include delicate frills or flounces or a simple stretch band.

Placket openings

Unless an elastic casing or a knitted-rib or band is made, some form of placket is needed to allow the sleeve to slip on and off and still fit snugly at the wrist. Three styles are shown here. Some are easier to sew than others and your choice may depend on the style of the garment you are making or the weight of fabric you have chosen.

FACED OPENING (EASY)

This is an easy method and best for a beginner to use. Working with a natural fiber such as cotton or silk will be easier to manage than a synthetic material like polyester.

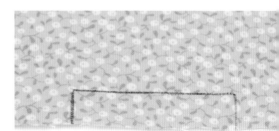

1
Cut a rectangle of fabric measuring approximately 1 in. (2.5 cm) longer and wider than the placket opening. The placket may be a slit or a box cut from the sleeve. Press under a ¼ in. (6 mm) hem to the wrong side on three sides.

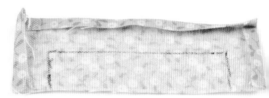

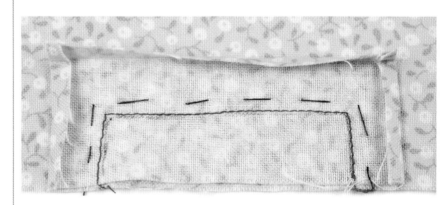

2
Place the right side of the placket to the right side of the sleeve over the marked opening. Baste together to hold the layers while you sew then shorten the stitch length (to make a stronger seam and strong corners). Follow the outline of the placket and stitch to the sleeve.

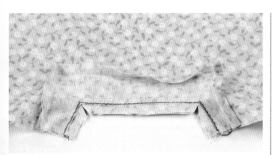

3
Cut into the placket corners and trim away excess fabric from the center to reduce bulk and produce a flat finish.

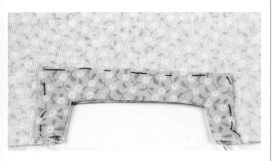

4
Turn through and press flat, then pin and/or baste the placket facing to the sleeve.

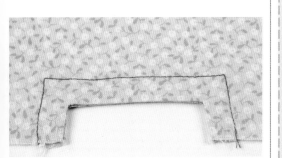

5
Topstitch from the right side of the sleeve, catching the folded hem of the placket facing on the inside to prevent it moving or twisting during wear. The placket is now ready for a cuff to be attached.

CONTINUOUS LAP (INTERMEDIATE)

This is a neat way to make a placket, but practice is needed to achieve the best finish. It is particularly difficult if the fabric frays badly. A fabric made from a natural fiber is easier to control than a springy and less manageable synthetic.

TIP
It is important to reinforce the top of the placket when you stitch it. Take a small horizontal stitch at the top of the opening and do not pivot the needle at the top to allow more space for turning and reinforce with a second line of stitching, over the first, at the top.

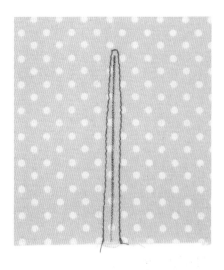

1
Mark the line of the placket and stitch to reinforce the opening before cutting into the sleeve. Shorten the stitch length to 16 spi (2 mm) and sew from the base to the point and back, tapering to a single horizontal stitch at the top.

2
Cut through the center of the opening, and up as close to the point as you dare without snipping any stitches.

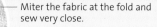

Miter the fabric at the fold and sew very close.

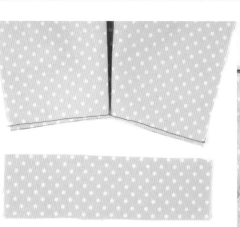

3
Open out the sleeve placket and cut a strip of fabric 1 ½ in. (4 cm) wide by the length of this opening.

4
Place the fabric strip to the opened placket with right sides together. Make sure the initial line of stitching lies in a straight line parallel to the edge of the strip and approximately ¼ in. (6 mm) away from it. Sew through the sleeve opening and the placket strip adjacent to the stitching.

5
Fold the placket strip edges to the wrong side of the sleeve and fold under. Pin to hold it in place.

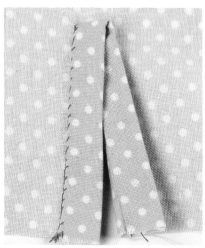

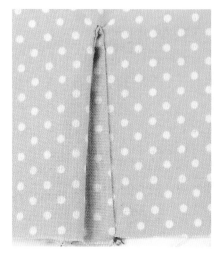

6
Hand stitch with hemming, or stitch in the ditch using a sewing machine, to hold the placket in place. You can now attach the cuff.

Reverse side of finished placket.

Right side of finished placket.

CLIP 6
Shirt placket
http://qr.quartobooks.com/vgss/clip6.html

TIPS
- If your commercial pattern does not include a pattern piece for a traditional shirt placket, dismantle a worn-out shirt and unpick the stitches. Iron it in place and make your own pattern using the fold lines to guide you.
- Make sure the plackets face the correct way with the opening and cuff toward the back of the sleeve.

SHIRT PLACKET (INTERMEDIATE TO ADVANCED)

Accurate measuring, stitching, and folding are necessary for a shirt placket, but it is worth the time spent on it for a great-looking placket and cuff finish.

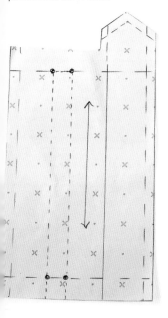

1
A traditional shirt pattern will have a placket pattern piece included in the envelope. Cut out the shirt placket piece and, with wrong side uppermost, fold the left and right hems in and the top corners down to form a triangle.

2
Place the right side of the facing over the placket position on the wrong side of the sleeve. Pin and sew around the stitching box. Cut through the center and close into the corners without snipping any stitches.

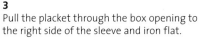

3
Pull the placket through the box opening to the right side of the sleeve and iron flat.

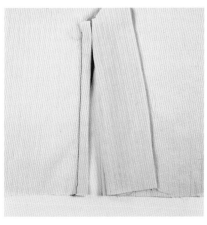

4
Press the short side of the placket over the raw edges and edge stitch in place. Press toward the opening.

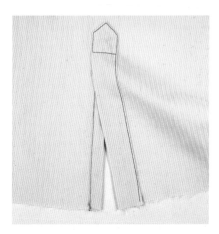

5
Fold the longer side into position, placing the triangular top over the opposite side. Press flat and topstitch in place. Now add your shirt cuff (see page 106).

CLIP 7
Shirt cuff
http://qr.quartobooks.com/vgss/clip7.html

Shirt cuffs

A standard shirt cuff has a button and buttonhole fastening, while a dress or French cuff is double with buttonholes to take cuff links rather than a sewn-on button. This means that the cuffs lie together rather than being lapped with one side over the other. For casual shirts and blouses, a softer interfacing is used on the inside.

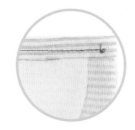

1
For each cuff, cut out a cuff piece of collar-and-cuff canvas interfacing in a suitable weight and remove the seam allowance on all sides. Cut a layer of fine, heat-adhesive interfacing the same size as the cuff and use this to hold the stiff interfacing in the center of the wrong side of the cuff. Use the iron to heat and fix the cuff interfacing in position.

2
Press the seam allowance on the top edge of the cuff over the stiff interfacing to the wrong side. Topstitch the cuff front.

3
Place the cuff to its facing with right sides together and the raw edges level. Sew on the seam line following the edge of the stiff interfacing. Stitch very close but not through the canvas, otherwise it will be difficult to turn through to the right side.

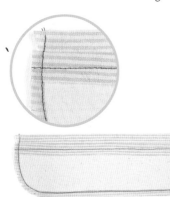

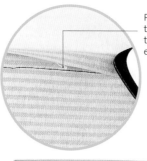

Press facing over the front cuff then tuck in for easier sewing.

4
Trim and layer the seam allowances and turn through so that the remaining seam allowances will sit behind the crisp interfacing and give a smooth finish on the front. Cut tiny notches at the curved ends and stagger them so that they do not weaken the seam.

5
Fold the facing seam allowance over the front of the cuff and press a crease with the iron. Now tuck the seam allowances inside the cuff. This makes it slightly longer than the cuff front, so that when it is edge stitched in place from the right side the facing will be caught easily by the stitching.

6
Mark the seam allowance on the lower sleeve edge and slide it into the cuff. Pin in place and edge stitch to hold the layers together. Add any other topstitching to suit the design and sew buttons (see page 86) and buttonholes (see page 88) in place.

Jacket sleeve hem finish

A jacket sleeve hem may be plain and straight, but often it has a vent. This is usually closed with buttons and buttonholes but these are normally just decorative and left uncut so they are not functional. Interfacing supports the hem and this can be applied traditionally with hand stitching, or ironed into place if you choose a fusible type.

1

Cut out the sleeve pieces. There is usually more than one section for this type of sleeve to improve the shape and follow the line of the arm. Cut out and apply interfacing on the lower edge and a placket extension on the sleeve.

2

Make up the sleeve, joining the panels together, but leave the placket seam unsewn. Press the seam open when completed.

3

Press up the hem along the lower edge and fold the placket into place. The vent, when finished, will face toward the back of the sleeve. Snip the seam allowances at hem level to encourage the hem to lie flat at the seam.

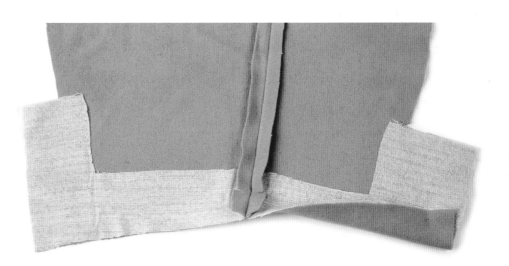

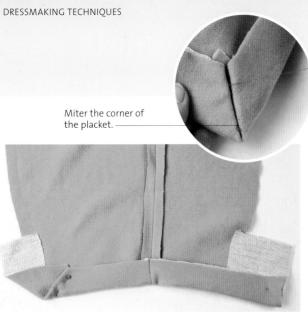

Miter the corner of the placket.

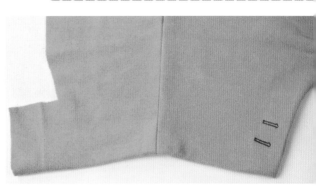

4
Press up the hem of the sleeve and miter the corner of the placket. To do this, fold in place and slip baste the diagonal seam, then turn to the inside and machine stitch over the slip basting. Remove the temporary stitches, trim, and turn to the right side.

5
Make the buttonholes but do not cut them open. Keyhole buttonholes are usually used for tailored jackets, but if you do not have this function on your sewing machine, a standard buttonhole with a bar at each end can be sewn and the button can be positioned carefully to cover one end. For hand-sewn buttonholes, see page 45.

6
Line up the seam with the raw edges level and lower hem in line. Pin then sew from the top of the placket to the armhole. Snip into the seam allowance where the stitching ends at the top of the placket, so that the vent can be folded toward the back of the sleeve, and the seam allowance can be pressed open.

Tubes of ribbing are available in limited colors.

Ribbing
Ready-made tube ribbing can be used to neaten cuffs. Cut a length twice the required depth of the cuff band and fold it so that the right side faces out. Attach the two raw edges of the folded rib to the right side of the base of the sleeve and stitch together as described above. Tubed ribbing is available in a limited range of colors so choose a contrast if you cannot find the exact shade.

7
Sew the buttons in position over the buttonholes, catching all the layers of fabric below. This keeps the plackets closed. This is purely a decorative cuff and the button fastening will not be used.

Stretch band cuff

A band or rib is the perfect way to finish the lower sleeve edge of a casual, stretch knit garment. The stretch in the cuff eases over the wrist without the need to add a placket. It is easy to construct whether you choose a contrast rib or the same fabric for the cuff.

Mark seam allowances.

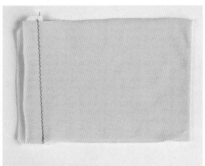

1
Cut out the sleeve and cut the cuff band to size: twice the depth of the finished cuff plus seam allowances by 80 percent or $\frac{4}{5}$ of the length of the lower sleeve edge.

2
Use tear-away stabilizer to prevent stretching the knitted fabric. Sew the sleeve seam and finish the raw edges—a serged seam is an ideal way to neaten stretch knit fabric as the stitches will move with the fabric when it is pulled and the threads will not break.

3
Sew the cuff band into a circle. Sew this seam with a sewing machine for a flat finish and use a stretch stitch with a tear-away stabilizer below to prevent the seam from stretching. Fold the cuff in half so that the raw edges are on the inside and the right side of the fabric faces out.

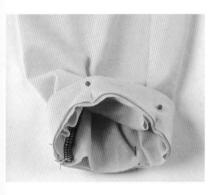

4
With the sleeve right side out, slide the sleeve inside the cuff, placing the raw edges level and the seams in line. Pin the three layers together at the four quarter points. The edges will not be the same length.

5
Using a serger or a stretch stitch on the sewing machine, sew the cuff to the sleeve, stretching the cuff to match the length of the sleeve in the process. Work a few inches at a time to make handling easier. Using this quarter pinning method means that the stretch will be evenly spread around the cuff.

6
Press the neatened seam allowances up into the sleeve when finished so that the cuff extends over the wrist.

Flounce or frilled cuff

A pretty way to finish the lower edge of a sleeve is to add a flounce or a frill. These differ in their construction—a flounce is cut as a circle with an opening and the smaller edge is sewn to the cuff, leaving a wide draped piece around the wrist. A frill is made from a long rectangle that is gathered on one side then attached to the sleeve. Both provide a feminine finish to a sleeve.

Snip into the seam allowance.

MAKING A FLOUNCE

1
Cut the flounce so that the curve or circle opening has the upper inside edge the same circumference as the sleeve it is to be attached to.

2
Snip into the curve of the seam allowance to allow the edge of the cuff to fit the lower sleeve edge then pin together on the seam line.

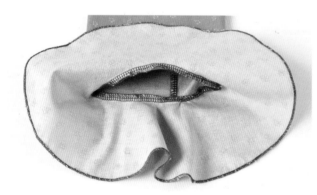

3
Sew the cuff to the sleeve with a sewing machine or a serger, and press the neatened seam allowance up toward the sleeve so that the flounce falls down over the hand. Neaten the lower hem of the flounce with a narrow, rolled finish (see page 65).

Finished flounce.

MAKING A FRILL

1

With right sides together, sew a seam to form a circle of cloth to make the frilled cuff. A French seam works well or use a narrow serged seam for a delicate finish. Neaten the lower edge with a narrow hem or add an edging lace for a pretty finish.

2

Set the sewing machine to the longest straight stitch and sew two rows of gathering at the top edge of the frill, either side of the stitching line. Pull up the gathering stitches so the top edge matches the circumference of the sleeve.

3

With right sides facing, place the gathered edge of the frill level with the sleeve edge. Match any seam allowances or pattern markings. Pin and sew the layers together on the seam line, then neaten with serging or zigzag stitching.

4

Press the neatened seam allowance up into the sleeve, allowing the frill to drape over the wrist.

Pockets

Pockets are a practical addition to any garment, and provide a handy space in which to carry our small belongings, but they are also a great opportunity to add detail and decoration to a piece of clothing, making it more interesting to look at.

If pockets are carefully cut and neatly sewn in place they will look great no matter whether they are big and obvious and stitched to the front with pleats or flaps, or discreetly inserted into seams. Follow the step-by-step guides and consider the tips for perfect pockets every time.

TIPS

- Cut pockets accurately, and if placed in pairs, make sure they are identical. Consider making a card template to help make two identically sized and shaped pockets.

- Use the correct seam allowances when making pockets. Cutting the pocket pieces out accurately then sewing inconsistent seam allowances will create matching and fitting problems when you make up the garment.

- Transfer pattern markings accurately using tailor's tacks, chalk, or a temporary marker pen. If the pockets are sewn in the wrong positions or very slightly askew, this will be glaringly obvious.

- Pin, baste, and sew pockets in position on single fabric pieces before constructing the entire garment. It is easier to sew them to a small piece of fabric than a large and heavy completed garment, with sleeves or legs getting in the way.

- When sewing with a patterned fabric (stripes, checks, or bold prints) cut and place pockets with care. Match the pattern where possible, or deliberately use diagonally positioned stripes and checks for effect.

- Before attaching a pocket or flap to a garment, apply a fusible interfacing to the wrong side of the fabric. This supports and stabilizes the fabric so that the pocket will not drag or pull away from the piece of clothing when filled.

- Stitch the top corners of pockets with strengthening triangles or bar tacks to prevent them from being pulled off the garment.

Pocket flaps

A simple pocket flap sewn to a garment (with or without an actual pocket beneath) adds detail to a piece of clothing. This may cover a patch or integrated pocket, or simply act as a mock-pocket effect for decoration. Careful positioning is essential, whether the pockets are functioning or fake, so take time to cut, make, and place them on your garment.

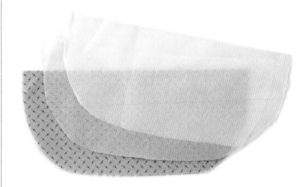

1
Cut a front pocket flap, with seam allowances included, from fabric, fusible interfacing, and lining. Fuse the interfacing to the wrong side of the fabric layer.

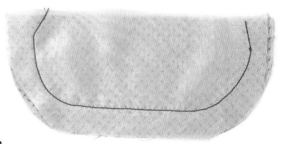

2
Place the right side of the pocket front to the right side of the lining and pin the outer edge, leaving the top edge free. Sew along the seam line of the flap, removing the pins in the process. Note that if you take a larger seam allowance at the top of the pocket—5/8 in. (1.5 cm) —this will be out of sight when the flap is stitched in place.

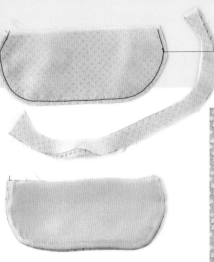

Trim away excess seam allowances.

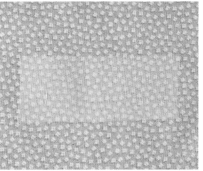

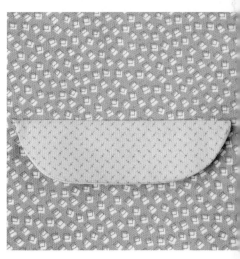

3
Trim the seam allowances to approximately ⅛ in. (3 mm). This eradicates the need to layer, snip, and notch the seam allowance. This is acceptable as it is a completely enclosed seam that will not receive wear and tear. Turn through and press the edges of the flap so they become flat and sharp.

4
Cut a rectangle of fusible interfacing and apply it to the wrong side of the garment where the pocket will be sewn. This will take the weight of the flap and provide support.

5
Press the seam allowance of the upper edge of the flap to the wrong side to form a crease, and place the upturned flap in position on the sewing line with right sides facing. Stitch across to hold it in place, securing the ends so that the flap will not pull off.

Zigzag over the cut edge.

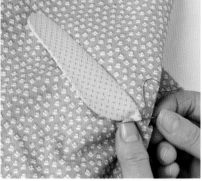

6
Trim the seam allowance to approximately ¼ in. (6 mm) and zigzag over the cut edge to hold it down. Note: The seam allowances do not extend beyond the flap if a larger seam allowance was taken in Step 2.

7
Thread a needle and sew a few stitches at each end of the flap to hold it to the garment and prevent it sticking out.

Finished pocket flap.

Patch pockets

A patch pocket is applied to the surface of a garment. It is generally edge stitched and/or topstitched to the garment and may or may not have a flap. It is the simplest type of pocket to create and can be sewn on at the start of construction or added later, if necessary.

1
Press a ¼ in. (6 mm) hem to the wrong side of the top edge of the pocket. Fold the fabric along the top crease of the pocket so that the right sides are facing and pin or baste, then sew the sides on the seam allowance. Remove pins or basting.

2
Trim away the excess seam allowance next to the stitching and turn through to produce two, neat, 90-degree top corners. Press flat.

Remove card template.

5
Slide the card out from beneath the gathers. Topstitch the upper hem in place, sewing from the right side and catching the edge of the hem below. Secure and neaten the threads at both ends by taking them to the wrong side and finishing into the back with a needle.

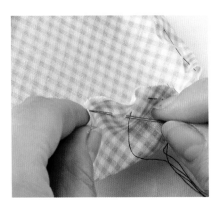

3
Hand sew a row of gathering stitches inside the seam allowance of the sides and lower pocket edges. Leave the thread tail loose and do not secure at this stage.

4
Make a card template of the finished pocket with the seam allowances removed. Slide this inside the folded top edge so that it fits snugly. Turn over and place on the ironing board. Press the raw edges over the card to shape the pocket sides and lower edge, pulling up the gathers to distribute the fullness.

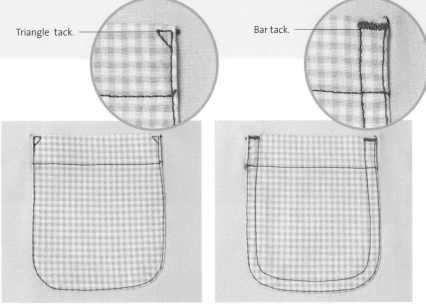

Triangle tack.

Bar tack.

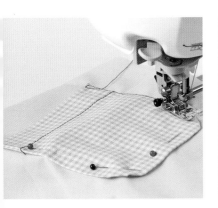

6
Place the pockets on the garment and pin or baste in position. Edge stitch and/or topstitch the pocket to secure it to the garment.

7
Sew triangles or bar tacks at the top corners for added strength. Take the thread ends to the wrong side and, with a needle, sew them in.

TIP
For jackets and coats, cut a piece of fusible interfacing just larger than the pocket and iron it onto the reverse of the fabric in the pocket position. Use a good-quality woven interfacing to give a light support that will not be visible from the right side. This is not necessary for lighter-weight cotton and polyester fabrics when making shirts and blouses.

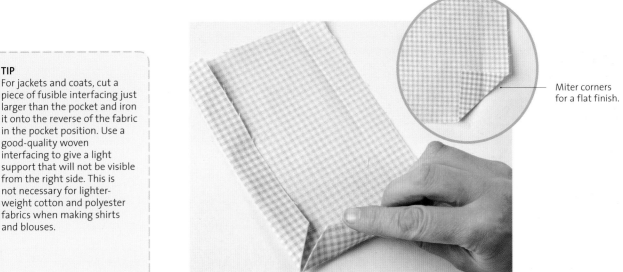

Miter corners for a flat finish.

If the bottom corners of a pocket are square, miter the seam allowances for a flat finish. Fold diagonally across the corner to the wrong side then fold each side to the middle.

Breast pockets

A well-crafted breast pocket, sewn onto a jacket, provides an extra special detail and gives a great finish. This type of pocket is a little like a flap (see page 112) but is sewn onto the garment on three sides in an upturned position. A faux effect can be produced, but adding an actual pocket bag in the process of construction is simple and makes it functional too.

1
Cut out the pieces to create the pocket. You will need to cut a rectangle of jacket fabric measuring twice the depth by the length of the finished pocket plus seam allowances, and interfacing for the band (half the above) and also for the jacket to support the pocket (slightly larger than the finished pocket). Lining will be required for the pocket bag—approximately 6 in. (15 cm) by 8 in. (20 cm).

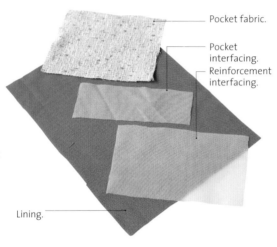

Pocket fabric.

Pocket interfacing.

Reinforcement interfacing.

Lining.

2
Apply the supporting fusible interfacing to the wrong side of the fabric where the pocket band will be sewn. Choose a light- or medium-weight interfacing that will not show through to the right side.

3
Fold the pocket band in half to create a crease. Apply the fusible interfacing to half the pocket band, up to the crease, on the wrong side. Iron it in place, with steam, for a strong hold.

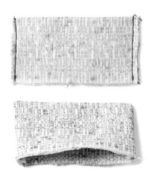

4
Fold the band at the crease, with right sides facing, and sew the short edges on the seam lines. Trim the seam allowances to approximately 1/8 in. (3 mm) then turn through and press, creating a crisp finish.

5
Place the prepared pocket band to the right side of the jacket between the positioning marks. The seam allowance and raw edge should extend above the line. Sew the band in place with a row of straight stitching and secure then ends neatly. Sew right to the end of the pocket band but not onto the jacket. Trim the seam allowance to 1/8 in. (3 mm).

Cut close into the corners. ——

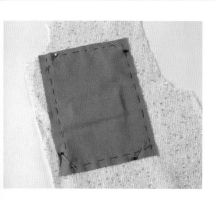

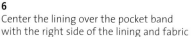

6
Center the lining over the pocket band with the right side of the lining and fabric together. Pin the outer corners of the lining to hold it in place and baste around the outer edge.

7
Turn the work over and sew exactly over the visible stitch line that holds the pocket band in place. Sew a second row of stitching ¼ in. (6 mm) above this, making it slightly shorter than the lower one. Feel for the trimmed band inside and do not catch it as you sew.

8
Cut the layers of fabric between the two rows of stitching. Snip close to the ends of the lower row of stitching to allow the band to sit flat. The interfacing will help to prevent the fabric from fraying when cut close to the stitches. Pull the lining through the opening. The lining will be on the inside of the jacket and the band on the outside.

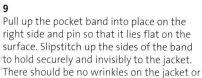

9
Pull up the pocket band into place on the right side and pin so that it lies flat on the surface. Slipstitch up the sides of the band to hold securely and invisibly to the jacket. There should be no wrinkles on the jacket or obvious stitches or threads on view.

10
On the inside of the jacket, level up the lining edges and sew together to produce a pocket bag. Neaten the raw edges with a serger or use a sewing machine and zigzag stitch.

Finished breast pocket.

CLIP 8
Welt pocket
http://qr.quartobooks.com/vgss/clip8.html

Welt pockets

A welt, or jetted, pocket looks a little like a large bound buttonhole with two neat, narrow bands bordering the pocket opening. This type of pocket offers a flat, formal finish to a tailored garment.

As with all pockets on tailored garments, an interfacing applied to the wrong side of the fabric in the pocket position adds support. A fusible interfacing is commonly used today, but a piece of linen is sewn in place to stabilize traditional tailored jackets and coats. The welts are created to edge the pocket and may be the same fabric as the garment or a contrast—a stripe, a check, or a satin weave are popular options. A lining is then added to produce the pocket bag.

1
Cut a piece of interfacing approximately 8 in. (20 cm) by 3 in. (7.5 cm). On the wrong side of the fabric where the pocket is to be sewn, fuse with an iron or hand-baste the interfacing in place.

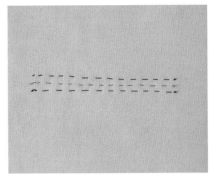

2
On the front of the jacket, mark the length of the pocket through the center with a line of basting. Mark two more lines on either side of the first, ¼ in. (6 mm) away from the center. Your basting stitches should be neat, straight, and visible from both the right and wrong sides. The pocket length will vary depending on the jacket design or whether it is intended for a woman or a man, but will range from approximately 4 ½ in. (11 cm) to 7 in. (17.5 cm).

3
Cut an 8 in. (20 cm) square of fabric on the cross or bias for the pocket welt. Place this over the pocket outline on the right side of the garment with the wrong side of the square facing up. Position the square so that two thirds of it sits above the center pocket line and one third below. Baste this to the garment on the outer edge to hold it still when machine stitching.

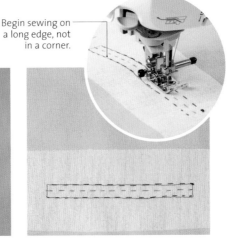

Begin sewing on a long edge, not in a corner.

4
Working from the inside of the garment, shorten the stitch length and sew a letterbox shape over the upper and lower basting lines and join them at the sides. Do not start in a corner as this is a weak point—instead, start and finish somewhere on a long edge, overlapping the first few stitches with the last ones for a secure join.

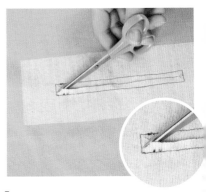

5
Cut through the center of the pocket opening and close into the corners without snipping the stitches. Cutting close to the corners will give flat and neat corners when the welt is completed. Remove all the basting threads.

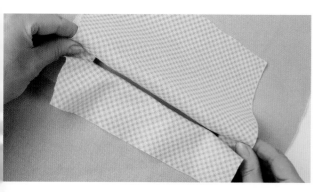

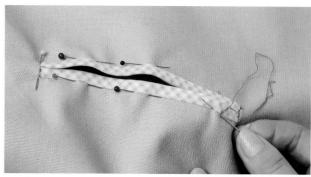

6
Pull the bias-cut welt through the opening to the wrong side. Tug at the short ends of the pocket opening and pin back, then carefully wrap the welts with the bias fabric and pin in the ditch. Adjust until a smooth finish is achieved.

7
Using hand-prick stitch or stab stitch (see page 49), hand sew through the ditch, catching the welt behind to keep the smooth appearance created in Step 6. Machine topstitching could be used for this step and would be stronger, but a neater finish is produced with hand stitching.

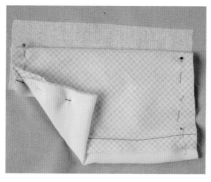

8
Cut a lining 8 in. (20 cm) wide by 7 in. (17.5 cm) deep. Join the upper and lower edges of the excess welt to the lining with right sides facing and sew them together.

9
Hold up the garment and allow the top edge of the welt to fall naturally into place. Pin and sew the sides of the pocket together to create an enclosed pocket bag.

10
Neaten the raw edges using whichever method you prefer.

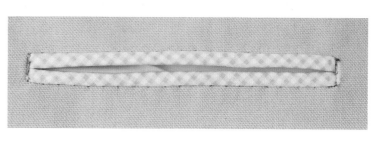

Finished pocket from the right side.

CLIP 9
Pants pocket
http://qr.quartobooks.com/vgss/clip9.html

Pants pockets

Pants and jeans often have front pockets that sit at an angle, or that are curved into the side seam just below the waist. The front opening edge of the pocket is cut off grain so it needs to be stabilized to prevent it from becoming stretched through wear. In pants, these pockets are generally functional, but in jeans, the shape of the pocket edge and added topstitch detail make them very much part of the design.

The front leg of the pants has the pocket cut into it and a separate part is added for the back pocket bag and to complete the front leg. They are joined by a front pocket bag piece and are then sewn together.

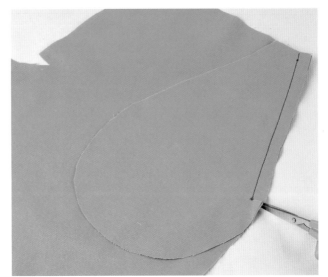

1
Sew the front pocket bag to the front of the pants with right sides facing. Match the pattern markings and sew accurately to the dot on the side seam, finishing the threads securely with reverse stitches. Do not sew beyond this into the side seam and make sure both front legs are identical to ensure symmetry. Snip into the seam allowance at the dot on both legs.

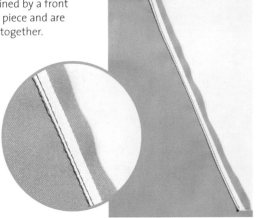

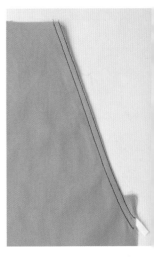

2
Place a narrow cotton or polyester tape to the seam just sewn. Pin it adjacent to the seam line inside the seam allowance and stitch close to the side of the tape nearest the seam. Sew through the seam allowances but not the front leg of the pants, and not beyond the dot and snip mentioned in Step 1.

3
Turn through and adjust the seam so that it sits slightly to the inside. Press flat and pull out the side seam at the base. Cut the excess tape but make sure it is long enough to be anchored into the side seam when it is sewn.

4
If topstitching and/or edge stitching are to feature in the design, sew the pocket edge now. This is popular on jeans or casual pants, but is not normally seen on tailored pants.

TIPS

- In Step 7 when sewing the side seam, make sure the stitching goes directly through the center of the base of the pocket. If you take a narrower seam allowance, fibers will be seen in the finished seam. Too large a seam allowance will result in the pocket being shorter.

- To reduce bulk, cut the front pocket bag from thinner lining fabric. Only the back of the pocket will be seen so this is cut from pants fabric.

- Stitch the tape to the pocket not the pants front, so that when turned through it is the farthest layer from the front and will not produce a ridge when pressed.

5
Place the prepared front pants leg over the back part of the pocket to complete the shape of the leg piece. Match up any pattern markings on the waist or side seam. At this stage it does not matter if the pocket bag pieces are not level on the inside, since the most important factor is ensuring the front lines up well and looks good. Secure the waist and side seam with pins or basting.

6
Lift up the front leg to reveal the pocket bag pieces below and pin them together. Sew the curved pocket outer edge from the waist to the side seam and neaten the raw edges with your preferred method.

Sew accurately at the pocket base to trap in seam.

7
Place the back leg to the prepared front leg with the right sides together and pin on the side seam. Sew on the seam line, catching the lower part of the pocket bag in the side seam in the process. Make sure you sew with an accurate seam allowance so that the stitching travels directly through the dot or pattern marking mentioned in Step 1.

Finished pocket.

Waists

A waist finish must fit well and be comfortable. It should anchor the garment in the correct position on the body, be wrinkle-free, and be neither too tight nor too loose. A strip or band is the most common way of neatening a waist on pants or skirts, but a facing or the addition of elastic are popular alternatives.

Finding your waist

Fashion plays a part in waist level and it may be low—sitting just above the hip—one season, and higher—closer to the rib cage—the next. However, knowing where your own waist sits naturally makes it easier for you to make clothes that look and feel good.

It is difficult for an onlooker to say where exactly your waist level is but you will instinctively place your hands on it if asked. For measuring, the best tip to follow is to tie a length of narrow elastic around your middle (see below). As well

as knowing where to measure your waist, all other measurements can be taken from this point, so making your own patterns or adapting commercial ones become easier tasks (see page 166).

You can also learn more about your own figure if you stand in front of a mirror. Here you can see whether your waist is parallel to the floor or whether it rises up at the front or back. This helps you to understand how to make level hems and adjustments that might be necessary to get a perfectly fitting and looking skirt or pair of pants.

Straight waistband

The most common method of neatening a waist edge is to add a folded strip to cover the raw edges. This strip is interfaced with a soft or a stiff layer, depending on the finish needed. For strength, the grain of the fabric runs around the body and the waist band extends beyond the waist length so that a suitable fastening can be incorporated on the underlap. The depth of the band may range from ½ in. (1 cm) to 2 in. (5 cm) and depends on the fashion of the moment and also personal choice.

There are different ways to construct a basic straight waistband, and you can sew the whole process on a sewing machine or finish it with hand stitching. Choose the method that suits you best.

TIP
You can find your waist by loosely tying a length of elastic around your middle—it will naturally rest at your waist. This is useful when you have a friend helping you take your measurements. It shows them where your waist is and gives a base line from which to take other measurements.

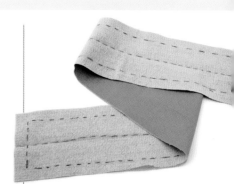

1
Cut the waistband to the correct length and depth with seam allowances and a 1 ¼ in. (3 cm) underlap added. Apply the interfacing to the wrong side of the strip. Fold the waistband in half and press a crease through the middle.

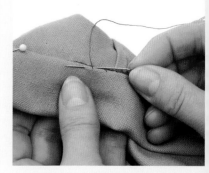

WAYS TO NEATEN A WAISTBAND.

To neaten the waistband by hand, tuck under the seam allowance along the inner edge of the waistband and fold at the level of the stitches. Use hand hemming (see page 59) and sew down the folded edge to the inside of the garment. Slipstitch the ends of the waistband.

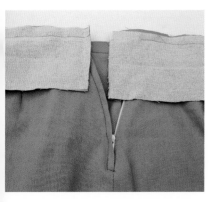

2
Position one long edge of the strip against the waist of the skirt or pants and match up any pattern markings at the seams if there are any. One end of the waistband should extend ⅝ in. (1.5 cm) and the other approximately 1 ¾ in. (4.5 cm for the underlap). Sew on the seam line.

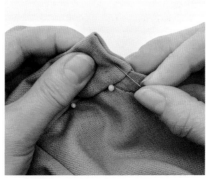

3
Bring the waistband over the raw edges, fold in the seam allowances on the end of the waistband that will lie flush with the opening, and pin to hold it in place.

4
Fold in the seam allowances at the extension end of the waistband and pin this too. Trim away any bulk from the seam allowances on the inside for a flatter finish.

To neaten the edge with a sewing machine, tuck under the seam allowance along the inner edge of the waistband so that the fold sits over the stitching then turn over and pin in the ditch from the right side.

With a straight stitch and using a zipper foot, stitch in the ditch at the base of the waistband, catching the fold on the inside. Edge stitch the waistband ends.

Neaten the raw edge of the waistband with a serger and place it flat against the inside of the garment. Turn the work over and stitch in the ditch to hold in place.

CLIP 10
Firm waistband
http://qr.quartobooks.com/vgss/clip10.html

Firm waistband

Use a firm interfacing to retain the shape of a waistband, preventing it from creasing without making it uncomfortable to wear. The stiff interfacing is sewn directly behind the front of the band so that any ridges formed by the trimmed seam allowances are hidden. Use belt backing or petersham and the technique suggested here for a stiff finish. The permanently smooth band will not crease and crinkle when it is worn and keeps a garment looking smart.

1
Construct the garment—a skirt is shown here—with zip and seams, and add a lining if your skirt needs one. Prepare the waistband, adding a 1 1/4 in. (3 cm) underlap for the fastening and 5/8 in. (1.5 cm) seam allowances on all edges.

2
Place the right side of the waistband strip to the right side of the skirt, matching the waist edges. Leave 5/8 in. (1.5 cm) extension on the flush end and 1 3/4 in. (4.5 cm) on the underlap end. Pin and sew on the seam line.

3
Lap the stiff waistband interfacing over the seam allowances on the side closest to the band (not the skirt). Place the edge adjacent to the stitch line and sew the interfacing to the seam allowances close to the edge.

4
Trim the seam allowances behind the interfacing and cut the ends of the interfacing to the correct length at each end.

5
Fold the waistband fabric over and around the stiff interfacing and tuck the seam allowances inside to conceal them. Manipulate the fabric to create a smooth finish and pin to hold it in place.

6
Slipstitch both ends of the band with tiny stitches to neaten and secure the waistband. The stiff interfacing gives a crisp edge when the fabric is pulled over it.

7
Move the pins to the right side and place them in the ditch below the waistband, making sure they catch the fold of fabric behind the band. Fit a zipper foot to the sewing machine and stitch in the ditch to hold all the layers together.

9
Sew hooks and eyes to the ends to fasten the waistband as the stiff interfacing will be too harsh to sew a buttonhole in it. If you want a button finish, sew a decorative button on the top with functional hooks and eyes underneath.

8
Alternatively, hand sew the back of the waistband in place.

Finished firm waistband.

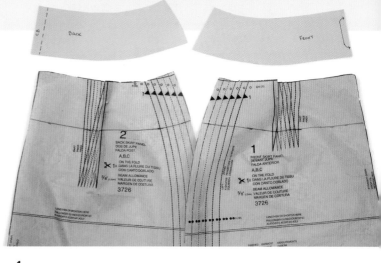

Faced waistband

A faced finish at a waist is smooth and comfortable to wear. The completed facing follows the shape of the figure over the waist and upper hip and sits on the inside of the skirt. It conceals the raw edges, creating a neat finish, and forms a comfortable waist finish.

If a commercial pattern does not have a faced waistband finish, it is easy to adapt a pattern with a waistband and make your own facing. When creating a facing, the darts are removed and this reduces bulk at the waistline.

1
Make your own facing pattern using the front and back pattern pieces. Draw a line approximately 3 in. (7.5 cm) below the top edge of the skirt pattern (front and back). Fold out the darts and trace off this curved band, transferring any important information, e.g., place to a front fold or straight grain.

2
Cut out the facing pieces in fabric and fusible interfacing and iron the interfacing to the wrong side of the fabric. This adds support to the waist facing. Join the parts to form the complete facing and neaten the lower edge with three-thread serging, or use a binding (see page 66) or Hong Kong finish (see page 218).

3
Place the facing to the waist of the skirt with right sides together and match up the seams. Pin on the seam line then sew the two layers together.

4
Position a narrow ribbon or tape on the seam allowance adjacent to the seam line to stabilize the waist edge of the skirt. Sew close to the seam line through the allowances and not through the skirt. Sewing the tape separately in this way is less bulky than sewing it at the same time as the waist seam, meaning that it lies flat on the inside.

5
Trim the seam allowances, grading the layers for a flatter finish. For the smoothest finish, trim the seam allowance farthest from the front the most.

6
Turn the facing to the inside and under stitch the facing to the seam allowances. This helps to keep the facing on the inside and prevents it rolling to the outside.

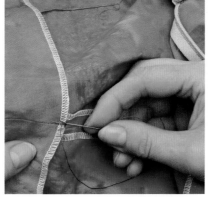

7
Turn under the seam allowances at the ends of the facing next to the zipper opening. Sew this to the zipper tape with some hand slipstitches to control the ends and prevent them catching in the zipper teeth.

8
Catch a few hand stitches at the seam allowances and darts to hold the facing in place. This stops it moving around during wear.

Finished waist facing.

Elastic casing waistband

Historically, simple garments were held at the waist with a belt, or a length of cord/lace was threaded through a stitched-down casing. When the first elastics were developed, these were fed through the casing and improved the comfort of skirts and pants. Today, we have high-performance stretch tapes made from elastic and spandex, and these are generally attached directly to the edges of garments to keep them in place comfortably. As well as waists, directly applied elastic is an ideal technique for finishing legs, armholes, and necklines where elastic is used for sportswear, swimwear, and lingerie.

In factories today, elastic is most often sewn to the fabric edge, but making a casing is still a popular method used at home, mainly because it can be more easily adjusted to fit the wearer. A waist finished with an elastic casing is ideal for children's clothing as the elastic can be adjusted to suit the child as he or she grows. It forms a comfortable edge and may be a single casing or made up of three or four channels for a wider finish.

1
Prepare the garment and press under a 1/4 in. (6 mm) turn to the wrong side on the waist edge. Press over again to create a casing. The casing should be just wider than the elastic but not too wide as this will allow the elastic to twist during wear.

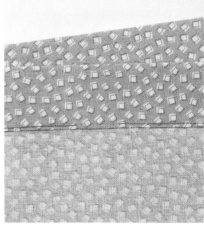

2
Pin or baste according to your preference then edge stitch the casing in place. Stop stitching 1 in. (2.5 cm) before you reach your starting point.

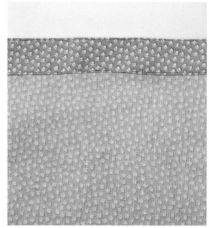

3
Edge stitch the top of the waist all the way around. This helps to give a flat finish and prevents the elastic from twisting.

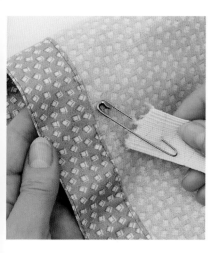

4
Tie a length of elastic around the waist to establish a comfortable fit. Add ½ in. (1 cm) excess and cut this length. With a safety pin attached to one end, place the elastic into the gap left in the stitching and feed it all the way through the casing.

5
Secure the two ends with some machine stitching or a few hand stitches sewn with a double thread.

6
Return the skirt to the sewing machine and sew up the gap with edge stitching.

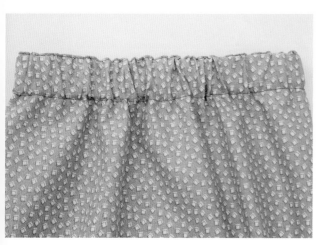

Finished waistband.

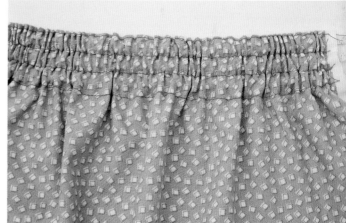

ALTERNATIVE
For a broad finish using narrow elastic, make a large casing and divide it into narrow channels. Feed the elastic through each of these.

CLIP 11
Attached elastic
http://qr.quartobooks.com/vgss/clip11.html

Sewing elastic to an edge

This technique used to attach elastic in a factory can be replicated at home to give clothing a manufactured finish. With a bit of practice, it is a quick and easy process, giving a neat finish.

The elastic is generally applied using the "quarter pinning method," where fabric and elastic are divided into four, matched up, pulled, and then sewn. This distributes the tucks evenly.

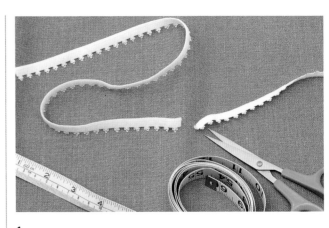

1
Sew up the seams to create the main part of the skirt. This may be a simple tube or an A-line shape.

Measure your waist and calculate 80 percent of this. Cut the elastic to this length. This may seem tighter than necessary, but the process of stitching the elastic to the fabric will extend it.

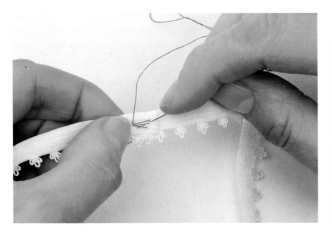

2
Make the elastic into a circle by lapping the edges and stitching them together either by hand or machine. This produces a flatter waist finish that is more comfortable to wear.

3
Divide both the elastic and the skirt waist into four equal sections with pins. Match up the quarters and pin the elastic to the waist with the wrong side of the elastic to the right side of the skirt. The fancy edge of the elastic (if there is one) will face into the garment and the straight edge will be level with the raw skirt waist.

4

Set the sewing machine to a three-step zigzag stitch and extend the stitch length. Set the width of the stitch to the width of the elastic (not including the pretty edge). Lower the needle into the waist at one of the pin positions. Stitch two or three stitches to anchor the threads then pull the elastic flat to match the fabric. With your left hand, hold the fabric behind the presser foot and place a finger of your right hand 3 in. (7.5 cm) in front of the needle, holding the elastic to the fabric, and sew a short length. Continue to sew in this way all around the waist, sewing a small amount at a time.

5

Fold the elastic to the wrong side, letting the fancy edge sit up just above the waist. Hold the fabric in this way under the presser foot with the right side of the skirt facing upward. Stitch a new row of zigzag stitches, pulling the elastic flat as you sew. This holds the elastic flat.

6

The finished waist is suitable for a lightweight fabric and is great for petticoats or waist slips.

TIPS

• When positioning the elastic to the waist, do not place the lapped ends on a seam as this will be very bulky.

• Extend the length of the three-step zigzag so that when the elastic relaxes, after it is sewn, the stitch shrinks to a standard length. If it is sewn at a standard length, the zigzags will be very close together when finished.

• Overstretching the elastic while you zigzag will result in unsightly rippling and the finished edge will be bigger than required.

• You can stretch the elastic as you go without quarter pinning in advance, but you may find you get an irregular finish with the tucks bunched in one area and flat areas elsewhere. Quarter pinning ensures an even arrangement of gathers.

Carriers and loops

Waist details are important for comfort and to keep garments looking good. Carriers allow a belt to be held in place, and may be purely functional or add style too, while hanging loops make it easier to care for a skirt by providing a way to hold it on a hanger.

BELT CARRIERS

Carefully spaced loops are often sewn to the waistband of pants to hold a belt in place. Make them up and sew them into the seam when joining the waistband to the body of the pants and finish them securely at the top edge. There are usually five, equally spaced belt carriers sewn to a waistband—two at the front, two on the back close to the side seams, and one at the center back. These may be simple ¹/₂-in. (1-cm) wide loops or wider strips. They may even be narrow and made up in pairs depending on the designer's inspiration.

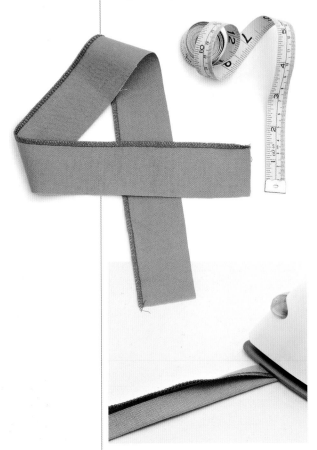

1
For five standard belt carriers, cut a strip of fabric (following the grain) approximately 1 ¹/₂ in. (4 cm) wide by 20 in. (50 cm) long. Neaten one long edge with serging or zigzag stitching.

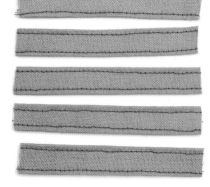

2
Using an iron to help fold the strip into three, tuck the raw edge into the crease with the neatened edge on the outside. Sew from the right side and edge stitch or topstitch down both sides of the folded strip, trapping the layers together.

3
Cut the strip into five equal pieces. You can adjust the length later and trim and sew to a perfect size.

4
Pin the waistband to the top edge of the pants and slide the five short strips into place. Make sure there is one trapped at the center-back seam and two placed symmetrically on the front. The remaining two must be placed between the front ones and the center back.

5
Now sew the waistband in place and catch the carriers between the garment and the waistband.

6
Complete the waistband construction then fold up each carrier to meet the top edge of the waistband. Tuck under the raw edge and sew through all the layers to hold it in place. Use a strong, size 14 needle or a jeans needle and a slow speed for best results. If there is any excess loop end, trim this away.

Finished carrier.

ALTERNATIVE METHOD
Make up the waistband and anchor the carriers to the top edge and the body of the pants. This may make construction easier but the belt carriers may pull off the single layer of fabric it is attached to and possibly rip the cloth.

HANGING LOOPS

It is important that loops are sewn to the waist of a skirt so that it can hang on a coat hanger and not become creased. These may be made from ribbon or woven tape, or you can sew strips from the remaining skirt fabric, although they may be quite thick.

CONCEALED HANGING LOOPS

Standard hanging loops have a tendency to flip out and be seen, so a clever alternative is to place them horizontally. This way when you are wearing the skirt they lie flat against the inside of the waistband, but they sit up and over a coat hanger when in the wardrobe. This method cannot be used when a skirt has a side fastening.

1
Buy a suitable color of ¼ in. (6 mm) tape or ribbon. You will need approximately two 10 in. (25 cm) lengths.

1
Cut a 6 in. (15 cm) length of narrow ribbon or tape and center over the side seam. Tuck under ¼ in. (6 mm) at both ends.

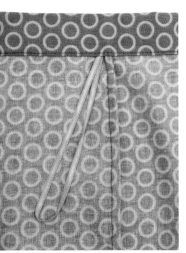

2
When neatening the inside of the waistband, either by stitching in the ditch by hand or machine, trap the cut ends in the seam allowance and sew securely in place.

2
Hand sew through the fold into the waistband below to secure each end.

3
Pull the loop up above the waist to hang the skirt from a coat hanger.

3
Lift the skirt by the loops and slide onto a coat hanger.

CLIP 12
Dress yoke
http://qr.quartobooks.com/vgss/clip12.html

Yokes

The yoke is the part of a garment that sits across the shoulders and upper back and joins the front and back pieces. Use it instead of shoulder seams when an alternative style is required.

A yoke is occasionally made from a single piece of fabric, but more often, two layers (a yoke and a facing) are used and they are sewn in a way that traps and conceals the raw seam allowances. This provides a smoother and better-looking finish.

Choose a contrast fabric for the yoke or just the yoke facing, or use bias-cut fabric when working with stripes or checks for a more interesting design. Alternatively, embellish the yoke with tucks, beads, or embroidery for added detail.

The term yoke refers to the upper, supporting part of a garment that holds a lower part; for example, at the waist and hip of pants or across the shoulder of a shirt.

Traditionally, the yoke facing was secured in place with hand stitching but this is never seen in manufactured clothing today. This method shows a simple way to construct a yoke with machine stitching only, eradicating the need for any hand sewing at all.

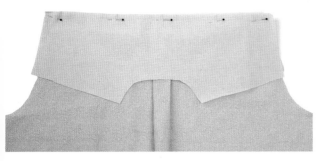

1
Having cut out the fronts, back, and yoke pieces, place the right side of the yoke to the right side of the back. Form any tucks or pleats in the back if required. Pin the two layers together.

2
Place the right side of the yoke facing to the wrong side of the back, removing and replacing the pins to catch all three layers. Sew on the seam line to hold the layers together.

3
Layer, or grade, the edges so that the seam allowance next to the facing is shortest. This produces a smoother line with no obvious ridge visible from the outside.

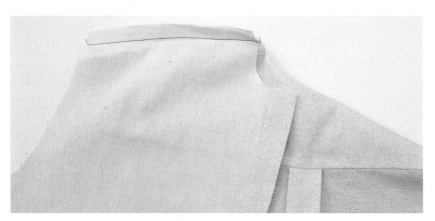

4
Sew the front pieces of the garment to the front edge of the yoke with right sides together. Make sure you have the center fronts in the middle and the armholes on the outer edge.

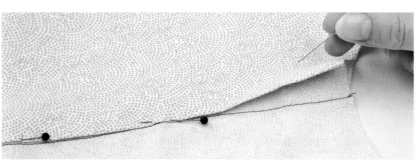

5
Take the yoke facing and fold under a ⅝ in. (1.5 cm) edge to the wrong side on the free edge. Pin this to the line of stitching just sewn on the inside of the garment. Place the pins close to the fold.

6
Working on one front yoke seam at a time, pull the facing through the yoke (6a) so the wrong side is on the outside and transfer the pins to the sewing line, grabbing only the seam allowances (6b). Working almost within the garment, sew along the pin line, removing the pins as you go (6c). Follow the existing row of stitching (6d).

6a

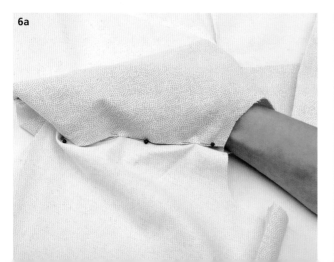

6b

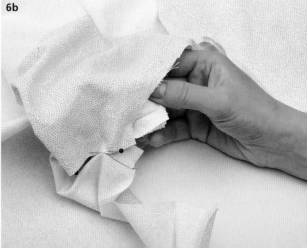

6c

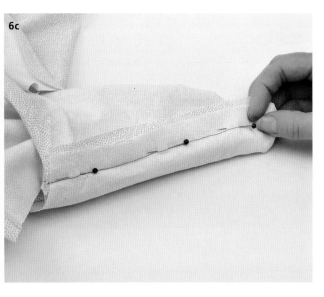

6d

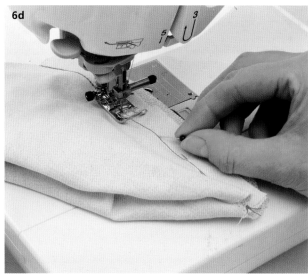

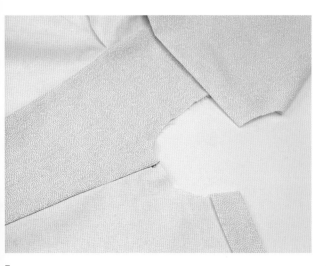

7
Trim and layer the seam allowances as you did with the back and turn the facing to the outside again. Press it flat and repeat with the other side.

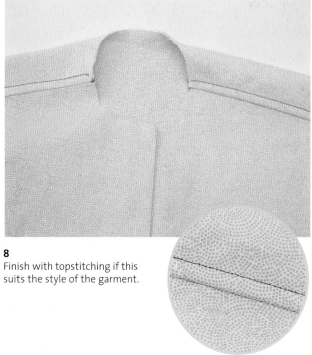

8
Finish with topstitching if this suits the style of the garment.

Setting in sleeves

Sometimes inserting sleeves can be difficult, but with the correct handling skills, and a few tips and hints, you can set in sleeves with ease.

Clever pattern drafting enables a two-dimensional piece of fabric to be cut and shaped to produce a three-dimensional shoulder that fits closely to your body while allowing you to move. Knowing how the shape is achieved can help you to sew it in neatly and easily.

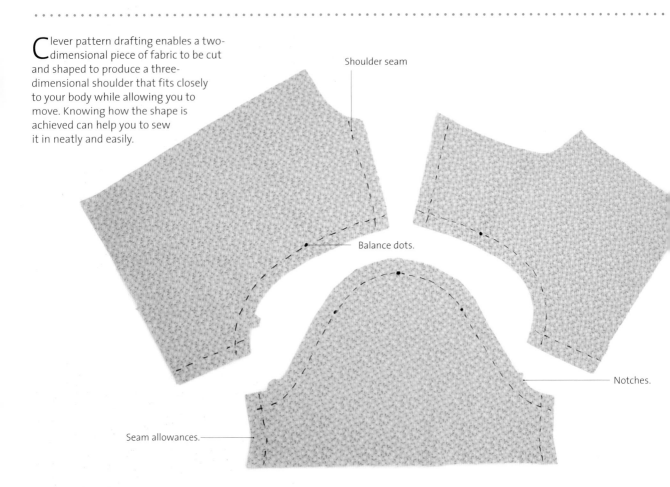

Shoulder seam

Balance dots.

Notches.

Seam allowances.

To create a pattern that fits well, the front and back armhole pieces are drawn before the sleeve is drafted over it. Points are marked and distances measured to make sure that the finished sleeve will fit the armhole perfectly. Only after the bodice and sleeve pattern pieces have been drafted are the seam allowances added. This means that although the outer edges do not appear to match or fit the seam lines you are working with, they will do. If you remember that you are following the seam line rather than the outside edge, you will find setting in sleeves a much easier task.

Sleeve styles vary but the head (or cap) of the sleeve must be reduced in size to fit the shape of the armhole. This is generally achieved with gathering stitches, but pleats (see page 144), tucks (see page 149), or darts (see page 68) are sometimes used. The gathering stitches may ease a small amount of fullness into the shoulder for a smooth, tuck-free finish, or a larger amount to produce a fuller, more puffy effect. This will depend on the style required and the pattern pieces will have been cut accordingly.

Gathered sleeve

This is the easiest type of sleeve to insert and is perfect for beginners—the only tricky part is managing to distribute the gathers evenly.

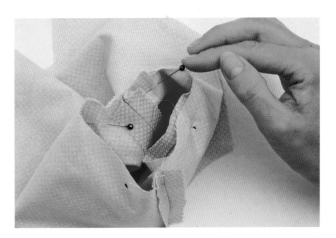

1

Cut out the pattern pieces in fabric. Sew two rows of machine gathering stitch (longest straight stitch) around the top curve of the sleeve between the notches. These should be placed at either side of the seam line and are best sewn with the right side of the fabric facing. This makes it easier to pull up the gathers from the wrong side later.

2

Make up the bodice and sleeves, neatening the seams in your preferred way. Make sure you have transferred the important pattern markings on the sleeve and armhole so that they can be matched.

3

Slide the sleeve into the armhole with the right sides facing and pin the underarm seams together.

4

Working from the inside, pin the sleeve to the bodice between the notches in the lower part of the armhole. Place the pins parallel to the seam line.

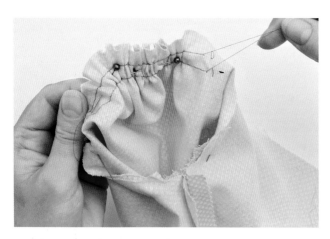

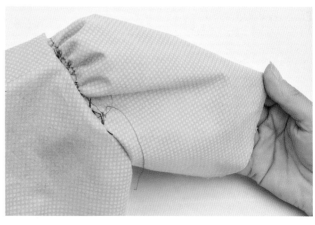

5
Pull up the gathers in the upper part of the sleeve by pulling the tails on the wrong side of the fabric. Match them to the size of the armhole and spread them evenly across the top of the shoulder. Hold them in place with a row of pins on the seam line.

6
Turn the sleeve to the right side (you can do this since the pins are making a temporary seam) and check that the gathers are evenly distributed and in the right place at the head of the sleeve.

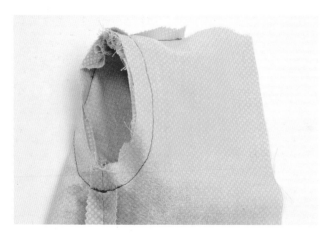

7
Adjust the gathers if necessary then stitch on the seam line (removing the pins as you sew) to join the sleeve to the bodice. Remove the basting stitches and tailor's tacks.

Finished gathered sleeve.

Eased-in sleeve head

A smooth, tuck-free shoulder is made with the same temporary gathering stitches as the gathered sleeve head (see page 139) but the sleeve head is smaller and cut to fit the armhole with no extra fullness. This means the gathers just ease in any excess fabric for a smooth finish.

1
Cut out all the pieces in fabric for the garment. Sew two rows of machine gathering, each ¼ in. (6 mm) either side of the sewing line, across the sleeve head. Sew from the right side and pull up the gathers from the wrong side for best results.

2
Construct the bodice and sleeves. Make sure the pattern marking dots and notches are marked so that the parts will go together correctly.

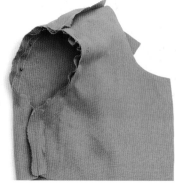

3
Insert the sleeve into the armhole and match up the seams and main balance points with pins. By pulling the tails on the wrong side of the fabric, ease up the gathers at the head of the sleeve very slightly so that it curves and fits into the armhole. Pin on the seam line.

4
Sew on the pinned line, removing the pins as you reach them. It can help to sew with the needle on the left (not the center) so that the foot flattens to the seam allowance and controls it while you sew.

5
Neaten the raw edges and press into the sleeve (away from the bodice). This helps to support the head of the sleeve and gives a good smooth shape.

Finished eased-in sleeve.

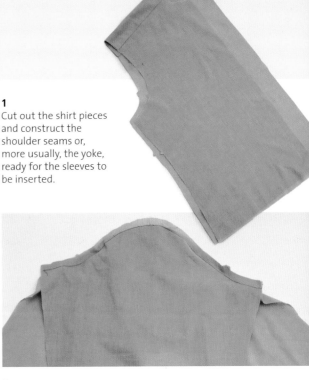

Shirt sleeve

A traditional shirt sleeve is sewn into the armhole flat before the side and sleeve seams are joined. As well as being constructed in a different order, flat-fell seams (see page 51) are used rather than plain seams. This finishes off the raw edges beautifully and creates a smooth finish throughout the garment.

1
Cut out the shirt pieces and construct the shoulder seams or, more usually, the yoke, ready for the sleeves to be inserted.

2
Take the appropriate sleeve (right or left) and place to the open armhole with right sides together and raw edges level. Match up the single and double notches and pin on the seam line.

3
Sew the sleeve to the armhole and remove the pins.

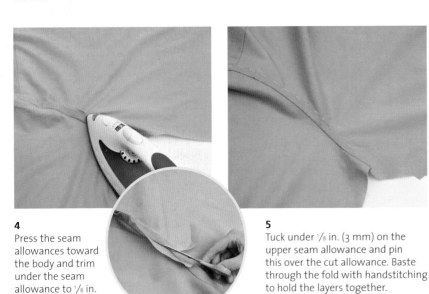

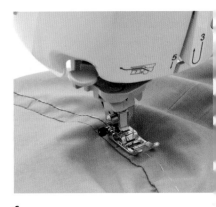

4
Press the seam allowances toward the body and trim under the seam allowance to ⅛ in. (3 mm).

5
Tuck under ⅛ in. (3 mm) on the upper seam allowance and pin this over the cut allowance. Baste through the fold with handstitching to hold the layers together.

6
Turn the shirt over and topstitch the seam from the right side. Use the basting as a guide to ensure you catch the fold underneath. Remove the basting threads.

TIP
If you do not feel comfortable making flat fell seams try the mock jeans seam (see page 52) as this is a little easier but creates a similar effect on the outside.

7
With wrong sides together, match up the side and sleeve seams, making sure the underarm seams are together. Pin on the seam line then sew the two layers together. Sew with the front uppermost as this line of stitching will be on show when the seam is completed.

8
Press the seam allowances toward the back of the shirt and trim the under seam allowance (shirt back) to 1/8 in. (3 mm).

9
Tuck under 1/4 in. (6 mm) on the upper seam allowance and pin this over the cut allowance. Topstitch close to the fold and sew through the layers below. Take care that you only stitch the seam when sewing into the narrow part of the sleeve. Remove the pins as you reach them, and sew a small part at a time.

The sleeve is now ready for a cuff to be added (see page 106). This will complete the shirt construction.

Pleats

Pleats are folds of fabric incorporated into clothing to add style, but they also create fullness and allow more movement. They may be crisp and sharp, or softly draping, depending on the fabrics used to make them. They may also be loose, partially stitched, or fully stitched, creating different textured effects and styles.

Accurate measuring and marking are essential, especially if the pleats are grouped or repeated in a garment. Choose them for tailored skirts, pockets, sleeve heads, and the backs of shirts.

TIPS

- Follow the grain line when cutting out fabric pieces so that the pleats lie exactly on the grain of the weave. If they are slightly off the grain they will not hang straight.

- Measure and mark the pleat positions and lengths accurately, again following the grain.

- For crisp pleats, press with steam and a pressing cloth to protect the surface of the fabric and prevent ridges.

- Cut a length of thin card into narrow strips and place these inside the pleats when you press them with the iron. This prevents any unsightly shiny lines forming on the surface due to ridges underneath.

- Consider edge stitching the folds of pleats to keep them sharp.

- Use beeswax or soap to help keep the pleat folds in place. Press the fold then open up the fabric and slide the beeswax or soap over the crease on the wrong side of the fabric. Press again to "stick" the fold. Repeat every four or five washes.

Knife pleats

These pleats all lie in the same direction and are often grouped to create a textured effect as well as to control the fullness of the fabric in a practical way. They may be soft folds or sharp creases, but they are made in the same way.

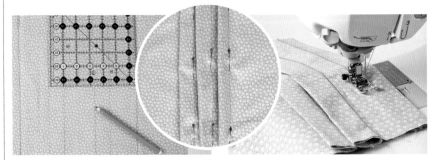

1
Mark the size and position of each pleat on the wrong side of the fabric. Use temporary marker pen, tailor's chalk, or basting. Match the pattern markings and pin the pleats with right sides together.

2
Using the longest sewing-machine straight stitch, baste the fold line of each pleat. Do not secure the thread ends as these are only temporary stitches.

3
Press the stitched pleats in one direction to form creases on both sides. Check that there are no wrinkles and the pleats lie in neat folds across the fabric.

4
Continue with the construction of the garment and when the top of the pleats are held in place with a seam, a waistband or a yoke, remove the temporary machine basting.

Inverted pleats

Inverted pleats are created by two equal folds of fabric that face each other. They may be held at the top as with the back of a shirt where the yoke controls them, or they may be stitched part of the way, releasing the fullness at the bottom—this is often seen in a tailored skirt where the pleat is released to give stride room.

End stitching here.

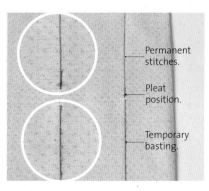

Permanent stitches.

Pleat position.

Temporary basting.

1
Mark the pleat positions and their length with temporary pen, chalk, or tailor's tacks. Do this on the wrong side of the fabric so that they are easily seen when working.

2
Fold the fabric with right sides together to form the pleat. Carefully match the pattern markings so that the pleat will lie flat and even. Pin then sew on the stitch line, securing the ends of the threads with a reverse stitch to prevent the pleat from opening up. Remove the pins as you reach them.

3
Increase the stitch length to maximum and sew from the base of the pleat to the hem, but do not fasten the threads at the ends as these are only temporary stitches.

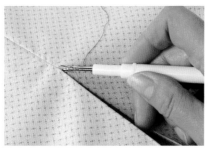

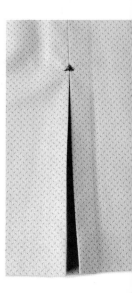

4
Open the pleat and match up the seam with the center fold. Work on an ironing board, and with the pleat on the underside, arrange the seam directly over it along its length. Press the pleat to flatten the folds.

5
Baste across the top of the pleat and remove the temporary machine basting to release the pleat.

6
On a skirt, sew a triangular tack at the base of the pleat where the fullness is released. This strengthens a potentially weak area of the garment. Use embroidery thread and create a decorative triangle with stitching.

Box pleats

A box pleat is a reversed inverted pleat. The two folds of fabric face away from each other to produce a broad vertical pleat that sits on the surface of a garment. Use it on the back of a shirt where the back meets the yoke, or on pockets for added texture and interest.

Tailor's tacks mark pleat positions on the fabric.

1
Mark the position and length of each box pleat on the surface of the fabric. Transfer the pattern markings from the paper pattern using tailor's tacks, chalk, or temporary marker pen.

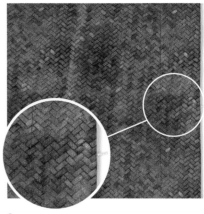

2
With the wrong sides of the fabric together, match the pattern markings. Pin and sew on the sewing line, securing the thread ends carefully to prevent the pleat opening up when being worn. Use temporary machine basting and sew from the secured stitches of Step 2 to the hem.

3
Lay the work face up on the ironing board and open up the pleat so that the center of the box pleat sits directly over the seam. Press to form creases down each side of the box pleat.

4
Remove the machine basting from the lower part of the box pleat to allow it to open.

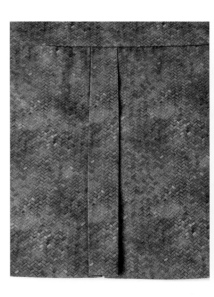

5
Secure the top of the box pleat with a yoke or band as appropriate.

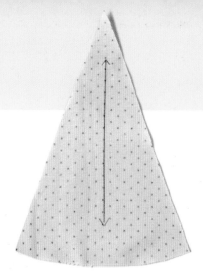

Godets

Although a godet is not technically a pleat, it creates a similar effect by releasing fullness at a controlled point. It provides stride room and creates a gently draping effect when inserted into a seam at the hem of a skirt or dress. It is a wedge of fabric sewn into a gap in the seam or a slash cut into the fabric to give flare and fullness to an area of a garment.

SEWING A GODET INTO A SEAM

1
Cut the godet with the grain line through the center with both sides equal to the seam length they will be sewn to.

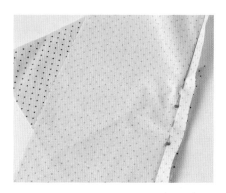

2
Sew the seam of the garment to the point where the godet will be inserted and secure the thread ends. Press the seam open and extend this to the hem so that ⅝ in. (1.5 cm) is pressed all the way.

3
Place the godet face up on the work surface then lay the open seam on top of it with the right side facing down. Lift up the front to reveal the seam allowance and match up the raw edges. Pin the crease of the pressed seam, catching the godet below.

4
Sew from the point of the godet to the hem, making sure you start exactly where the seam finishes to continue the join. Keep the layers separate and feel for folds of fabric under the work while you sew to make sure that tucks don't form at the top of the godet.

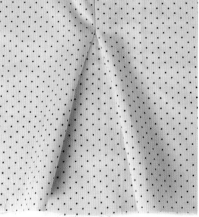

5
Iron the godet and seam when completed to produce a smooth, wrinkle-free finish on the front.

Match the pattern markings accurately for a smooth join.

SEWING A GODET INTO A SLIT

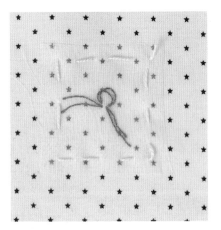

1
When sewing a godet into a raw slit in the fabric, you need to stabilize the point first. Cut a 1 in. (2.5 cm) square of silk organza and center it over the top of the godet position on the right side. Hold the organza in place with temporary stitching and mark the point where the godet will fit with a tailor's tack.

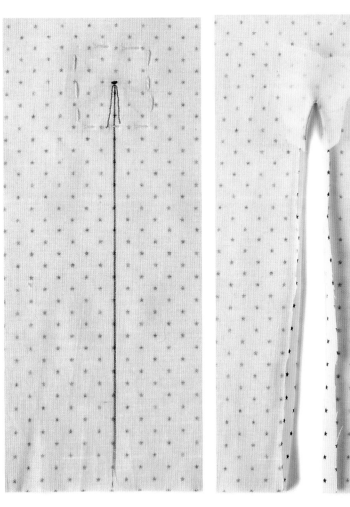

2
Turn over and sew a small upturned V-shape at the point where the top of the godet will fit. Reduce the stitch length to approximately 12 spi (1.5 cm) to create a strong line of stitching that will hold the point securely. Sew two tiny stitches across the point rather than pivoting at the top.

3
Cut through the fabric to the point and take the organza square to the wrong side. Press flat so that the seam is turned slightly to the wrong side and is not seen from the right side. Press creases on either side of the slit (from the point to the hem) then sew the godet in place (as for a godet in a seam) using the creases as a guide to follow.

Tucks

Tucks are tiny folds sewn on the surface of fabric that produce a delicate, textured detail. They are generally sewn in groups and are regularly spaced.

TIPS

- Work with a fabric made from a natural fiber. It is easier to control a natural fabric by using an iron to form creases, and these folds are easier to follow. A synthetic fabric is springy and therefore more difficult to handle.

- Fold tucks along the grain to keep them straight and true. They may curve or ripple if sewn slightly off the grain.

Tucks vary from edge-stitched folds only $1/16$ in. (2 mm) wide to perhaps $1/2$ in. (12 mm)—the size of small knife pleat. As with pleat-making, accurate marking and measuring are vital for a good finish. Make the tucks run along the grain as otherwise the fabric may stretch and result in a rippled tuck. Use groups of tucks to control fullness in the yoke area of a blouse or dress, or at a cuff for shaping.

Make a tuck guide from cardboard with regular marks made along its length. Use this to mark the size and position of the tucks on the flat fabric to ensure they are equally spaced and consistently sized when sewn.

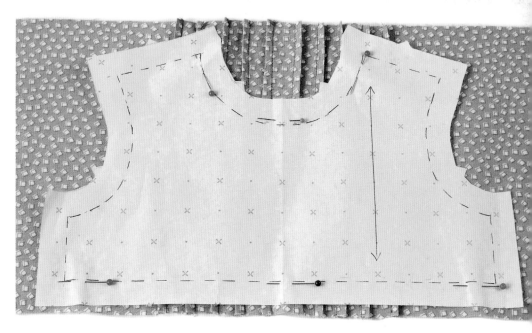

To form tucks you need more fabric than the finished width. Pin tucks use only a small amount of excess fabric, but three times the amount is required to make each standard tuck. Because of this, when making a yoke (see page 135), it is a good idea to prepare the tucks on a rectangle of fabric before placing the pattern piece on the fabric and cutting it out. This ensures the finished garment will fit well.

Standard tucks

Standard tucks are regularly spaced folds sewn along the full length, or left free at one end. Use horizontal tucks above the hem of a skirt as an interesting detail, or vertical tucks at the yoke of a nightdress.

1
Measure and mark the tucks on the surface of your fabric. Use tailor's chalk, temporary marker pen, or a line of basting so that the fabric will not be permanently marked.

2
Fold the fabric along each marked line to create the tuck and pin at intervals to hold the fold together. Use an iron to help crease these folds so they will be easier to see when you start to sew.

3
Set the sewing machine to straight stitch and sew parallel to each folded edge. Use the presser foot edge as a guide or choose a mark on the throat plate so the distance is consistent on each tuck.

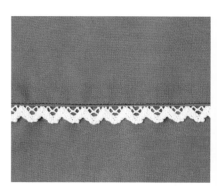

4
Press the tucks in the same direction. Hold the edge of the fabric in your left hand as an anchor and slide the iron from left to right to encourage the tucks to lie flat.

Finished horizontal tucks above a hem.

For a pretty alternative, catch an edging lace under a stitched-down tuck. Press the creases as shown in Step 2 and press each tuck flat. Slip the plain edge of the lace under the tuck and pin then topstitch in place.

Pin tucks

Pin tucks are dainty edge-stitched folds that remove a little fullness but add a surface textured detail. Use this technique for antique effects with white cotton and linen material, and combine with beautiful laces.

Alternatives
ZIGZAG PIN TUCKS

Sew the tucks with a zigzag stitch to create an interesting effect. Use a contrast thread or if you prefer, something more subtle, such as a metallic floss, to catch the light and give a bit of sparkle.

1
Mark the tuck positions on the surface of the fabric with chalk or tailor's tacks and press the folds with an iron to form creases. Make sure the wrong sides of the fabric are together when making the folds.

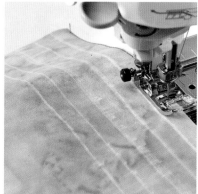

2
Set the sewing machine to straight stitch and sew each tuck ¹/₁₆ in. (2 mm) from the edge. Sew all the tucks in the same direction, from top to bottom, to prevent twisting.

1
Prepare the fabric for pin tucks and fold with wrong sides together. Set the sewing machine to zigzag stitch with the longest and widest option and feed the fabric under the foot, catching the edge of the fold only when the needle swings to the left.

3
Place a soft towel on the ironing board and lay the work with tucks side down and then press lightly with a steam iron. This irons the tucks without flattening them.

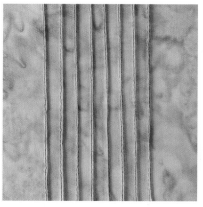

4
Turn the fabric over and on the right side the tucks sit upright, creating tiny parallel ridges on the face of the fabric.

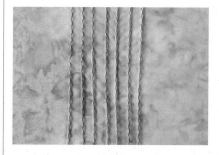

2
When finished, pull the fabric open gently and the tuck sits on the surface with a crisscross of threads over the top. It is important to catch just the very edge of the fold so that the tension is loose enough for the thread to lie flat on the tuck. If you sew too much of the fold, the tuck will pull up and crinkle.

CORDED PIN TUCKS

Sew a fine cord into the fold while you sew to give a more prominent ridge to each tuck and more of a texture to the finish.

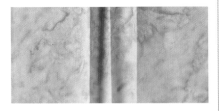

1

Measure, mark, and press the tucks as before with the wrong sides together.

2

Set the sewing machine to straight stitch and fit a zipper foot. Place a length of cord inside the fold of the first tuck and lay the fold on the throat plate with the zipper foot up close to it. Sew the length of the tuck, keeping the zipper foot pushed up next to the cord.

3

The finished tucks are filled with the cord and give a stronger, more ridged effect.

TWIN-NEEDLE PIN TUCKS

Tiny tucks can be created using a twin or double needle. The two needles combine with the bobbin thread to form two parallel rows of stitching on the surface and a zigzag below. By adjusting the tension, the resulting ridges can be made more prominent.

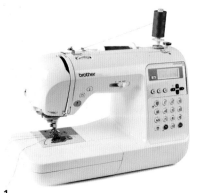

1

Choose a $\frac{1}{16}$ in. (2 mm) twin needle (this refers to the distance between the needles) and set up the sewing machine with two reels of thread—place one on the spare bobbin. Keep the two threads apart where possible, sharing the guides when it is essential. Fit a pin tuck foot to the machine.

2

Mark the first tuck position with a crease and lay the fabric right side up under the pin tuck foot (in the center groove). Follow the marked line, sewing along its length. If the resulting tuck is too flat, use a thicker, topstitch thread in the bobbin and the next tuck will be more prominent.

3

For the next and subsequent lines of twin-needle stitching, use the grooves in the underside of the presser foot to space the lines regularly and act as a guide. Providing the first twin needle tuck is straight, the others will follow and be parallel.

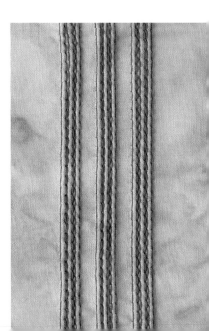

Finished twin-needle tucks.

Rouleaux and piping

Fine tubes of fabric with the raw edges enclosed within are referred to as rouleaux and used for straps or button loops. Piping is a covered cord inserted into seams and edges to add definition or to give a decorative finish.

Bias cut strips of fabric are used to make rouleaux and also to cover cord for piping as it curves and shapes without creasing. When a straight grain strip of fabric is used for either of these purposes crinkles appear at piped corners and where the rouleaux loops. It may seem appropriate to cut strips of fabric on the grain for economy but the results will never be as good as when cut on the true cross.

Rouleaux

Rouleaux are made from bias-cut strips of fabric that are sewn and turned inside out. For the daintiest tubes, a rouleau turner is an essential tool, although broader tubes can be produced with a bobby pin.

1
Cut a bias strip of fabric measuring 1-in. (2.5-cm) wide. Use scissors or a rotary cutter, ruler, and self-healing mat for sharp, clean edges that will be easier to work with.

2
Fold the fabric strip in half lengthwise with the right side on the inside. Shorten the stitch length to 12 spi (2 mm) and sew a line of stitching ¼ in. (6 mm) from the fold. Do not trim the seam allowances, as when turned through, the raw edges fill the gap to make a tube.

3
Make a small snip in the folded side of the tube ¼ in. (6 mm) from one end. Feed the rouleau turner through the tube from the uncut end to the snipped end and clasp the snipped end with the latch.

4
Carefully pull the rouleau turner back through the tube, easing it little by little and smoothing the creases in the process—if the creases build up at one point the tube will get stuck.

5
The resulting tube is smooth, even, and round. Use it for shoestring straps on evening wear, or cut into short lengths to make button loop fastenings.

TIP
If you do not have a rouleau turner, use a bobby pin. Follow Steps 1, 2, and 3 (below) and make a snip near the end. Slide the bobby pin through the snipped end and ease it through the tube, pulling the remainder behind it.

1

2

3

TIPS
• Snip into the seam allowance of the piping cord when you reach a corner so that the piping will be released and sit around the corner comfortably.

• The fabric strips covering the cord are cut on the bias so that no wrinkles or tucks form at corners and curves.

Match the two strips at the seam line, not the raw edge.

Piping

To make piping, use a bias strip of fabric over a plain cord and trap the seam allowances of the fabric strip in the seam.

1

Measure the circumference of the cord and add 1 ¼ in. (3 cm) for seam allowances. Cut bias strips of this width for covering the cord (see below).

2

Join the bias strips together to make a continuous length and press these seams open. Place the ends at right angles to one another with the seam allowances overlapping. Sew across the strips where the edges cross.

3

Set the sewing machine to straight stitch and lengthen the stitch for temporary basting. Fit a zipper foot. Wrap the cord with the long bias strip, leveling up the cut edges. Place the seam allowances of the fabric strip under the zipper foot with the cord inside adjacent to the foot. This allows you to sew close to the cord.

4

Lay the covered cord on top of the first layer of fabric it is to be applied to. Place the covered cord toward the center of the fabric and keep the raw edges level at the edge. Pin and then sew the cord to the fabric with temporary basting stitch as before.

5

Place the second layer of fabric over the cord with the right side down, and level up the edges once more. Place pins perpendicular to the seam line to hold the layers together with the piping sandwiched in between.

6

Turn the work over and return the stitch length to 10 spi (2.5 mm). Sew a new row of stitching even closer to the cord than before. Use the existing basting as a guide and keep to the left of this so that the temporary stitches are hidden. Remove the pins as you reach them.

Inside of piped seam.

Finished piping.

Linings

A lining adds a finishing touch to a garment. As well as concealing all the raw edges, it lengthens the wear and improves the overall effect. A satin-weave lining allows clothes to slide on and off smoothly, adding body to the fabric, improving the shape, and making the garment look more luxurious.

A lining is not always included in the envelope of a commercial pattern, but one can be added using the main pattern pieces. You can also add linings to unlined shop-bought garments or replace ones that are worn out.

Lining fabrics

Choose a lining that works with your garment and fabric. Fabrics made from silk, polyester, viscose, and acetate fibers are popular for linings as they are smooth and slide over the garments worn beneath the lined one. The weave plays an important part—satin, twill, and plain weaves are common for linings.

LINING EXAMPLES
Lightweight: habotai silk, China silk, and silk charmeuse for delicate blouses and dresses, or soft pants.

Medium weight: polyester, rayon, silk taffeta, silk broadcloth, and Jacquard silk for jackets, skirts, dresses, and pants.

Heavyweight: polyester and acetate linings in twill and satin weaves for coats and jackets.

LINING A SKIRT

Skirt linings are generally secured at the waist but left free at the hem. A lining hides all the raw edges of the seams and is hand stitched to the side zipper so the lining edges do not get caught in the zipper teeth. As with all garments, a lining prolongs its life, improves the shape, and allows skirts to slide on and off comfortably.

1
Construct the skirt with side seams and darts and insert the zipper (see page 77). Neaten the raw edges of the seams and press them open. Press darts to the side seams or the center. Whichever direction you choose, be consistent throughout the garment. You do not need to neaten the hem or the waist at this stage.

2
Cut out the main skirt pieces in lining fabric. Unless a lining pattern is provided in the envelope, use the main skirt pattern pieces, cutting them 1 in. (2.5 cm) shorter. There is no need to transfer the pattern markings for the dart but do mark the base of the zipper position.

3
Sew the seams of the lining, leaving a gap where the zipper will be inserted. Press the seams open and neaten the raw edges with zigzag or three-thread narrow serging (see tip opposite). Press the seam allowances of the opening to the wrong side.

4
Turn the skirt inside out and slide the lining (right way out) over the skirt. Match up the side seams and make tucks in the lining to take up the excess at the dart positions. Fold the tucks in the opposite way to each pressed dart. Baste the skirt and lining together on the waistline.

5
Treat the skirt and lining layers as one and attach the waistband with your preferred method. Tuck the seam allowance to the wrong side beside the zipper and catch the tucked darts with the waistband.

6
Slipstitch the folded edge to the zipper tape to hold it in place.

TIPS
- The lining conceals the rough fabric edges inside, but as the hem is left free and not stitched down, you may decide to neaten the seams.

- Neatening the raw edges with zigzag stitching or serging adds unnecessary bulk so to avoid this, fold up a double topstitched hem and trim the lower vertical seam allowances with pinking shears.

- Leave the edge next to the zipper unfinished as the lining will be stitched down here.

7
Shorten the hem of the skirt to the required length then fold up and stitch the lining hem with a narrow, double-folded, topstitched hem. Make the lining hem $1/2$ in. (1 cm) shorter than the finished hem.

8
Control the lining at the hem with French tacks at the seams. This holds it in place but leaves it free so that it does not pull or constrain the skirt.

Lining a dress

Adding a lining to a dress undoubtedly improves its finish. If there are no instructions for a lining inside a pattern envelope, it is easy to add one using the main pattern pieces.

The style of a lined dress will affect the way it is constructed. A dress with a waist will have a join in the lining, while a princess-seam design with vertical seams will be sewn at the shoulder only. Sleeve linings will normally be made up separately and joined at the armhole; however, sometimes a dress will be lined but the sleeves left unlined, depending on the fabric and style.

LINING A DRESS WITHOUT A WAIST SEAM

The lining and dress are joined at the neckline and armholes before the side seams are sewn. There are other techniques but this is the most straightforward and least fussy method for a dress with no waist seam.

1
Construct the dress and the lining (see page 156), sewing the shoulder seams and leaving the side and center back seams open. Press the seams open.

2
Neaten the lower vertical seams with pinking shears, zigzag stitch, or serging. Match the lining and dress at the neck edge and armholes with right sides facing. Pin and sew on the seam line. Grade/layer and notch where necessary (see page 240).

3
Turn through to the right side and roll the seams, using your fingers, to the outer edge. Understitch the lining to the seam allowances where possible to prevent the lining from rolling to the outside and being seen. Stop sewing short of the side and back seams to allow access to these for the next step.

4

Match the underarm point where the lining meets the dress and place the right sides together with edges level. Pin and sew from the underarm point to the hem on both the dress and the lining.

- When lining a dress or skirt with pleats, there is no need to make the lining in the same way—simply leave the lining seam behind the pleat free below the knee to allow stride room.

- Trim $\frac{1}{16}$ in. (2 mm) off the lining seam allowance at the neck and armhole, then keep the lining and dress edges level when pinning. This makes the lining slightly smaller than the dress so the seam line turns to the inside and is less visible from the dress side.

- If you have a dress with a waist seam, make up the skirt and skirt lining and baste them together at the waist with wrong sides facing inward (see lining a skirt on page 156 for details). Sew these two layers to the bodice at the waist. Pull the bodice lining down over the waist seam and tuck under the seam allowance. Pin through the fold to the layer below and hand sew to hold it in place.

5

Press the side seams open and turn the dress through to the right side. The seams will lie flat under the arm with the seams lying open.

6

Complete the center-back seam and insert a zipper if required. Turn under the seam allowances of the lining at the zipper and hand sew it to the zipper tape. This avoids the lining catching in the zipper teeth.

7

Turn up and sew the hem of the dress and the lining leaving approximately $\frac{1}{2}$ in. (1 cm) of the dress hem showing beneath the lining. Sew a French tack at each seam to keep it in place.

Finished tunic dress.

Lining a jacket

Traditionally, jacket linings were sewn in by hand, but as we are now accustomed to manufactured techniques, jacket linings are often "bagged through" so that nearly all the stitching is sewn by machine. If you are following a commercial pattern there are likely to be full instructions on inserting a lining. However, you can use our step-by-step guide to add a lining to an unlined jacket (made or bought) or to replace the worn-out lining of an existing jacket.

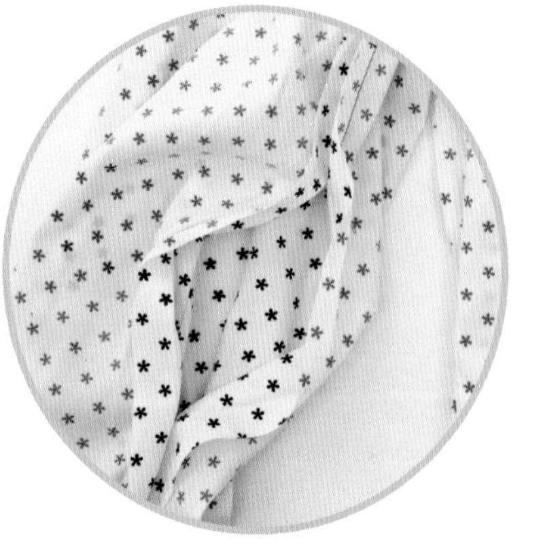

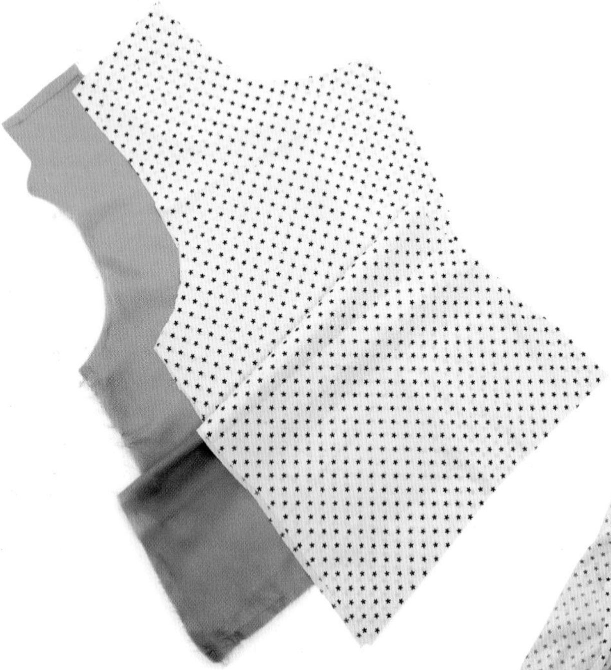

1

Cut out the parts of the lining using the main pattern pieces provided, or if remaking a lining for an existing jacket take the shape and size of each panel from the worn-out lining. Carefully unpick each piece, press out the seam allowances, and use this as a pattern. Remember to add your own seam allowance from each stitch line, as the existing seam allowances will have been trimmed.

2

Construct the body and sleeves of the lining. Sew darts if they form part of the shaping, baste the tuck or pleat in the center back (if there is one), and press the seams open but do not neaten the raw edges. Leave a 4 in. (10 cm) gap in one of the sleeve seams so that the lining can be pulled through the jacket to the inside.

3

Pin the new lining to the front edges and back neck facing of the jacket with the right sides facing. Match up the seams and sew on the seam line. If the fabric creeps due to the satin lining and different thicknesses of layers, start from the back neck and sew to the front left then front right. Sew the lining to the jacket and remove the pins.

4

Turn the lining through the right way and slip the lining sleeves into the jacket sleeves. Press the join between the lining and jacket facings and press up the lining hem to approximately $1/2$ in. (12 mm) above the jacket hem.

5

Cut two pieces of lining measuring $5/8$ in. (1.5 cm) wide and $2 1/3$ in. (6 cm) long. Use these to attach the underarm of the lining to the underarm of the jacket with approximately $1 1/4$ in. (3 cm) apart. This will control the seams without pulling or distorting the jacket.

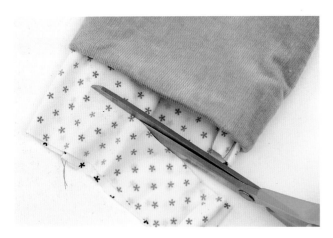

6
Let the sleeve lining drop below the cuff and trim level if necessary.

7
Tuck up the sleeve lining hem so that the raw edge is level with the jacket edge inside and ½ in. (1 cm) of jacket fabric shows below the lining. Slip baste the fold of the lining hem to the inside of the jacket cuff.

8
Pull the sleeve up and through the jacket then drop it below the gap in the hem so you have room to work on it. Stitch on the seam line of the cuff all the way around. The slip basting will hold it in place while you sew.

9
Slip baste the lining hem to the jacket hem as you did with the cuffs in Step 7. Sew the lower lining fold to the jacket, making sure you do not catch any extra layers inside.

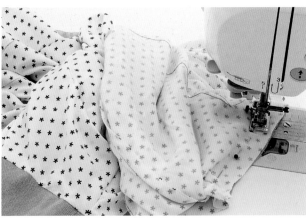

10
Locate the gap left in the sleeve lining seam and pull the hem through.

11
Manipulate the layers to make sure you are sewing through only the jacket hem and lining hem allowances and join these layers.

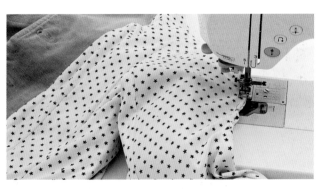

13
Find the gap in the sleeve lining again and fold along the seam. Pin the edges together then edge stitch with straight stitch or slip stitch the seam closed if you prefer.

12
Pull the hem back through and remove the slip basting. The lining at the hem and cuff will now be secured at the correct level.

TIPS
- Use the same basic technique to line a coat but leave the hem of the lining free. Anchor it at the seams with French tacks as you would a skirt (see page 157).
- Always examine a shop-bought garment when you are deconstructing it. Seeing how the garment has been put together and the materials used on the inside will give you ideas for your future sewing projects.

Lining a bag

It is not only garments that need to be lined, but accessories too. Whether you need to replace a worn-out lining of a favorite bag, or you decide to make your own lined purse or handbag to match an outfit, it is easy to do. Choose good-quality and strong fabric to line a bag as items inside a bag can damage the lining.

Finished lined bag.

REPLACING A LINING

1
Unpick the existing worn-out lining and remove it from the purse or bag, then separate each panel. Do this as carefully as possible to retain the shape so that you can take a pattern from it. Iron each section.

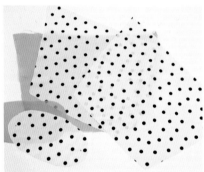

2
Use each panel as a template to cut out the new lining pieces. Transfer important information to the new lining, e.g., where seams meet or the zipper position.

3
Construct the lining, leaving the part that will be sewn to the bag open. This may be around a zipper or on the upper edge, depending on the type and style of the bag or purse.

4
With the bag the right way around and the lining inside out, drop the lining into the bag.

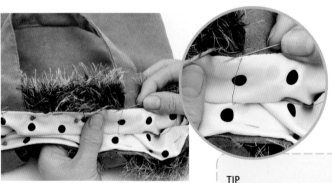

5
Fold back a ⅝ in. (1.5 cm) seam allowance to the wrong side of the fabric. Pin around the upper edge and slipstitch in place, through the fold of the lining to the bag beneath.

TIP
For a stronger lining, reinforce the lining fabric with an iron-on interfacing on the wrong side before sewing the pieces together, and sew to the bag or purse with topstitch thread or a double length of standard thread.

Finished bag.

LINING A BAG IN CONSTRUCTION

When making a bag or purse it is easier to machine sew the lining in place—this produces a stronger finish compared with hand sewing. There are innumerable designs of bags so adapt the following instructions as required, using the basic principle that a gap is left in the lining to allow the main body of the bag to be pulled through.

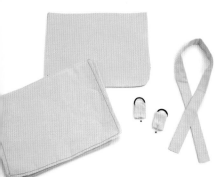

1
Construct the bag and gather the other parts together, e.g., the strap, flap, and fastening. Stiffen the bag with iron-on interfacing on the wrong side if necessary, before sewing the parts together. Trim the seam allowances but do not neaten any raw edges since the lining will conceal them.

2
Make up the lining of the bag, leaving the top edge free to attach to the main bag fabric and a 4 in. (10 cm) gap in part of the seam in the base.

3
Pin the flap and straps in place at the top edge of the bag. With the lining inside out, slide the bag into the lining.

4
Replace the pins around the top to catch all parts and sew through the layers on the seam line. This will sew the bag and add the lining at the same time.

5
Pull the bag through the 4 in. (10 cm) gap in the internal seam so that the lining sits inside the bag with the wrong sides hidden on the inside.

6
Find the unsewn part of the seam in the lining and fold along the seam so that the raw edges are inside. Pin the edges together then stitch (with machine straight stitch) very close to the fold or slipstitch the seam closed if you prefer.

Working with patterns

You will find all the information you need about selecting, adapting, and making patterns for your own well-fitting clothes in this chapter. Whether you are using a commercial pattern or making one of your own, all the advice you need is here.

Choosing a pattern

When buying clothes "off the rack" from a store, you can tell instantly if they fit well and suit you. When making your own clothes, however, you need to put more thought into the choice of style, and the size you cut out and construct.

There is nothing more disappointing than trying on a garment after hours of sewing to discover that it does not fit and the style does not do justice to your figure. Before you start, take some time to look at yourself in a full-length mirror to recognize your figure type, and enlist the help of a friend to give honest advice about your shape.

Having established your silhouette type and the kind of garments to select or avoid, the next vital step is to choose the correct size. Always follow the size chart on the pattern envelope and never assume you will be the same size as garments from a store—this is seldom the case. It is also important to remember that few people fit into a standard size and most of us have figure variations that range between sizes.

After choosing a suitable style in an appropriate size, minor adjustments can be made to achieve a perfect fit.

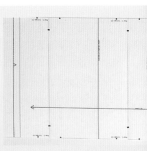

Flicking through a pattern catalog is an easy way to get ideas.

PRINTING AND ASSEMBLING A DOWNLOADED PATTERN

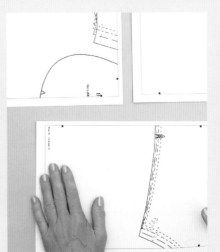

3
Now you are ready to glue the sheets together side-by-side to form rows. It is important to pay special attention to matching the black boxes. Be as accurate as possible.

1
The downloaded pattern prints on your normal home printer on 8 ½ x 11 in. (21.5 x 28 cm) sheets with a heavy black border. On each sheet are column and row numbers along with small black boxes to help when matching up the sheets.

2
First, organize and divide the sheets of paper by rows, numbers, or letters, and cut off the margins on the top and left sides.

Where to buy patterns

Pattern catalogs are often handily grouped into themed collections.

PATTERN CATALOGS

These thick, glossy books show photographs or illustrations of the finished garments with information on the sizes available, and the type and amount of fabric required to create them. Grouped into categories, this makes choosing a suitable outfit easy. They are generally updated with new styles two or four times a year.

MAGAZINES

Some companies publish monthly or quarterly magazines with pull-out patterns and garment construction details. You can trace these patterns and follow the instructions to create fashionable designs in your chosen material.

DOWNLOADS

The most obvious advantage of downloading a pattern from the Internet is that you receive it immediately, but it can take time to print the many parts and even longer to put them together accurately to achieve your pattern pieces.

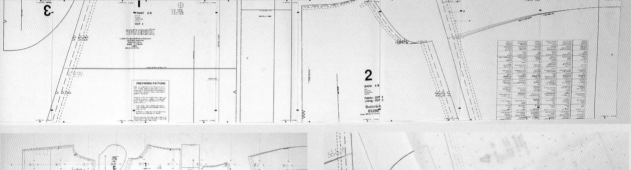

4
Once all the rows are finished, paste them together lengthwise. The pattern is now complete.

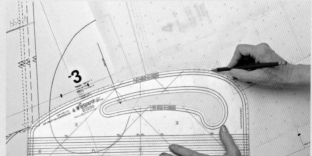

5
Once the pattern is complete, it is a good idea to trace it onto pattern tracing paper. This will make the pattern easier to pin to your fabric because tracing pattern paper is made for that purpose.

Pattern envelope information

You will find the essential information you need on the outside of the pattern envelope (before opening it up and fighting with the tissue paper that never seems to go back in the envelope quite the same way again!). The pattern information includes advice on the type and quantity of fabric to choose, and any other extras you need to buy to complete the piece of clothing illustrated, as well as how to choose the correct size.

Pattern envelope front

The front of the pattern envelope displays the initial vital information to help you select the right pattern for your shape and size.

PHOTOGRAPH OR ILLUSTRATION (1 AND 2)

The front of the pattern envelope usually shows a photograph or sketch of each item of clothing, complete with variations. This might be a skirt in two or three lengths, or a shirt with a choice of collar styles, but all views will be shown, usually from the front. A photograph gives a more realistic idea of how the finished garment will look, while an illustration may use a certain amount of artistic license by elongating the model. Always remember your own shape when choosing a pattern and do not be fooled by the elegant model in the illustration, whether a photograph or a sketch.

SIZE (3)

The size or sizes included in your envelope are stated on the front, and a chart is often printed on the flap of the envelope, though sometimes this information is contained inside the envelope. Generally there will be a range of at least three sizes offered by the pattern, but some multi-size patterns may include ten or twelve options. Make sure you buy the pattern in the size range that best covers your measurements.

PATTERN NUMBER (4)

This identifies each pattern, making it easy to order your selection.

Sizes (3) shown in more detail on back of pattern.

Pattern number (4).

Photograph (1).

Illustration (2).

Sizes (3).

The pattern envelope
The back of the envelope carries a lot of essential information, including how to calculate the amount of fabric you will need.

Pattern envelope back
On the back of the pattern envelope you will find detailed information about your pattern.

SILHOUETTE KEY (5)
Some companies suggest the figure types a garment style is suitable for by using a very simple key of triangles and rectangles. This supports the knowledge you have of your own figure (see page 168) and helps with pattern selection.

DESCRIPTION (6)
A short written description of each item of clothing is given with details such as how it should fit, whether a lining is included, and information about fastenings. This, in addition to the outline view and main illustration, will give a complete vision of the finished garments.

NOTIONS/HABERDASHERY (7)
This is where the extra requirements needed to complete each garment are included. If a zipper is necessary, it will state the length and type, or the number and size of buttons required. Lining and underlining requirements are also listed.

FABRIC (8)
Information about suitable fabrics is always included to help you to choose appropriately. This will suggest the weight or stretch required for a good fit. You may already have a fabric in mind and this will confirm its suitability, or make you aware of other aspects of the design you had not considered.

GARMENT MEASUREMENT DETAILS (9)
Measurements of the completed garments are included to help you to

Silhouette key (5).

Description (6).

Notions/haberdashery (7).

Fabric (8).

Diagrams showing garment detail (10).

Fabric quantity guide (11).

Garment measurement details (9).

visualize how the finished item will look. For example, the skirt length, or the hem circumference on a pair of pants, are useful pieces of information to know before buying a pattern. These details are not always evident from the outline diagrams or illustrations, and this allows you to choose or reject a particular pattern, or be aware that alterations will be required to achieve the look you want.

DIAGRAMS SHOWING GARMENT DETAIL (10)
The front and back views of each item included in the pattern envelope are illustrated, showing seam and dart positions and fastenings. This adds to the

visual information given in the photograph or sketch on the envelope front.

FABRIC QUANTITY GUIDE (11)
As well as offering suggestions for choosing suitable fabric, charts are also included to show how much you need to buy for each view and size. Since fabric can be bought in a range of widths, following this chart will help you avoid buying too little or too much material.

Inside the pattern envelope

Inside the pattern envelope, you will find information pages to guide you through the construction of your new garment. Sheets of tissue paper with the pattern pieces printed on one side are included and will need to be prepared before use.

Pattern instructions

Having chosen suitable fabric and notions, the next step is to read the information pages to gain an overview of the steps to creating your new garment. It is a good idea to check over all the stages of construction before cutting into your fabric. The instructions show how to lay out the pattern pieces and cut out the fabric both economically and to give the best finish. After this, step-by-step instructions advise on the order of construction and the techniques involved in combining the fabric pieces. When you are satisfied with the information gleaned from the pattern, it is time to get started.

Different pattern manufacturers will display information in slightly different formats.

LINE DRAWINGS (1)
Line drawings show details of the finished items included in the pattern with a number or letter to indicate the view you plan to follow. The pattern pieces may look similar to each other, so this helps to differentiate between, for example, a knee-length or a calf-length skirt.

PATTERN PIECES (2)
All the pattern pieces are listed or shown as small-scale diagrams and are numbered to make it easy to identify them when cutting and selecting the tissue pieces.

MEASUREMENT CHART (3)
This is often included on the instruction sheet but may be printed on the tissue itself. It helps to identify the correct size you need to cut out. (See pages 176–179 for advice on selecting the most appropriate size.) Some indicate how and where to take your body measurements.

FABRIC CUTTING LAYOUTS (4)
Various layout options are given as a guide to how to best fit the pattern pieces on the fabric, depending on the width of the cloth and the view you've chosen. This may also include interfacing, underlining, and lining.

INFORMATION KEY (5)
A key is also included to make sense of the layout guide, indicating the right and wrong sides of the fabric and whether lining or interfacing have to be cut out, too.

STEP-BY-STEP GUIDE (6)
Brief instructions provide the necessary information, along with diagrams, to make each step clear and comprehensive. Some basic sewing knowledge is required, but these instructions are all that is needed to construct the garment, providing they are followed carefully and in order.

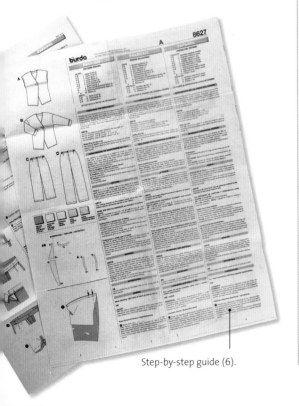

Step-by-step guide (6).

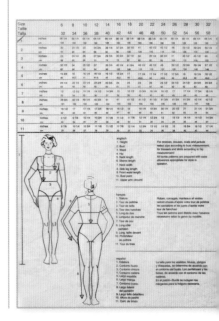

Line drawings (1).

Measurement chart (3).

Fabric cutting layouts (4).

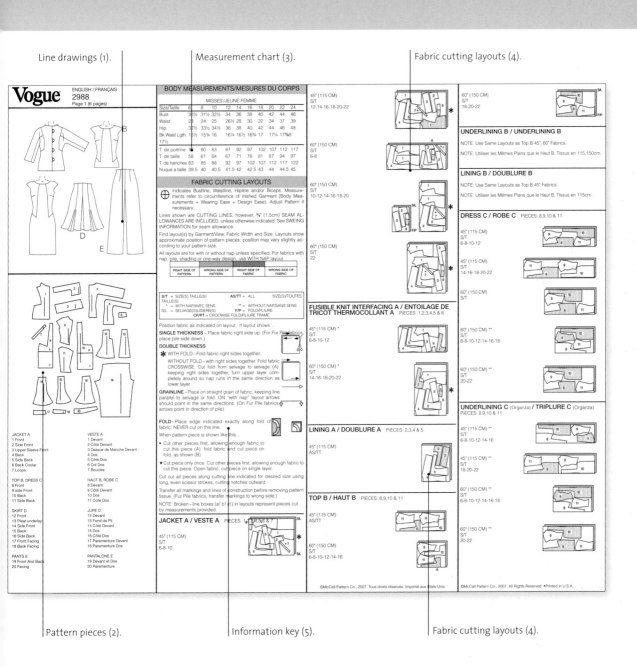

Pattern pieces (2).

Information key (5).

Fabric cutting layouts (4).

The size chart details the average measurements of the figure for a range of sizes. See page 178 for how to use this chart.

Understanding pattern symbols

The symbols printed on the pattern pieces may seem like an elaborate code, but this shorthand is easy to follow when you know how to decipher the shapes and marks.

What it all means

Commercial pattern companies tend to use the same symbols, and so it should only take a short time to learn what the information means and how to use it. Once you can recognize the message given by each printed shape or mark and how to use it, you can sew with any pattern easily. Some of these symbols help in laying out the pattern on the fabric, while others need to be transferred to the fabric to accurately match pieces later in the construction.

PATTERN NUMBER (1)
Each pattern piece shows the company that produced it and includes a number identifying it from all other patterns.

PART NUMBER AND DESCRIPTION (2)
Each piece will be named and have a number indicating its part in the finished garment, e.g., front, collar, sleeve, pocket, etc.

NUMBER OF PIECES (3)
Information will be included to state how many pieces you should cut out in fabric, lining, and/or interfacing.

SEAM ALLOWANCE (4)
This is the name given to the border added to the edge of a pattern, between the cutting line and the sewing line so that the fabric pieces can be sewn together and the edges folded and finished.

SHORTENING/LENGTHENING LINES (5)
A double line drawn horizontally through a pattern piece shows where it is best to shorten or lengthen a garment to achieve an appropriate length.

BALANCE MARKS (6)
Dots and spots printed on a paper pattern are important in helping to place the fabric panels together. These are often used for marking dart or tuck positions and should be transferred with tailor's tacks (see page 42).

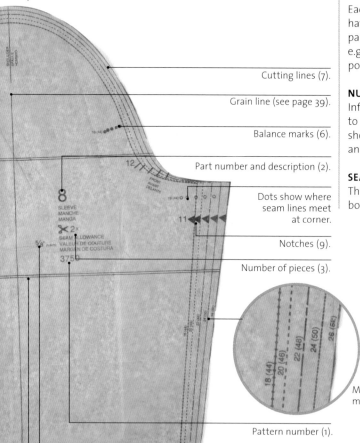

Cutting lines (7).

Grain line (see page 39).

Balance marks (6).

Part number and description (2).

Dots show where seam lines meet at corner.

Notches (9).

Number of pieces (3).

Multi-size markings.

Pattern number (1).

Seam allowance (4).

Shortening/ lengthening lines (5).

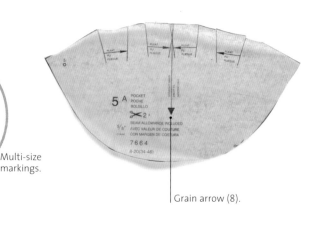

Grain arrow (8).

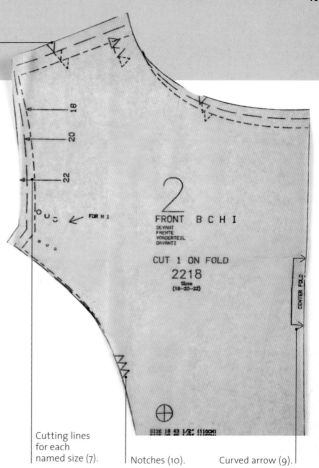

Notches (10).

CUTTING LINES (7)

Traditionally, patterns were produced for individual sizes and the cutting line was indicated with a solid line and the sewing line by a dotted line. On most patterns today, where several size options are included, a range of lines is used to identify different sizes and the sewing line is assumed to be a seam allowance width inside this. Work out which line is used for your size (dots, dashes, solid, etc.) then cut along these lines for each pattern piece.

GRAIN ARROWS (8)

Arrows printed on paper patterns show the direction the grain of the fabric should lie in when cutting out the pieces. This line must be parallel to the selvage edge (see page 39) for the finished garment to hang correctly.

CURVED ARROWS (9)

An arrow with curved ends pointing to a solid line indicates that the pattern piece should be placed against a fold. This ensures the fabric piece will be perfectly symmetrical when laid out and is often used for the back of a jacket or the front of a skirt where there is no seam.

NOTCHES (10)

Notches are used on the cutting lines to show where fabric pieces will be joined. This ensures that skirt panels are put together correctly and longer, shaped seams can be eased together in the right place; for example, through the bust point of a princess seam. Similarly, when sewing a sleeve into an armhole, single (front) and double (back) notches are used so that the arms are inserted in the correct armholes.

Cutting lines for each named size (7).

Notches (10).

Curved arrow (9).

USING NOTCHES

When laying the pattern pieces on the fabric, cut around the notches to help match seams together. It is better to cut around these than snip into the seam allowance as this avoids weakening the seam.

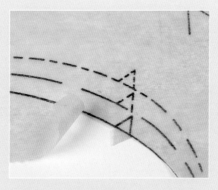

Cutting around a notch
Cut notches "out" rather than "in" to prevent weakening the seam.

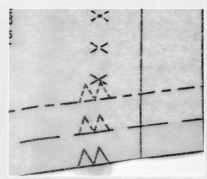

Matching up notches
Make sure you link up double notches with the corresponding double notch, and likewise with single notches.

Measuring

For clothes to fit our three-dimensional bodies we need to have a good idea of our general shape, along with detailed figure dimensions. With accurate measurements, personal patterns can be created to fit an individual perfectly. This type of styling is expensive and most home sewers, who do not have an in-depth knowledge of pattern cutting, must rely on commercial patterns produced from standard measurements. This allows us all to create pieces of clothing that almost meet our body shape requirements. After some tweaking, we can achieve a great fit.

General measuring rules

When using a standard pattern, you must have accurate body measurements so that you can choose the size closest to your own silhouette. Follow the rules below for easy and precise measuring:

- Get a friend to help you take your measurements. It is hard to reach certain areas and to make sure the tape measure is level where you cannot see it. This also makes the process more enjoyable and less of a chore.

- Use a full-length mirror to check that you are placing the tape measure in the correct places and between the right points. Even if you have a friend to help, a mirror is helpful for you both.

- Wear well-fitting undergarments when taking measurements and do not take your measurements over clothing. You need to have complete access to every limb and body part to find out its length and circumference.

- Stand tall, with your feet together, and do not breathe in. You need to have truthful figures to work from.

- Measure accurately, making sure the tape is flat and starts and finishes at the proper points. Use the fitting guide opposite to help you to know how to take each measurement.

- Place the tape firmly (but not too tight) around the body and do not leave any slack. Ease is built into the pattern for comfort and style, so there is no need to add any more.

Body landmarks

HORIZONTAL:

1 Bust: Hold the tape level and measure the fullest part of the bust. A well-fitting bra is essential in achieving this.

2 Waist: Tie a length of soft elastic lightly around your middle and it will automatically fall into the waist position. Measure at this point.

3 Hip: This is the fullest part of the bottom, and its position varies from one person to another.

4 Chest: Measure across the center front, just above the bust, from armhole to armhole approximately 3 in. (7.5 cm) below the neck level.

5 Back width: Measure across the center back between the armholes, approximately 6 in. (15 cm) below the prominent neck bone.

6 Shoulder: Take this measurement from the neck edge to the shoulder bone.

7 Upper arm: Place the tape measure around the bicep, while the arm is slightly bent, with your hand on your waist or hip.

8 Wrist: Measure the wrist with a small amount of ease.

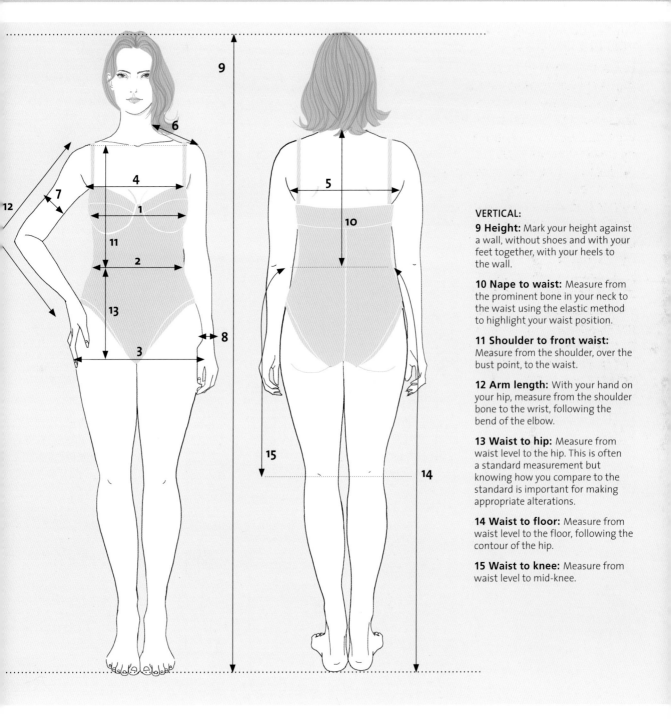

VERTICAL:

9 Height: Mark your height against a wall, without shoes and with your feet together, with your heels to the wall.

10 Nape to waist: Measure from the prominent bone in your neck to the waist using the elastic method to highlight your waist position.

11 Shoulder to front waist: Measure from the shoulder, over the bust point, to the waist.

12 Arm length: With your hand on your hip, measure from the shoulder bone to the wrist, following the bend of the elbow.

13 Waist to hip: Measure from waist level to the hip. This is often a standard measurement but knowing how you compare to the standard is important for making appropriate alterations.

14 Waist to floor: Measure from waist level to the floor, following the contour of the hip.

15 Waist to knee: Measure from waist level to mid-knee.

Size charts and measurements

Selecting the right size for your body measurements is vital to achieving a good fit.

Landmark	Standard measurement	Personal measurement
1 Bust		
2 Waist		
3 Hip		
4 Chest		
5 Back width		
6 Shoulder		
7 Upper arm		
8 Wrist		
9 Height		
10 Nape to waist		
11 Shoulder to front waist		
12 Arm length		
13 Waist to hip		
14 Waist to floor		
15 Waist to knee		
16 Crotch depth		

Measure accurately

Stand in front of a full-length mirror while you, or a friend, take your body measurements. Keep the tape measure parallel to the floor for horizontal measurements and make sure the tape is flat with no twists. Keep the tape measure snug but not tight, and remember to breathe.

Record your measurements

Photocopy the chart provided here and write down all your measurements in the right-hand column. Use the diagrams on pages 176–177 to help you know where to take your body measurements. Compare your measurements with those given by the pattern company. These can be found on the outside of the envelope, but they are sometimes printed on the tissue paper inside. Decide the size you are closest to and write those measurements down in the central column. Highlight any anomalies (for example, bust measurement or back length) and be aware of these when cutting out and adapting your paper pattern.

MULTI-SIZE PATTERNS

Patterns normally offer a choice of sizes, making it easier to create a well-fitting garment for a variety of figures. This may be three or four sizes, although some multi-patterns offer a much larger range.

The advantage of such a large size range is that it makes it possible to buy just one pattern and to choose the cutting lines to achieve a good fit. Since most of us are of a non-standard size, we can use the pattern lines to create an individual fit from a commercial paper pattern.

Measure the pattern pieces

Check your measurements against the actual pattern before deciding which size to cut out. To do this, select the relevant pattern pieces and measure the actual size of the pattern without seam allowances and darts. Ease will be included so bear this in mind and compare pattern size with your measurement.

Choose your size

Make a decision about the size that best suits you and cut out the tissue paper. If you need to adapt the pattern, do this now (see page 180).

As a general rule, choose skirts and pants using your hip measurement, and tops and jackets with your bust measurement in mind. However, this is not always the case and it is important to have a feeling for your general build. For example, if you have a small frame yet a large bust, using this measurement will result in a garment that may fit at the bust but will be too big elsewhere. Here, use the measurements based on your shoulders, back, and chest, and make a bust enlargement to the pattern.

MEASURE THE PATTERN PIECES

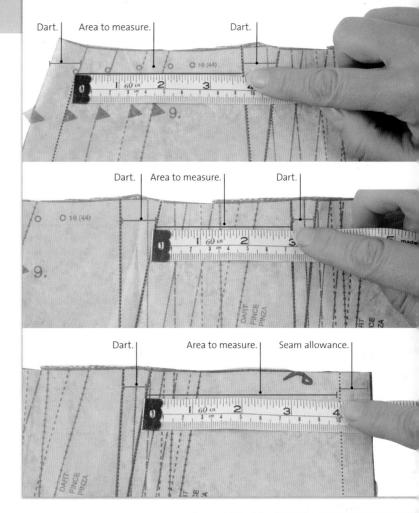

Dart. | Area to measure. | Dart.

Dart. | Area to measure. | Dart.

Dart. | Area to measure. | Seam allowance.

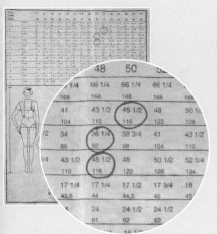

1 Mark your own measurements onto the size chart and take note of where they lie in relation to the standard measurements. Make a decision on the size or sizes required. If one of the measurements appears as an anomaly, the pattern will need to be adjusted separately in this area.

2 Find the relevant pattern pieces and lay them out flat, noting the cutting line key for the size or sizes needed (see page 175).

3 Go over the cutting lines required with a colored pen or pencil and draw new lines to join or merge between sizes, creating a smooth line. Where seams join, make sure the lines on both pattern pieces follow the same angle. A French curve is a useful tool for this task (see page 13). When the lines are completed, cut out the pattern pieces and continue with the construction.

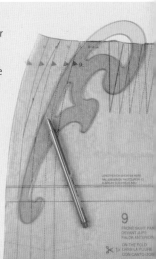

Adapting a pattern

Commercial patterns are based on standard measurements, but very few people correspond exactly to these, so it is often necessary to make small alterations to improve the fit.

For best results, make any changes to the paper pattern and then construct a toile in muslin (see page 184)in order to check the fit. Transfer any further alterations back onto the paper pattern, before cutting out and making the final garment.

Length

Changing the length of pattern pieces is relatively easy to do. Simply measure the body: A side-pants measurement (required length) would be taken from the waist to the hem, for example, and a back measurement would be taken from the nape to the waist. Compare these body measurements with the actual pattern size, and tuck a fold in the pattern paper to shorten the length or cut and separate the piece to add length if necessary. Use this method to adjust sleeve length too.

Adapting a pants paper pattern

Measure the length of the side seam from the waist to the hem and alter the pants paper pattern accordingly. Fold up excess length to shorten or cut and move the pattern pieces apart before inserting paper pieces to lengthen them.

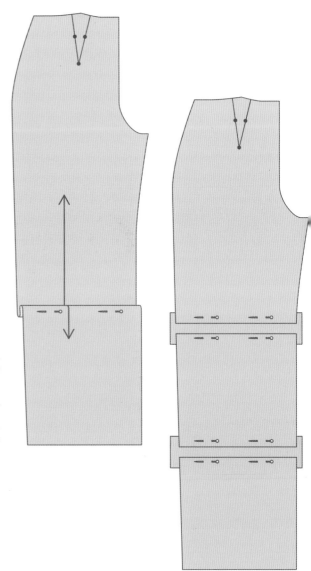

Horizontal parallel lines through a pattern suggest the best place to lengthen or shorten a garment. Simply cut and move apart to lengthen pattern pieces or make a fold to shorten them. It will normally be necessary to finish the adjustment by smoothing the sides of the pattern. Be aware that sometimes it is better to make smaller length adjustments in more than one place than one large alteration.

Waist

The most obvious solution to altering a waist is to alter the size of the darts. More, or less, fabric can be pinched away at the waist and if necessary the darts can be lengthened or shortened to improve the shaping.

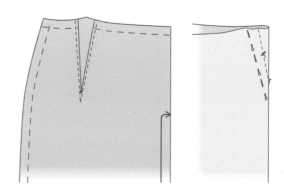

Large stomach

To adjust a pattern to create more room in the front stomach area, cut into the paper pattern both horizontally, at the widest part, and vertically through a dart. Pivot this at the side seam—to retain the length of the side seam and enlarge the dart. Smooth out the side seam and reshape the dart.

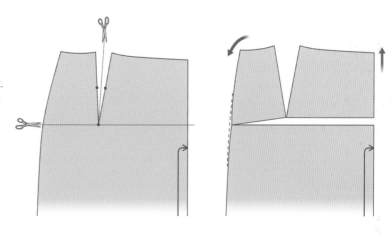

Small stomach

If there is excess fabric in the stomach area, this can be removed by cutting into the pattern as above. In this case, fold the pattern in on itself to remove excess fabric and reduce the size of the dart. Reshape the side seam and dart.

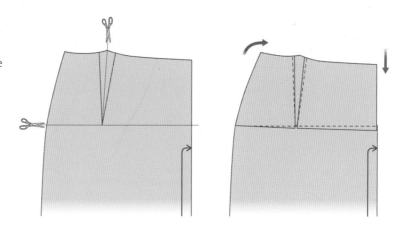

Large seat

More fabric can be built into the seat of a skirt or dress by cutting into the paper pattern. Cut horizontally at the largest part of the hip and also vertically through the dart. Pivot this at the side seam to enlarge the dart and create more fabric for the seat. Smooth the side seam and reshape the dart.

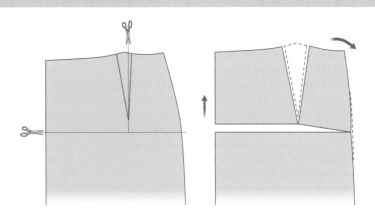

Small seat

To reduce excess fabric in the seat, cut horizontally through the paper pattern in the problem area and vertically through a dart. Fold the pattern in on itself and reshape the side seam and dart.

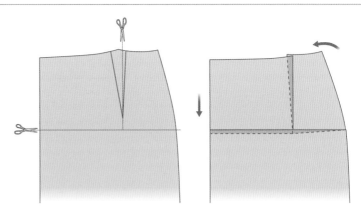

Back adjustments

Accommodate a broad or narrow back by cutting into the back armhole area. Make a horizontal and a vertical cut in the shoulder and armhole.

• To allow more fabric for a broad-backed and wide-shouldered figure, move the cut pattern piece out and reshape the shoulder and armhole.
• For a broad back but narrow shoulders, pivot on the shoulder seam and reshape.
• For wide shoulders but narrow back, pivot on the armhole and reshape.
• For a narrow back and shoulders, move the cut pattern piece into the pattern.

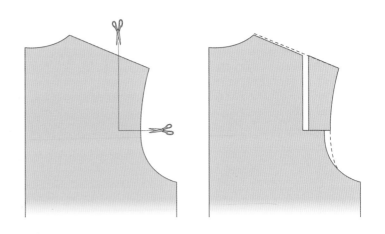

Large bust

First, choose a pattern with waist and armhole darts or a princess seam, which will allow adjustments to be made.

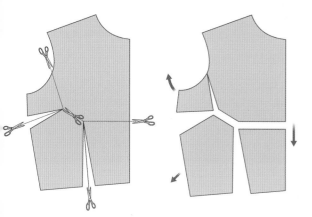

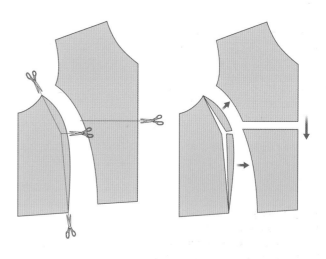

BODICE WITH DARTS
Cut the pattern through the darts, the center front, and the armhole. Pull the pattern pieces apart to create more space for the bust, pivoting at the armhole. Reshape the darts.

PRINCESS LINE BODICE
Cut horizontally through the bust point and lengthen to add space for the bust. Cut and move the side front pattern piece as shown to allow more fabric and to retain the seam shaping.

Small bust

Start with a pattern close to the body measurements to minimize alterations.

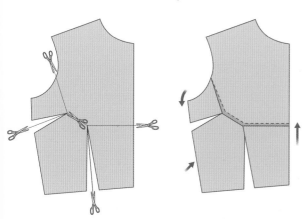

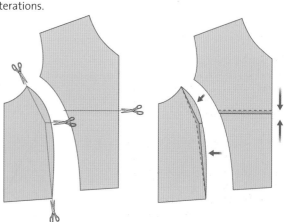

BODICE WITH DARTS
Cut into the darts and overlap the pattern pieces, taking care not to alter the seam lengths. Reshape the darts.

PRINCESS LINE BODICE
Cut horizontally through the bust point and overlap the pattern pieces. This will take up the excess fabric in the length. Pivot at the armhole to avoid disturbing the armhole measurement.

Making and fitting a toile

A toile is an early version of a garment made in inexpensive fabric to test a pattern—a kind of fabric prototype. You may make multiple toiles during the process of perfecting your pattern.

Preparation

First, you need to press the creases from some medium-weight muslin with a steam iron. Fold the muslin in half with the grain. Place the pattern pieces on the muslin parallel to the grain line, and trace around them with a pencil. Mark on the center front (CF) and center back (CB), and draw in the bust lines, waist lines, the biceps line, and the elbow line. Mark in the hip line on the skirt and all the grain lines. It is important to mark these out on the muslin so that once you have made up the garment, you can see if the lines are balanced and in alignment with the body.

Sewing your toile together

Sew your toile together, beginning with the darts while the pieces are flat. Press the front darts toward the side seam. Next, sew the front and back bodice shoulder seams and side seams together and press them open. Sew up the underarms of both sleeves and then set the sleeves into the finished armholes (see page 138). Do not press the sleeve caps or you will flatten out the ease. For the skirt, make the darts first before sewing up the side seams.

Methodical working

When you are pattern cutting, it is good practice to work in a methodical manner. Create a history of how your pattern was drafted and all the stages that this involves. When a mistake becomes apparent, it is then easier to retrace your steps and identify where the mistake happened. Many mistakes are made by sewing pieces together the wrong way up. Working in a step-by-step way helps to keep mistakes and inaccuracies to a minimum. Never be tempted to ignore a problem. Chopping pieces off your patterns or toiles will usually show up on the finished article. So sorting out problems at the paper pattern stage will save valuable time and money.

TIPS FOR WORKING METHODICALLY

- Working methodically allows you more scope to be creative once you have learned the basic principles.

- Label everything thoroughly, with the name and date of the pattern piece i.e., Left Skirt Front (cut 1), Cuff (cut 4), Cut on Fold, and so on. Mark on the CB and CF lines, grain lines, balance lines, notches, and size of seam allowance. This will help to avoid confusion at every stage.

- Trace off the pattern pieces at every stage of pattern manipulation, and keep and label the stages.

- Always write on your pieces the right way up and on the correct side—if necessary mark "Right Side Up" (RSU) on pieces that can't be turned over.

- Notches are vital for matching up pattern pieces, for checking them at the pattern stage, and for sewing up—don't forget to put them on, as it will save you a great deal of time later (see page 175).

- Cut one pattern piece at a time, and check all the pattern pieces to ensure that they fit together where necessary.

- Mark on all the darts and details on your fabric pieces with tailor's tacks or chalk (see page 42).

- When sewing your toile together, always sew to the seam allowances. If you are inaccurate by even a fraction of an inch, the size of your toile will be altered considerably.

- Any alterations that you make on your toile should be copied to your pattern immediately, before you forget what or where they were. Don't forget to add seam allowances back on where you have chopped parts off your pattern.

TIP
To find the true CF, make a plumb line by tying a string loosely around your neck. Thread another length of string loosely through it and tie a slightly weighted object on the end. Arrange the plumb line at the CF neck and let it hang down. Mark the exact CF line with sticky tape on your undergarments or leotard, and repeat the process for the CB.

Try on your toile

Before trying on your toile for the first time, tie some elastic around your waist—this will mark the natural waistline—and mark the fullest part of the bust and low hip on your undergarments or a leotard with sticky tape to check that these points on your body line up with the relevant points on your toile.

What is balance in a garment?

Perfect balance is when a garment's CF, CB, waist line, and hip lines are aligned with the corresponding points on the body. It is important to balance your toile correctly, because all other garments will be produced from this base. Getting this right will remove the need to correct all subsequent garments that you produce using this pattern.

Using a dress form
If you have invested in a dress form, you could fit your toile to a dress form padded out to your own personal measurements (see page 178).

Assessing the fit of your toile

When you try on your toile, stand back and look at your garment in a long mirror. Assess the fit and notice the position of the balance lines on the toile. Check that the CF, CB, waist, bust, and hip lines align to your own body. It is important to stand straight and look forward. Ask someone to help you with this stage, as it can be difficult, particularly when trying to see the back. Looking down or twisting will render the assessment of fit inaccurate.

Be aware of how the garment feels on the body—the bodice should be fitted, but not tight. Notice any excess loose fabric or pulling across the garment. The armhole must not feel restricted, and you should be able to move your arm freely. Remember to look at the side seams and check that they are on your sides and not drifting forward or backward.

Taking your time to properly assess and alter the toile at this stage will be worthwhile. A perfectly fitted toile will ensure that the designs you produce subsequently will fit beautifully.

1 Tie a cord or length of elastic around your natural waist. Compare the tied line to the waist line marked on the toile. If, as shown here, the two lines are not the same, the waist line will need to be adjusted on the pattern.

2 Here, two alterations are needed. The bodice is too long and the waist is too small. To correct this, measure the difference between the elastic and the pencil line; this will give you the amount to shorten the bodice pattern by. The tightness at the waist is best adjusted by opening the side seams. Measure the amount of extra room required and add it to the pattern.

Fitting the sleeve

You can assess the sleeve fit when it is on the stand or on the body. The center grain running down the sleeve should line up slightly in front of the skirt or pant side seam. Look at the sleeve on the arm to see that the wrist is central within the sleeve hem, and check that the sleeve is not dragging up against the arm at the front or back. If dragging is present, take the sleeve out and readjust the sleeve cap by moving it around the armhole either forward or backward. This may be only a very slight adjustment, no more than ¼ in. (6 mm).

Incorrect sleeve alignment
This alignment would cause the sleeve to drift toward the back.

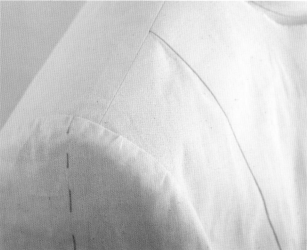

Correct sleeve alignment
The central sleeve grain should start ³/₈ in. (1 cm) behind the bodice shoulder line. The biceps line should be horizontal and the central grain should continue down slightly in front of the garment side seam.

Making simple toile adjustments

If the toile is too big:
Pinch out any obvious excess fabric through the seams and darts of your toile, making sure that the balance lines remain straight. Mark the adjustments with a pencil, and transfer them to your pattern.

If the toile is too small:
Unpick the restricted area, releasing the tension. Measure the gap that is created, and add in the amounts needed where necessary.

Making major toile adjustments

You will need to permanently alter your toile if any adjustments are major, and perhaps even make another. Always ensure you make the corresponding adjustments to your pattern. The toile is an important part of making your own patterns, and often several are needed before the fit is completely right.

Pattern making

There are simple ways to make your own patterns using existing clothes as templates or working with basic shapes. It is a great way be creative and produce your own unique styles.

Commercial patterns are expertly created with instructions and diagrams to help you to construct all sorts of garments. You can also learn the principles of pattern drafting to make your own unique designs, but it can take time to master these skills. With knowledge gained from using commercial paper patterns, it is easy to make your own clothes by cloning your favorite items from your wardrobe, or by joining simple shapes to produce a more complex three-dimensional piece.

The easiest way to copy a well-loved garment (where a replacement cannot be purchased) is to cut it up and use each panel as a template to create a brand new version. This, however, might not be appropriate if you still want to wear the original item or, for sentimental reasons, do not want to cut it up. If this is the case, it is still possible to flatten out each part of a piece of clothing and take a paper copy of it to use as a pattern. If you use an iron to flatten out any creases and a tape measure for accurate sizing, the process is simple.

For more original ideas, working to a formula is another option for creating your own patterns. By incorporating specific measurements for bust, waist, and hip, among others, a shape can be built up to fit your own body shape.

It is never acceptable to copy manufactured garments for commercial use. If you have a favorite, well-fitting item of clothing that has worn out and cannot be replaced then use either of these methods to replicate the design.

Cutting up a garment

When a piece of clothing is worn out but you love the style, use the panels as templates to produce a new garment. This process works for childrens' and adults' garments.

1
Cut the garment along the seam lines and separate the panels. Iron them flat so that they are easier to work with—flat, crinkle-free pieces will give a more accurate result.

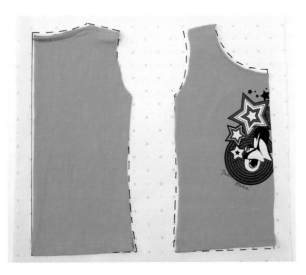

2
Place the pieces, one by one, on pattern paper and draw around each piece with a dotted line. Where the pieces are perfectly symmetrical, cut through the center and draw only half of the shape—for example, a center front or center back where there is no fastening or join.

4

Add seam and hem allowances to each piece where appropriate. This is generally 5/8 in. (1.5 cm) for seam allowances but hem depths vary; use the existing garment as a guide. Draw this as a solid line as this will be your cutting line.

3

Add facings and bands as necessary, using the cut-up garment as a guide. You may decide to measure the neckline circumference, but it is easier to get an accurate length using the actual band.

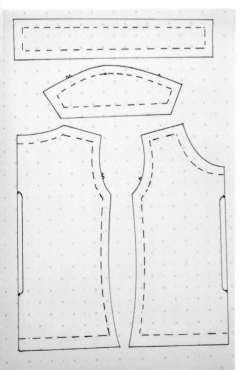

5

Add marks and symbols to the pattern pieces to transfer the necessary information for making up. Mark the straight grain, if any part should be placed to a fold, and dots and notches to show where panels will be joined. Also, name each piece and state the number of pieces that need to be cut out.

6

Make up the garment in appropriate fabric using the pattern symbols to match the pieces in the correct places.

Copying a favorite garment

If you do not want to cut up your favorite garment, you can trace each section onto pattern paper to achieve a copy of the garment. When you have added seam and hem allowances, you will have a good-fitting replica of the original.

Original shorts.

TIPS

With a complex shape, use the clues from the weave to see the direction of the grain.

- Don't forget about darts and areas that are eased or gathered. Allow for these in the panels and draw in new darts in the appropriate places.

- Measure curved seams on the garment and draw these accurately on paper to make sure the parts fit well.

- Mark topstitching lines and button and buttonhole positions.

- Make up a toile to make sure that the pieces fit together before starting with your chosen material.

- Take a photograph of the original garment and add it to the envelope where you will keep the pattern pieces so you can store them for future use.

1
Lay the garment on the pattern paper with the relevant panel directly on it. Hold the panel in place and draw around the outline. Adjust the panel to enable you to draw around all sides of the shape on the sewing line, lifting up the edges to give yourself a better view.

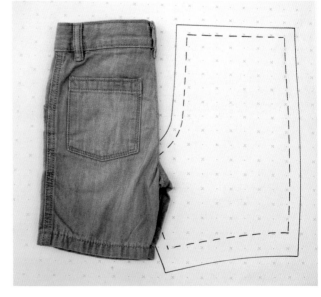

2
Add seam allowances (normally ⅝ in. [1.5 cm]) and hem allowances to the panel you have prepared so that it can be joined to the other parts.

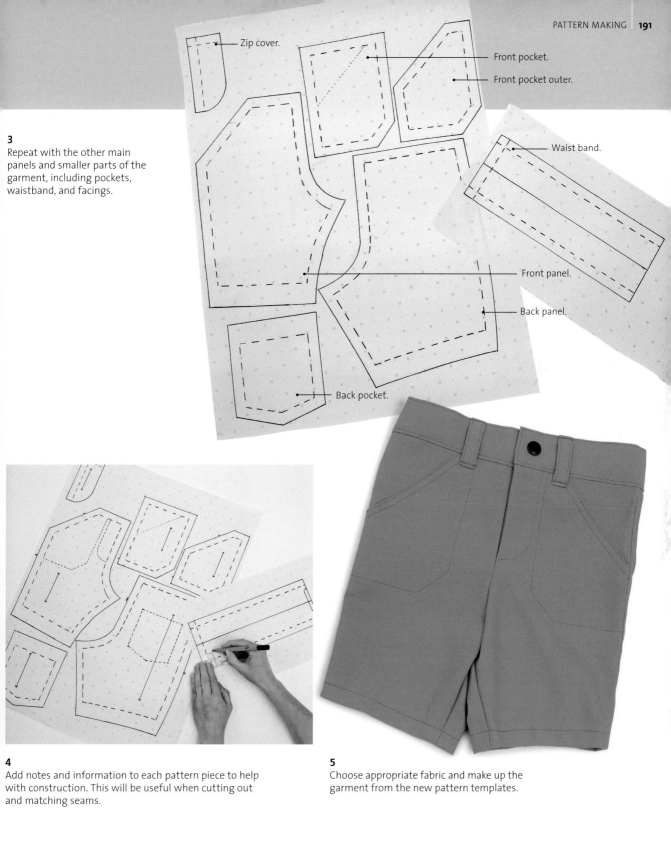

Zip cover.

Front pocket.

Front pocket outer.

Waist band.

3
Repeat with the other main panels and smaller parts of the garment, including pockets, waistband, and facings.

Front panel.

Back panel.

Back pocket.

4
Add notes and information to each pattern piece to help with construction. This will be useful when cutting out and matching seams.

5
Choose appropriate fabric and make up the garment from the new pattern templates.

Skirt formula

Make a basic, straight skirt that fits well by following a formula that uses your own measurements. You will need your waist and hip measurements as well as waist-to-hip and waist-to-knee measurements.

1
Draw a vertical line of your waist-to-knee length near the left of your pattern paper. This represents the center front and center back of your skirt. Mark the position of the waist-to-hip length on this line and draw a horizontal guideline from this point. Also draw horizontal lines from the waist and knee positions.

2
Take your waist measurement and divide it by four. Add ¾ in. (2 cm) for darts. Mark this point on the top horizontal guideline, measured from the left.

3
Take your hip measurement and divide it by four. Mark this point on the middle horizontal guideline, measured from the left.

4
Take your quarter hip measurement from Step 3 and add ¾ in. (2 cm). Mark the point on the bottom horizontal line, measured from the left.

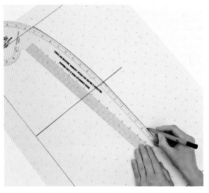

5
Draw a curved line joining the points at the waist to the hip level then continue straight to the point on the knee level in a natural line. This is the side seam position.

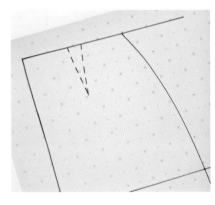

6
Mark the mid-point on the horizontal waist line and draw in a ¾-in. (2-cm) wide dart measuring 3 in. (7.5 cm) long.

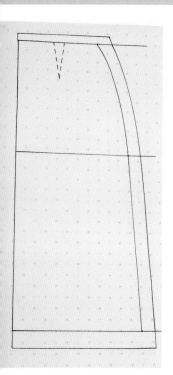

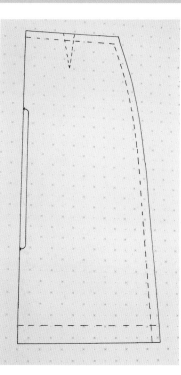

TIP
Alter the style to suit your taste and figure by moving the dart position and lengthening or shortening them appropriately or changing the waist level. Add patch pockets if you wish (see page 114), insert a front fly zipper (see page 77), or cut on the bias (see page 39). Your new, well-fitting, basic skirt pattern has lots of possibilities.

7
Draw a line 1 in. (2.5 cm) outside the side seam (⁵/₈ in. [1.5 cm] is for the seam allowance and ³/₈ in. [1 cm] for ease). Add a ⁵/₈ in. (1.5 cm) seam allowance at the waist and a 1 ¼ in. (3 cm) hem allowance.

8
Trace off the pattern information from Step 7 for your skirt front. When cutting out, the straight vertical line should be placed to a fold.

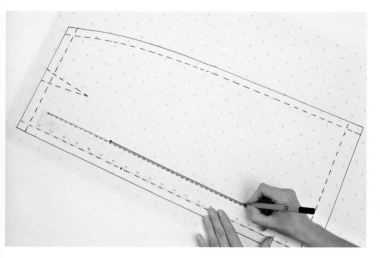

9
Trace off the same pattern shape for the back and add a 1-in. (2.5-cm) seam and ease allowance to the center-back seam. Draw in the new seam lines and mark the base of the zipper. Cut two pieces for the back.

10
Make up the skirt in your own choice of fabric. Insert a zipper in the center-back seam and finish the waist edge with a band (see page 122) or facing (see page 126).

Simple top

You can make a simple sleeveless top using a basic rectangular shape. You will need your bust measurement as well as your shoulder-to-hip length and shoulder-to-bust length.

1
Draw a rectangle with a length the same as your shoulder-to hip-length and width of half your bust measurement plus 1 in. (2.5 cm) for ease.

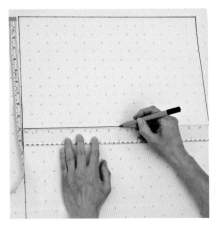

2
Measure your shoulder-to-bust length, mark this measurement on the vertical line taken from the top left of the rectangle, and draw a horizontal line that represents your bust level.

3
Find the middle of the horizontal lines and draw a vertical line that represents the center front and center back of the garment.

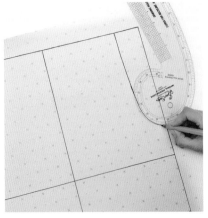

4
Draw in the armholes from a starting point 2 in. (5 cm) above the bust level to the top horizontal line (shoulder level) to suit your style. Use a French curve to create a smooth and natural shape.

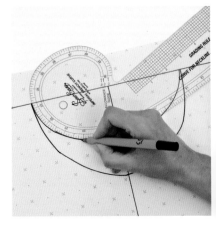

5
Draw in the front and back neckline shaping to suit your style. Use a French curve, and ensure the scoop is symmetrical.

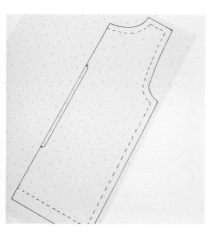

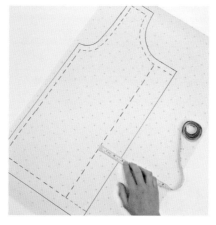

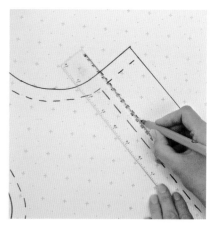

6

Trace off half the shape using the back neck shaping; this is the back of your top. Mark the center line with a curved arrow to represent placing the fabric to a fold and add seam and hem allowances to all the other outside edges.

7

Trace off half the pattern again with the front neck shaping for the front of your top. Add 2 ½ in. (6.5 cm) to the center edge for a stand for buttons and buttonholes, and add seam and hem allowances to the other outside edges.

8

On the front panel, mark vertical fold lines for the 1-in. (2.5-cm) wide front band where the fabric will be folded to create an integrated facing for the buttonholes and buttons. Mark the waist position at the side seam and a point 2 in. (5 cm) below for a vent at the lower end of the side seam.

9

To make up the top, choose a suitable fabric and cut out one back to a fold and two front pieces. Fold the front band into position and topstitch then finish the armholes and neck edge by binding with bias strips or facings. Make two narrow ties to insert in the side seams at the waist—when tied at the back, these will add shape to the garment by identifying the waist. Leave the lower end of the side seams open.

Customizing clothes

This chapter provides a reference for ideas and inspiration for embellishing and customizing fabrics, clothes, and accessories. Choose techniques like appliqué, couching, smocking, and decorative serging to turn your own designs into unique and special creations.

Decorative stitching

Machine stitching doesn't always have to be functional; it can be used to great decorative effect when embellishing fabrics and garments. Sewing with fancy, novelty, or contrasting colored threads and yarns create decorative finishes to make clothes unique.

Teacups (far left) stitched by Helen Dickson
Free-motion machine embroidery and appliqué can be combined to make pictures and embellish fabric. There's no need to neaten raw edges, the cut fabric and free-motion sewing produces quirky, contemporary motifs.

Figures (left and below) stitched by Rosemary James
Free-motion embroidery is a textile art in its own right. With practice, and an artistic eye, you can create wearable works of art.

Topstitching and edge stitching

Topstitching (see page 57) and edge stitching describe the process in which machine sewing is used on the surface of a garment to add decorative detail, although it may also be functional to make an edge crisp or control a loose facing. The two are often used together but may be used separately to either sharpen an edge or draw attention to a seam or a feature on a piece of clothing. To make topstitching more obvious, topstitch thread is often used as it is thicker and gives a bolder finish. If done well, topstitching can turn a homemade garment into an expensive-looking, hand-crafted, or designer outfit.

Topstitching (see page 57)

ALTERNATIVE TOPSTITCHING

Set the stitch to a stretch or reinforcement stitch if you only have standard thread and you want a stronger line. This sews backward and forward forming extra stitches to make the line appear bolder.

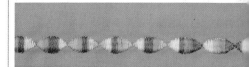

Choose a decorative stitch rather than a straight stitch if one is available on your sewing machine, and sew this parallel to the edge or seam. This is particularly attractive with variegated thread. Alternatively, use shaded thread with a broad satin stitch as this looks like a braid when sewn close to the edge.

1
Choose a suitable thread in an appropriate color, either to blend into the garment or, more likely, to contrast and show up on it. Choose topstitch thread, buttonhole twist, metallic thread, or even two standard threads together. Use standard thread in the bobbin.

2
Fit a specialist needle (topstitch or metallic) to the sewing machine and lengthen the straight stitch to 1/8 in. (3 mm). These needles will prevent the threads from splitting or shredding. Fit an edge stitch foot if you have one, as this will provide a guide to follow and help to produce a straight, professional finish.

3
For edge stitching, stitch very close to the edge or seam—1/16 in. (2 mm) away. To help achieve a perfectly straight edge if you do not have an edge stitch presser foot, try adjusting the needle position and mark a spot on the standard presser foot to follow.

4
For topstitching, decide how far from the edge you wish to sew—generally about 1/4 in. (6 mm) and find a guide to follow to keep your stitching straight. Use the edge of the foot or fit a quarter-inch or topstitch foot to the sewing machine.

TIPS
- Sew from the right side of the cloth for best results, as the tension is set up to produce a better-looking stitch this way.
- Do not secure your thread ends with reverse stitching but take them through to the wrong side and tie off or neaten with a needle.

Couching

Couching describes the process in which a thread or cord is held in position on the surface of a fabric with a second thread that is sewn over it. Decide whether you prefer to couch by hand or with a zigzag stitch on a sewing machine. Either way, use it to decorate a garment with lettering or cord embellishment.

COUCHING BY HAND

1
Mark the design on the surface of the fabric with a temporary marker.

2
Thread up a needle with a thread the same color as the cord being used to produce the design, and secure it in the back of the work with a knot or two stitches, one on top of the other. We have used different colors here to illustrate the technique.

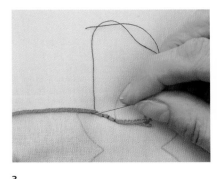

3
Lay the cord on the surface of the fabric over the guide line. With a tail extending beyond the start, bring the needle to the right side and take it back down, making a stitch over the cord at the beginning of the work.

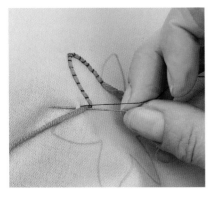

4
Make tiny stitches along the length of the cord, trapping it in place on top of the guide line and securing it to the fabric.

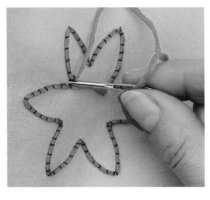

5
When the design is completed, thread the cord tails at the start and finish of the work onto a large-eyed needle and take them to the underside to neaten off.

Completed flower outline with the cord tails finished on the wrong side.

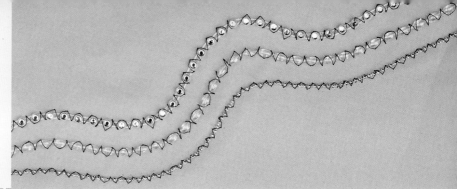

COUCHING BY MACHINE

1
Transfer the design to the surface of the fabric and add a support to the wrong side with a tear-away stabilizer. Choose a sticky variety, or use a temporary spray adhesive to hold the layers together while working.

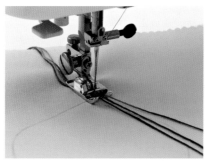

2
Set up the sewing machine with a zigzag stitch, adjusting the width so that it just covers the cord. Fit a cording foot to the sewing machine for best results, and use a suitable thread in the needle to couch the cord in place. Feed the cord through the foot and place over the starting point of the design. Lower the presser foot and zigzag over the cord, following the guide line.

3
Follow the outline of the design and the foot will automatically position the cords under the needle for stitching. Complete the design.

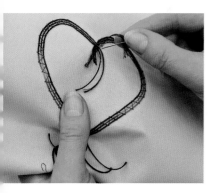

4
When the stitching is complete, take the threads and cord ends to the wrong side with a large-eyed needle and secure them neatly.

5
Remove the stabilizer from the wrong side of the work. It should tear away easily.

Finished example with thread tails pulled through to the wrong side and neatened.

Free-motion embroidery and quilting

When the feed dogs are dropped into the body of the machine and the standard presser foot is replaced with a darning foot, sewing control is over to you. The fabric is no longer moved steadily from front to back by the rotating teeth, but by moving the fabric under the needle yourself, you can decide where the stitches are formed, and how long or short each one should be. This makes it possible to quilt freehand or "paint with threads."

FREE-MOTION EMBROIDERY

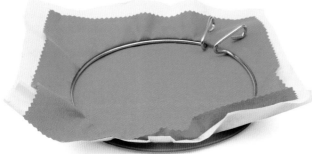

Pattern embellishment Select a printed cloth and highlight areas of the design with free machine sewing using rayon or polyester machine embroidery threads that reflect the light.

TIP
Free-motion sewing can also be used for darning. Apply a patch to the wrong side of the fabric with a heat-fusible film of glue, and with the right side facing, free-sew back and forward over the area to mend it.

1
Drop the feed dogs by moving a switch or lever on your sewing machine or by covering the teeth with a plate. The manual will show how to do this for your model.

2
For best results, place a stabilizer on the wrong side of the fabric and fix the layers into a hoop. This holds the fabric and prevents pulling and distorting. If the work is too large to hoop, use a stiff stabilizer to support the fabrics while you sew.

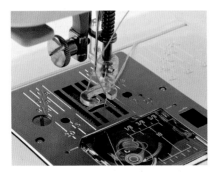

QUILTING

3
Fit a darning foot to the sewing machine and set the needle to sew in the center on a straight stitch. Thread up with standard thread in the bobbin and needle. (When you have mastered the technique, you can use decorative threads on the surface and bobbin, fill in the base, and play with zigzag stitch to achieve the effects you wish.)

4
Place the hoop under the darning foot. You may need to raise the take-up lever to a higher position to allow it to slide under. Lower the presser foot (although note it will not hold the fabric tight), and start sewing by moving the fabric while you have the foot pedal pressed. Sew steadily to create consistently sized stitches.

You will not need to use a stabilizer or a hoop for quilting, just grab the edges of the quilt and sew over the layers. Wearing latex gloves will help you to keep the work clean and help to grip the fabric layers while you sew.

Reverse stitching

Reverse stitching is simply explained as sewing upside down. Sometimes it would be nice to have a bold decorative thread on the surface of the fabric but the size of the eye of the needle limits the thickness of thread you can use. By winding a fine cord—stranded silk, stranded cotton, or crochet cotton—around the bobbin and feeding your fabric under the needle with the right side facing down, the needle thread will hold it on the surface, a little like couching. Choose a straight or pre-programmed decorative stitch, or sew freehand to achieve the style you want.

> **TIP**
> Use the same technique, winding thick threads and cords onto the bobbin, with pre-programmed stitches like simple flowers or leaves for a bold border on a hem or cuff.

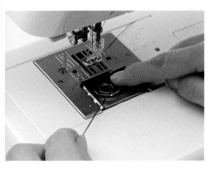

1
Select a suitable cord, thread, or yarn for the bobbin and wind it on carefully. Place the bobbin in the bobbin holder or race and adjust the tension until the cord runs smoothly. Set the machine to free-motion sewing then thread the needle with a standard thread.

2
Apply a tear-away stabilizer to the wrong side of the fabric—a temporary spray adhesive works well. The stabilizer improves the quality of the stitch. Draw the design on the stabilizer so that you can follow it while you sew.

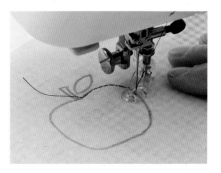

3
Place the work so that the right side of the fabric faces down and the stabilizer with the design outline faces up. Lower the presser foot and follow the design, sewing steadily and creating consistently sized stitches.

4
When your sewing is finished, cut all the threads with long tails and pull them to the wrong side to secure them.

5
Turn the work over to see the finished effect with the cord sewn to the surface of the fabric.

WARNING
It is important to have a separate bobbin holder that can be kept for decorative stitching when the tension must be changed so that you do not need to alter your main one. This avoids problems with poor tension when you return to standard sewing.

Appliqué

Appliqué is a decorative technique where fabric shapes are sewn, by hand or machine, to the surface of a background fabric. Traditionally the fabric pieces were basted in place before being sewn, but now adhesive products are available to make the task easier and quicker.

Hand-sewn appliqué

Generally, the raw edges are tucked under for a neat finish, and when in position, a blanket stitch or slipstitch holds the applied fabric shape permanently in place.

1
From your design idea, cut out each appliqué shape in your chosen fabrics with a 1/4 in. (6 mm) seam allowance around the outside.

2
On the wrong side of the appliqué shape, mark the sewing line with a temporary pen. Snip or notch the 1/4 in. (6 mm) seam allowance just short of the sewing line and then fold it to the wrong side so that the shape is flat with no creases or tucks below.

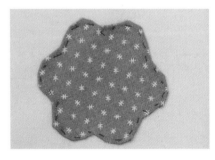

3
Arrange the appliqué shape on the background fabric according to your design idea, and baste in place ready for hand stitching.

4
Thread your needle with perlé cotton or stranded cotton/silk and tie a knot or secure the thread end in the back of your work. Bring the needle to the surface and sew around the edge of each shape with a blanket stitch (see page 45).

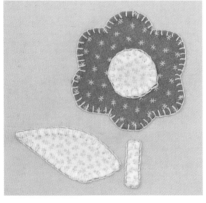

Finished design with blanket stitch.

Alternatively, sew the pieces in place with a slip stitch for an invisible join.

Machined appliqué

Attaching appliqué with satin stitch or zigzag is a quick and effective way of creating a bold design. It is good for adding lettering to garments or decorating children's wear. A paper-backed fusible adhesive is the best way to apply the fabric pieces.

1

Iron a paper-backed adhesive to the wrong side of the appliqué fabric. Draw the design on the paper backing (remember to draw the shape in reverse so that it will appear with the right side facing when in place).

2

Cut out the appliqué shape and peel away the paper backing. Discard the backing paper as the glue will now be on the reverse of the fabric.

3

Place the shape on the backing fabric and iron it in position to soften the heat-fusible glue to hold it in place.

4

Choose a contrasting thread to work as an outline to your appliqué shape and set your sewing machine to zigzag stitch. Adjust the width to suit and shorten the length so that the zigzag looks like a solid line and becomes a satin stitch.

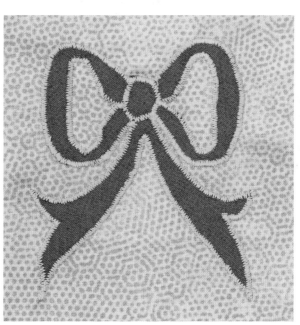

5

Carefully sew around the outer edge of the appliqué shape covering the join with the satin stitches to form a border. To finish, take the thread tails to the wrong side and neaten securely.

Alternative appliqué ideas

Stuffed appliqué

Padded appliqué is a good way to add depth and texture. While it may not be a regular embellishment on garments, it is useful for decorating bags and accessories.

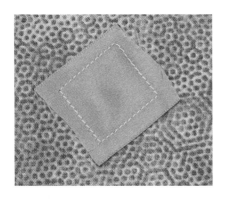

1
Cut out the appliqué shape ¼ in. (6 mm) beyond the outline and position on the fabric. With the sewing machine set to a straight stitch, sew on the outline of the shape through the fabric below it.

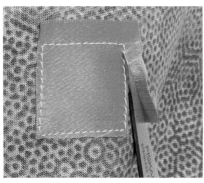

2
Trim the shape, snipping away the fabric just outside the outline, taking care not to cut the backing.

3
Change the sewing machine settings to satin stitch and sew over the stitching and raw edge to produce a bold neat outline. This defines the shape and secures the edge of it.

4
Turn the work over and cut a small slit in the background fabric behind the appliqué. Take care not to cut through or damage the top layer.

5
Stuff with padding to raise the design and finish by sewing up the slit with a few slip stitches.

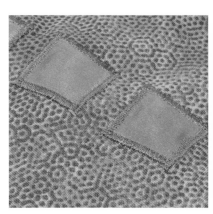

The finished appliqué squares are slightly raised from the surface of the cloth.

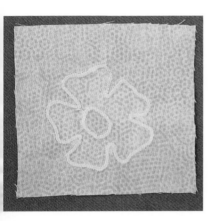

Reverse appliqué Place the right side of a contrasting fabric to the wrong side of your main cloth and baste together. Sew a satin-stitch outline of your chosen shape then cut away the surface material to reveal the fabric behind to create a reverse appliqué.

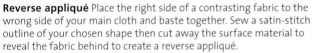

Straight-stitch free machining and appliqué Make simple pictures or flowers by applying small shapes of cloth and drawing in lines, or create texture and detail with free-machine stitching.

Using a print Use a printed flower or motif from a length of cloth as a ready prepared appliqué shape. Iron a fusible adhesive to the wrong side, cut around the outline, and iron then sew in place.

Smocking

Use this traditional craft for cushions, purses, and panels in evening bodices. A length of cloth is gathered up to form a bank of tucks or tiny pleats then hand embroidery or machine stitching is sewn over them. The result is a decorative panel with a small amount of stretch in it.

HANDMADE SMOCKING
The method below shows you how to create gauging stitches. It is possible, however, to buy sheets of transfer paper with regularly spaced smocking dots on, which are ironed on to the wrong side of the fabric to produce a guide to make it easier to sew even gauging stitches.

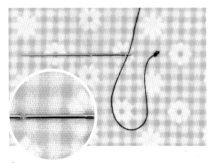

1
Having decided on the length of the stitch, secure the thread with a generous knot. Insert the needle into the fabric on the wrong side and make a tiny stitch of just a few threads.

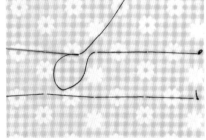

2
Work the first row, ensuring that all the stitches are evenly sized and spaced. Leave a long thread at the end of the row. Work a second row, making sure that all the stitches are exactly on the same vertical line.

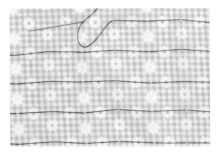

3
Work several rows of stitching, again making sure that all the stitches are exactly on the same vertical line.

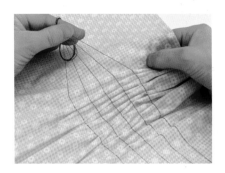

4
Carefully holding all the threads at the end of the rows, begin pulling up the gathers until you have the desired finished width.

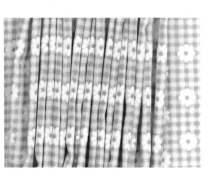

5
Place a pin at the end of each thread and fasten the thread around the pins in a figure eight.

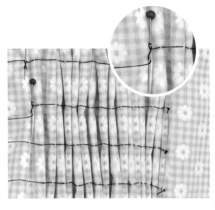

6
On the right side of the fabric, you will have produced rows of small, neat pleats that can then be smocked.

STITCHING YOUR GAUGING

Once the fabric is prepared with gauging, the embroidery stitches are sewn on the surface of the vertical tucks.

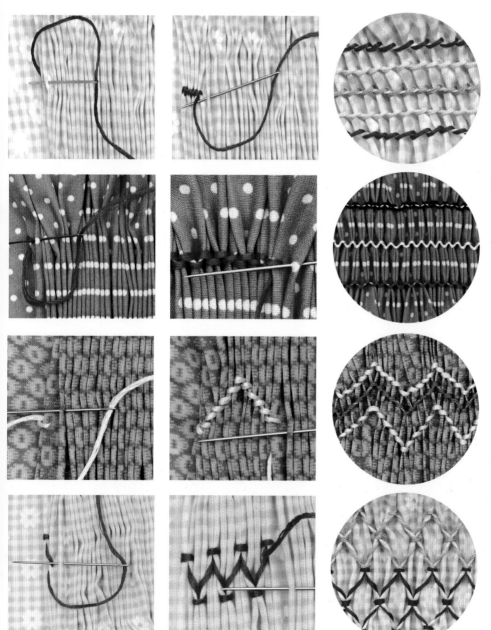

Stem stitch Bring your needle up on the left of a pleat and take it down on the right of the second pleat just a little above so that the slanted stitch grabs the two together. Bring the needle up on the left of the second pleat and take it down on the right of the third pleat and continue.

Cable stitch Create the stitches as above, except make the stitches horizontal rather than slanted to form one above and the next below along the row.

Chevron stitch Work stitches in blocks, sewing up and down to create a zigzag. Count carefully, to make the stitch repeat consistent. Several of these create a wave pattern.

Honeycomb stitch Working left to right, take a large diagonal stitch followed by a shorter horizontal stitch. Make these in pairs to form a zigzag and sew a second row below it mirroring the first.

Sewing machine smocking

Although machine smocking does not recreate traditional smocking, it is a quicker alternative that looks good in its own right. Sew the gathers by hand or use machine gathering with a long straight stitch. Start each row of machine gathering in line with the one above it to help to keep the tucks even.

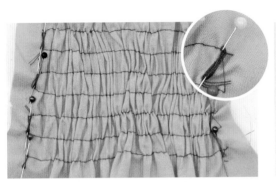

1
Prepare the panel of pleats by hand gathering them as on page 208 or by setting the sewing machine to the longest straight stitch and sewing several rows of gathering. Pull up the gathers to form the base for the smocking. Secure the thread tails at both ends by winding them around vertical pins.

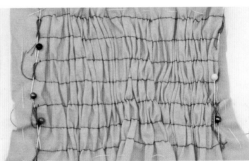

2
Apply a tear-away stabilizer to the wrong side of the prepared gathered fabric to support the work while you sew the decorative stitches. Baste this in place, or use a temporary spray adhesive.

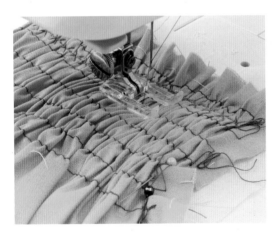

3
Set the sewing machine with two reels of thread fed through the guides and needle—two threads will give a bolder stitch. Fit an open-toe or clear-view foot to the sewing machine to make sewing easier. Sew parallel rows of stitches over the gathers and in between the temporary gauging.

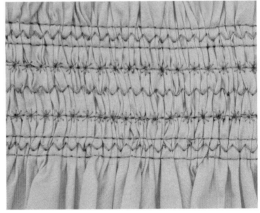

4
Remove all the temporary stitches and the stabilizer from the wrong side and ease out the stitches. Press lightly from the wrong side.

TIPS
- When working machine gathers as a base for smocking, start each row in a straight line so that the tucks line up across the fabric. This helps to prevent the tucks from twisting or looking uneven.

- Examine the decorative stitches available on your sewing machine and carry out a test piece to help select appropriate stitches for your design.

Decorative serging

Sewing with a serger is a great way to construct clothes quickly, since they sew seams and neaten edges at the same time. However, sergers can also produce very useful and attractive stitches by adjusting the tension and using decorative threads in the loopers. Use these alternative finishes for delicate hems and decorative seams.

Picot edge

This delicate edge is very similar to a rolled hem (see page 65) but it has a softer, more forgiving finish that works better on some fabrics. With virtually the same settings on your serger, a picot stitch has a slightly longer stitch length and this softens the edge and makes it less stiff. Providing the stitch coverage is still close enough to hide the narrow raw edge, making the stitches further apart is much more appropriate for chiffon and similar lightweight, soft materials.

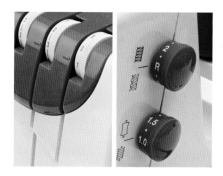

1
Prepare the settings on your serger for rolled hem but instead of making the stitches very close to one another, lengthen the stitch to increase the space between them. Place the fabric under the presser foot and serge to form the picot edge.

2
Adjust the stitch length as necessary—close enough to control the narrow hem yet far enough apart to soften the edge.

TIPS
- It can be difficult to grab the edge of a lightweight fabric like chiffon at the start of a hem, so place a small piece of tear-away stabilizer under the fabric at the start to provide the support needed to stitch.

- When making scarves using a soft, sheer fabric, use this stabilizer trick at each corner to prevent the stitches from falling off the fabric: Place a dot of fray-stopping glue on each corner chain, and when dry, snip off the excess chain for a neat finish.

The finished edge curls to create a delicate, feminine effect.

Lettuce edging

A lettuce-edge hem is a delightful way to neaten the edges of a garment made from a stretchy fabric. It is especially popular on dresses and T-shirts for girls. Simply set your serger to rolled hemming and stretch the fabric as you feed it under the presser foot to force more stitches onto the edge to make it curl.

1
Use standard thread on both loopers and needle, or place metallic or embroidery thread through the upper looper to give a special edge. Start serging so that the first few stitches attach to the edge.

2
When the stitches are anchored, continue to feed the fabric under the presser foot with the blade skimming off the raw edge, and hold back the fabric as the feed dogs drag it under the presser foot. With your right hand clasping the fabric in front of the needle, and your left holding the fabric edge behind, feed the fabric through slowly to ensure more stitches are sewn to the edge. This will encourage it to curl.

Serged tucks

A textured effect is created when rows of rolled hem are stitched on folds of fabric. Just like pin tucks sewn on a sewing machine, serger tucks can be formed over the surface of material to produce a raised, decorative finish.

1
Set your serger for rolled hemming and place a decorative or contrasting thread in the upper looper. Disengage the serger blade, if possible. Press folds into the fabric to show the spacing and positions of the tucks.

2
With right side facing out, feed the folded fabric under the presser foot, watching as the needle catches the fold. Adjust the position of the fold as it is fed under the foot to control the size of the tuck. Sew all the tucks, working in the same direction for each one.

3
When the tucks are formed, open the fabric and press lightly from the wrong side, taking care not to flatten them. You can create a lattice effect with crossed serged tucks as has been done here.

Fishing line hem

For a stiff, curled edge, sometimes seen on elegant, ballroom dance dresses, serge over a length of fishing line and manipulate the edge to form a firm and curving hem. Use 18-lb (8-kg) breaking-strain fishing line, or heavier, and set your serger for rolled hemming. This effect can only be created on a stretchy fabric, so choose a fine knit, or cut woven fabric on the bias or true cross.

1
Prepare your serger for rolled hemming and thread up accordingly. Use a decorative thread in the upper looper and choose the other cones to match the fabric color. Hold the fishing line under the presser foot and serge some stitches over it.

2
When the stitches have merged with the nylon line, place the fabric edge under the fishing line, in front of the foot, with ½ in. (1 cm) extending beyond the blade. Serge, cutting off the excess and watch as the line and fabric edge become encased in rolled hem stitches.

5
When you have finished stretching the stitches across the fishing line the curling is complete and a stiff, gently curving edge is created. Cut off the excess fishing line and use a dot of glue to hold the end in place within the rolled-hem stitches.

3
When the hem is complete, cut the stitch chain from the machine but not the fishing line. The edge is flat with the fishing line encased by stitches on the edge.

4
Manipulate the line through the rolled hemming stitches, stretching the fabric in the process. As the fabric stretches, the hem edge curls and is held with the stiff fishing line inside the stitches.

Flatlocking

Preparing a serger for flatlocking is not possible on all models and settings vary, so check your manual for details. Flatlocking involves loosening the needle tension so that when the seam is sewn, it can be pulled flat to sit on the surface. This leaves loops on the surface and a ladder of stitches on the wrong side. Using decorative thread in the loopers creates very attractive effects. Take time to play and experiment.

1
Set the serger to the settings for flatlocking. This involves removing one needle and using either the left (for a wide finish) or the right (for a narrow finish), loosening the needle tension, and tightening the lower looper tension. Run a test sample to check the stitching and adjust as necessary.

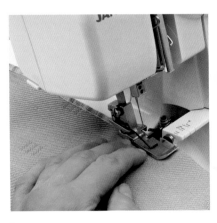

2
With wrong sides together, feed the fabric under the presser foot. Cut the excess from the seam with the blade as you go.

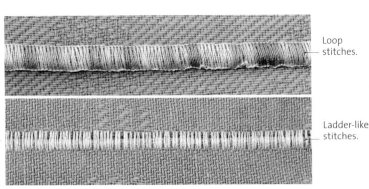

Loop stitches.

Ladder-like stitches.

3
When the seam is complete, remove it from the serger, leaving a length of chain—do not cut it short as it is likely to ravel. Carefully pull the seam apart so that the loops lie flat on the surface and the ladder stitches underneath.

4
When the seam has been pulled flat along its length, the loops will sit on the right side and the ladders underneath. If a decorative thread is used, it will appear on the surface.

TIPS
- Adjust the stitch length and tension to suit the thread in the serger. It is worth taking time to experiment on spare cloth so that your project will have perfect decorative stitching.

- If you remove a needle, tighten up the screw even though there is nothing to hold in place. If you do not, the screw is likely to rattle out and drop into the serger or get lost.

Decorative thread

Show off your serged edges! Using decorative threads can add contrasting edging to your projects. Don't just use matching threads, experiment with different colors and types of thread to add something different to your garments.

GREAT WAYS TO USE DECORATIVE THREAD

1. Add a luxurious silk thread edging: Use it only in the loopers so this expensive thread will go further.

2. Use wooly nylon in the needles and loopers to create a soft edge with great coverage.

3. Decorate an edge using 2mm wide silk ribbon in the upper looper to create a beautiful soft finish.

4. Create a braid-like finish by using a heavy, pearlized tapestry cotton in the upper looper only to make a heavier trim for heavier fabrics.

5. Use topstitching thread in a striking color or a medium-weight strong thread in a high luster. Thread the upper looper only for something a bit different.

1

2

3

4

5

SERGING WITH CROCHET THREAD

Crochet thread can be used to add a decorative edge to a project, forming a braid-like fabric edging. Choose the thread carefully—it must be soft, pliable, and narrow enough to go through the machine and upper looper.

1
Thread the upper looper with crochet thread and loosen the tension setting; use a needle threader or thread loop to do this.

2
Thread up the machine using regular threads in the needles and lower looper.

Set stitch length to the maximum setting, in this case 4.

Set the differential feed dial to 1.

3
Set the machine to the longest stitch settings and turn the handle to ensure stitches are being made. Test out on your fabric and adjust stitch length/tension setting until you achieve the desired result. Sew slowly until you have completed your edge.

Couture techniques

Special couture finishes are explained here for you to use on those distinctive garments where only the best will do. Here you'll discover what to do on the inside to make the outside look great.

Hong Kong finish

CLIP 14
Hong Kong finish
http://qr.quartobooks.com/vgss/clip14.html

This traditional method of finishing seam allowances with a binding is known as the Hong Kong finish. It is labor-intensive and therefore usually reserved for high-end garments.

This variation places the finished seam allowances on the outside of the garment; it's a nice way to emphasize line and add texture. For this technique, the wrong side of the fabric is exposed in the seam allowances, so use a reversible fabric, or one with a wrong side that you like. This finish is not suitable for curved seams for which the allowances need to be clipped to lie flat.

1
Cut enough 1 ½ in. (3.75 cm)-wide bias strips to bind the edges of all the seam allowances that you wish to finish. Because any joins in pieced strips would be glaring, make sure that you have enough fabric to make long, unpieced strips. The extra width of the strips makes the process easier and can be trimmed away later.

2
Stretch press the strips. Bind the seam allowance edge.

3
Place a garment section wrong side up. Lay a bias strip, right side down, along the edge to be bound. Sew in place, stitching ¼ in. (6 mm) from the edge (the width of your presser foot).

4
Using a pressing cloth, press the work as sewn to embed the stitches, then press the seam allowance and the bias strip away from the garment section.

TIPS
- The binding is applied to the seam allowances before the garment is constructed, so it is imperative to make a toile (see page 184) and correct your pattern as needed before beginning. Seams finished in this manner should not be altered.

- Try using prints, checks, or bold colors for the binding fabric. Have fun!

- Repeat the steps in this section on all edges to be bound.

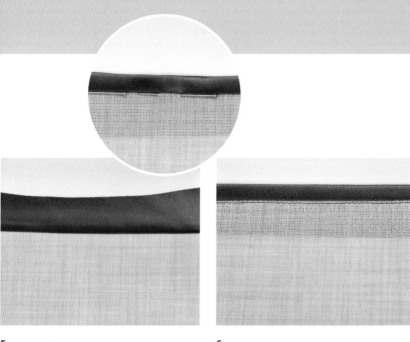

5
Fold the bias over the seam allowance edge onto the right side of the garment piece. Pin, placing the pins in the ditch of the seam.

6
With the garment section wrong side up, stitch in the ditch to secure the binding.

7
Turn the piece over. Trim the bias strip about 1/8 in. (3 mm) from the stitching. Assemble the garment.

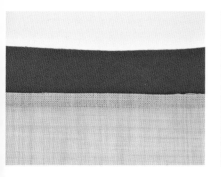

8
Refer to your pattern directions for the construction sequence. For each seam, place the garment pieces wrong sides together, aligning the bound edges. Pin and then stitch each seam.

9
Press the work as sewn to embed the stitches, then press the seam allowances open. On each allowance, stitch in the ditch over previous stitching through all thicknesses.

10
Follow your pattern directions to complete the garment.

Balanced dart

CLIP 15
Balanced dart
http://qr.quartobooks.com/vgss/clip15.html

A balanced dart is created by adding an extra layer of fabric on the inside. The additional layer allows the fabric layers to lie naturally giving a smoother finish.

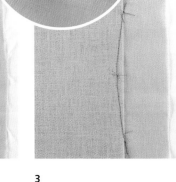

In the case of a conventional dart, the fabric is folded and sewn to remove fullness and pressed to one side. However, this leaves bulk on one side of the dart and, effectively, a seam sitting along one edge. By balancing the dart with extra fabric a flatter, smoother finish can be achieved, even though fabric has been added.

1
Transfer the markings from the pattern using tailor's tacks, and fold the dart through the center with right sides together—matching up the tailor's tacks. Pin the dart into position ready for sewing.

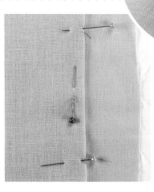

2
Cut a rectangle of the garment fabric, longer and wider than the dart. Place this under the dart and re-pin to hold all the layers together.

3
Start at one end of the dart in the excess cloth and stitch onto the point of the dart along the sewing line and off at the other end onto the excess fabric below.

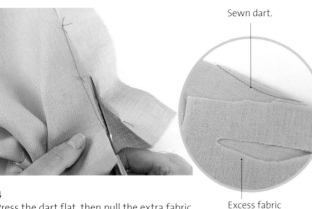

Sewn dart.

Excess fabric showing cutaway.

4
Press the dart flat, then pull the extra fabric away from the seamline toward the folded edge. Cut away the excess fabric (not the garment!) in line with the folded edge.

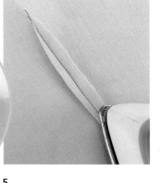

5
Press the dart one way and the extra fabric the other way using the point of the iron. Turn over and lightly press the surface of the garment using a pressing cloth to protect the fabric. You will achieve a beautiful smooth shape.

Use this balanced dart technique for a smooth finish on a close-fitting dress with bust and waist darts.

Single-thread dart

The "couture dart" is a wonderful method for sewing a dart that has been passed down through the generations. Surprisingly, it is not widely known, though it should be. This dart works well on all fabrics, and it is essential when working with sheers. There are no unsightly thread ends at the tip of the dart just a clean, graceful finish.

1
Mark the dart on the wrong side of the fabric.

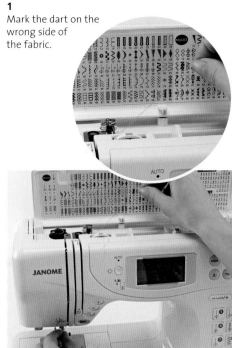

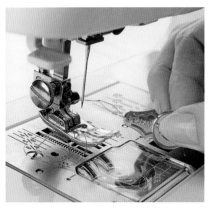

2
Next, thread the machine needle. Pull the bobbin thread through the needle from back to front.

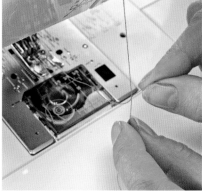

3
Tie the top thread to the bobbin thread so there is one continuous thread.

4
Then wind the thread back so that the knot won't get caught in the thread tension.

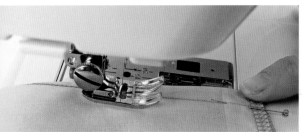

5
Start sewing the dart at its tip; do not backstitch. Once you have finished sewing each dart, you will have to rethread the needle for the next.

This technique creates a smooth dart.

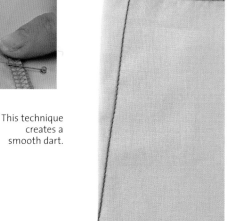

Finished dart.

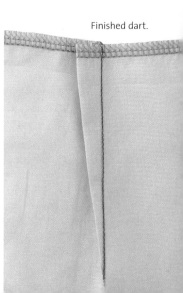

Horsehair braid hem

To support a hem and give it more rigidity, you can sew horsehair braid (or "crin trim") to the hem. Generally, it is sewn into the lining or petticoat of a skirt, but it can be stitched to the fabric itself.

Horsehair braid is made from bias-woven nylon and is available in wide and narrow widths. It supports the hem without adding bulk and keeps it from collapsing, giving a much softer effect than hooping a skirt with wire. There are various ways to apply horsehair braid. The two described here give neat finishes and are easy to sew.

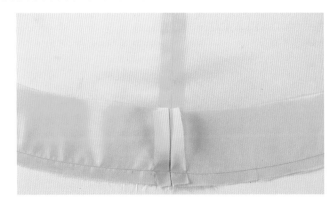

1
Prepare the skirt, and pin and sew the facing pieces to the lower edges of the hem. Before edge-stitching or pressing to the wrong side, go to Step 2.

2
With the wrong side of the skirt uppermost and the facings hidden below, pin the horsehair braid to the seam allowances; the edge of the braid should lie next to the stitching. Stitch close to the edge, sewing through the horsehair braid and the seam allowances, taking care not to stretch the braid in the process. At the end, overlap the horsehair braid and cut off the excess.

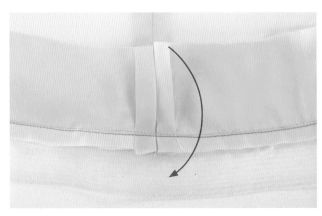

3
Fold the facing up into place on the inside of the skirt, enclosing the horsehair braid in the process. Press lightly with the seam and the understitching on the inside, leaving a smooth finish on the right side.

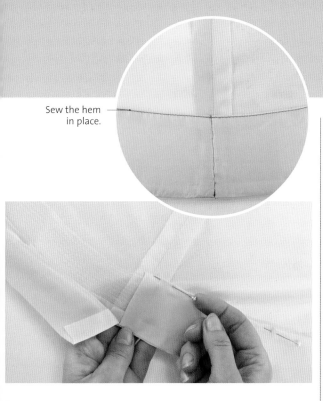

Sew the hem in place.

4
Slip-stitch the facings at the seams and tuck under a seam allowance on the upper facing edge. Pin and sew the hem facing in place, leaving the upper edge of the braid free. If the horsehair braid is being applied to a lining, machine edge-stitch it into position. If the braid is being sewn directly to the hem of a skirt or dress, hand-stitch it neatly to the underlining.

Final hem.

Concealing horsehair braid in the hem

The nylon threads of the horsehair braid have a rough texture that could snag pantyhose. For this reason it is best to ensure that it is wrapped fully and not just sewn to the inside edge of the hem.

1
Check the length required for the finished garment and mark this with basting or a chalk line on the wrong side of the fabric. Place the horsehair braid below the marked hemline and measure ¼ in. (6 mm) from the horsehair braid. Trim the entire hem to this newly marked length.

2
On the wrong side of the fabric, overlap the horsehair braid over the lower ¼ in. (6 mm) of the hem. Pin and machine-stitch the braid to the hem edge, taking care not to stretch the horsehair braid in the process. Overlap the ends and snip away the excess.

3
Fold the braid to the wrong side of the skirt hem, then fold again to hide the braid and raw edge within the hem. Secure the hem with machine topstitching or with hand slip-stitches as appropriate.

Organza "Bubble" hem finish

While a manufactured finish demands crisp, clean edges, a softer approach is needed for a couture finish. Silk organza provides this shaping and holds the structure of a straight skirt.

To prevent the lower edge of a sheath dress or skirt from collapsing close to the legs and inhibiting movement, slip a folded bias band of organza between the hem allowance and garment body. You don't press the fold of this band, so it makes a bubble-like spacer inside the hem. This clever, innovative, and very simple technique proves that versatile organza is an item of high standing in the well-stocked sewing armory.

1

Cut a 5 in. (12.5 cm)-wide bias strip of silk organza the length of the hemline plus extra for overlap. In this instance you may piece the strip because it is hidden from view and will not affect the function.

2

Fold the organza strip in half lengthwise. Do not press it—you want the fold to stay soft. Staystitch the raw edges together using a 1/2 in. (1.25 cm) seam allowance. Do not stretch-press before you fold, the curve of the organza helps the bubble to do its work.

The organza attached to the hem, seen from the right side.

Seen from the reverse side, the skirt hem is unfolded and the organza is attached to lining.

3

Mark, fold, and press the hem at the bottom of your garment; finish the top edge of the hem allowance as you wish. A 2 1/2 in. (6.5 cm) hem depth is ideal. Lay the garment wrong side up and unfold the hem.

4

Orienting the raw edges toward the hem fold, lay the organza strip on the hem allowance, overlapping by 3/4 in. (2 cm). If the bottom of the garment is a tube, lap the ends of the strip one over the other; do not join with a seam. Sew the organza to the hem allowance by machine, stitching along the staystitching.

5

Fold the hem allowance into place again. Sew the hem by hand, using a catch stitch or other hand stitch, and placing the stitches through the hem allowance along the seam of the organza—so that the folded edge of the organza remains loose.

The reverse side of the finished organza "bubble".

Couture waists

The flat and smooth, wrinkle-free finish of a couture waist is worth striving for.

The couture method of constructing a waistband results in a superior product. The band does not roll, yet it is comfortable, and lies flat. There is no extra bulk so it is particularly compatible with thicker woolens where a double layer of face fabric would simply not work. This technique is time-consuming but worth all the effort.

1
Cut a waistband to the finished length and width you need, plus seam allowances. Cut one in fabric and one in silk organza. Then cut a third band in tailor's canvas, and remove the seam allowances.

2
Mark the seamlines on the organza. Place the tailor's canvas between the seamlines. Channel stitch the canvas to the organza. Aim for 1/8 in. (3 mm) spacing in order to add stability without bulk. Press.

3
Place the stabilized organza on the wrong side of the waistband, and machine-baste in place. Press.

4
Cut a strip of Petersham ribbon the length of the waistband. It should be 1/4 in. (6 mm) wider than the finished band. Working on the right side of the waistband, place one long edge of the Petersham along the fold line of the band. Make sure it is a scant 1/8 in. (3 mm) away from the fold line so it will not show when the garment is completed. Stitch it in place. Press to emb the stitches. Press the band along the fold line.

5
With the right sides together, pin the waistband to the garment. Stitch, trim, and press.

6
On the reverse side of the garment, sew the Petersham ribbon down by hand.

A finished couture waist looks and feels good.

High-waist couture facing

This couture approach to constructing a waist facing works well on any waistline where a waistband is not desired. It is particularly well suited to pants and skirts with high waists. The channel stitching and the bones add structure and support while maintaining a clean line.

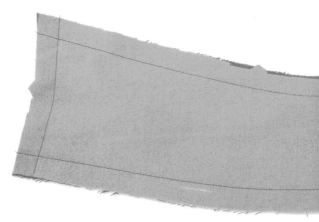

1
Prepare the garment as usual so it is ready for the facing. Now tape the waistline to prevent stretching during wear. This basic step is extremely important for all faced waistlines. Place stay tape over the seamline and stitch it in place.

2
Underline the facing with silk organza (see page 230) and mark the stitching lines.

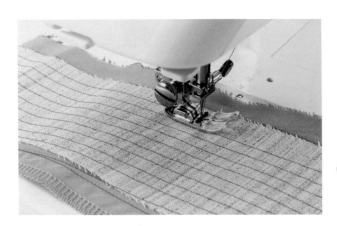

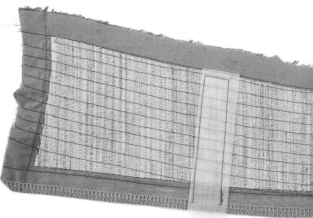

3
Remove the seam allowances from the interfacing and position it on the organza side of the facing, between the marked seamlines. Channel stitch through all thicknesses using ¼ in. (6 mm) spacing. A walking foot may be helpful.

4
Add boning channels where required. The important locations include seams and the areas of the facing that correspond to dart placement on the garment. The channels should stop a generous ⅛ in. (3 mm) short of any seamlines. Stitch through all the thicknesses, leaving the bottom end open.

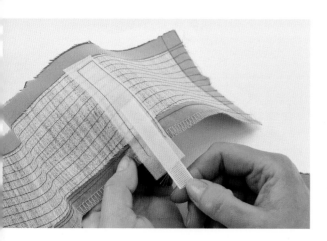

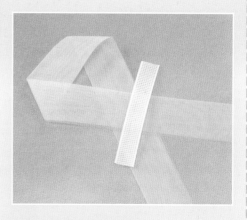

MAKING BONING CHANNELS
To make boning channels, cut a long, 2-in. (5-cm) wide strip of silk organza on the lengthwise grain and fold it in half lengthwise. Press and cut into the lengths you require.

5
Insert bones into the boning channels. Stitch the lower ends of the boning channels, encasing the bones. It is wise to singe the ends of the bones so that they are less inclined to poke through.

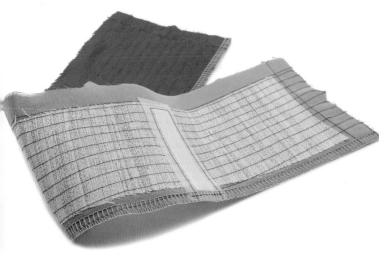

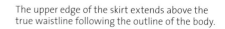

The upper edge of the skirt extends above the true waistline following the outline of the body.

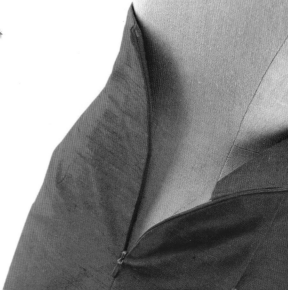

6
Trim away the excess channel, and finish the edge of the facing. Pin and sew the facing to the waist of the skirt to complete the process.

Lining/Binding skirt panels

This clever technique neatens the raw edges of the fabric and creates the lining all in one. It gives a beautiful, clean, and efficient finish.

This lining/binding technique works well on fairly straight seams with minimal curves. It is suitable for panel skirts, pants, and unstructured rectangular-shaped jackets. It results in the garment being lined and seams finished with minimal effort.

1
Cut the pieces of the garment according to the pattern. Cut the lining seams to be bound 5/8 in. (1.5 cm) wider than the pattern.

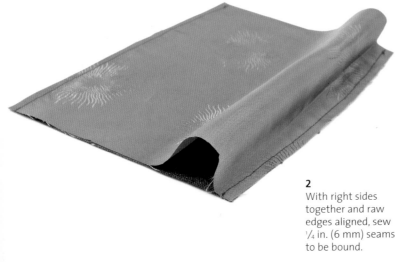

2
With right sides together and raw edges aligned, sew 1/4 in. (6 mm) seams to be bound.

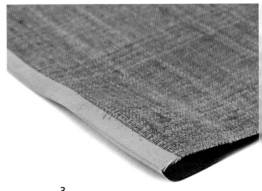

3
Press to embed the stitches. Press the seams away from the garment. Turn the garment section right side out and press again. Stitch the top edges together.

4
You may choose to stitch in the ditch if you are working with a slippery lining.

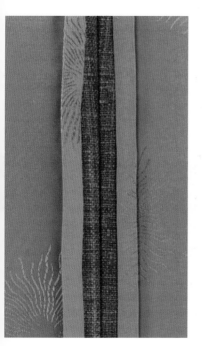

5
Sew the garment sections together as usual. Press to embed the stitches. Press the seams open.

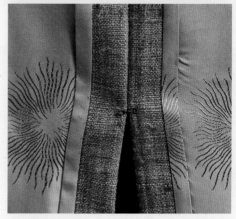

STYLE IDEAS
Top: The lining/binding. This technique results in an attractively finished lining and seams.
Bottom: Reinforcing the slit. This subtle, age-old designer trick provides maximum benefit from minimal labor. The "bar" from a hook-and-eye set is placed strategically at the top of the skirt slit to reduce the chances of the seam coming undone under stress.

Interlining

Interlining, sometimes referred to as underlining, is the technique of using an additional layer or layers of fabric behind your chosen fashion fabric to change its characteristics.

Unlike interfacing, which is used in small areas such as collars, cuffs, and facings to add support and strength, interlining is an entire panel cut in a separate layer of fabric and placed to the wrong side of the main fabric. It may be fused to the fabric but is more commonly hand placed and used in the couture world to improve the finish of a garment. The extra work involved in making a garment with an interlining is reflected in the construction time and cost.

As well as understanding why you would use an interlining, you need to know what fabrics to use and how to choose them. There are many reasons to add an interlining—for example, adding body or depth or preventing creasing—and here is a guide to help you make the best choices.

FABRICS SUITABLE FOR INTERLINING

When you buy a commercial paper pattern, instructions for interfacings are normally included. Interlining details, however, are not normally stated, so use the guide below to choose the most appropriate material for your design and combine it with your fabric with the step-by-step method shown here.

A. Bleached muslin: An ideal interlining to add a small amount of weight and control to a light, fly-away fabric.

B. Satin lining: Use satin to add weight behind the surface fabric.

C. Cotton sheeting: For medium-weight fabrics, sheeting is a useful interlining for adding depth and weight.

D. Fusible interfacing: These are available in different weights and are useful to support loosely woven fabrics that would otherwise ravel.

E. Cheesecloth: Use cheesecloth with its loose weave to add body and weight.

F. Silk charmeuse: Use this to improve the draping qualities of the surface fabric.

G. Lining: For a softer, fluid effect, use acetate lining. Its weight helps to make fabrics hang well.

H. Net: Use net when you want a stiff interlining to add structure.

I. Silk organza: Its strength and crisp nature make it ideal for supporting fabric without adding any depth.

J. Cotton lawn: Use lawn for backing silk because the fibers adhere to each other and hold the silk and cotton together.

Reasons for adding an interlining

TO ADD BODY
Add body to a garment by applying a firm extra layer. This will give a far better structure and will help to maintain the shape of a dress or jacket. One-hundred percent silk organza is an ideal interlining to add body because it is stiff and strong yet very thin, so it will not increase depth or bulk. Use it for day wear and evening wear for dresses, skirts, blouses, and jackets.

TO PREVENT CREASING
Some of the most beautiful fabrics are constructed from natural fibers that are prone to creasing. There are various ways of eliminating the creases but this will depend on the style. Some dresses will require weight to pull the creases out. A full, frothy, pure silk evening dress may get easily scrunched and creased, but a layer of stiff dress net below will help it to bounce back into shape. Use nylon net for light gathered styles, or a sculptured effect, or silk organza on less flamboyant styles.

TO ADD DENSITY
Light-colored fabrics may need more density to prevent shadowing from seams, shoulder pads, hems, and even underwear—for example, a white woolen coat, crêpe dress, or silk wedding dress. Without an interlining, the interior details will be seen. Choose a suitable layer of cotton, e.g., muslin, lawn, or sheeting for structured garments, or lining for softer, more fluid styles.

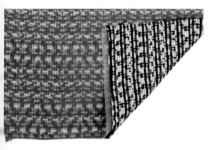

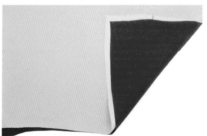

TO PREVENT SEATING
A tightly woven interlining will prevent an open-weave fabric such as Linton tweed from stretching, especially over the seat of a slim-fitting skirt or at the elbows on a fitted sleeve of a jacket. Once again, 100 percent silk organza is the perfect choice.

TO ADD DRAPE
A design requiring a soft draping effect needs to be backed with an interlining with a certain amount of weight for it to hang well and move fluidly. Interlinings made from acetate fibers have this quality but are still thin, and therefore do not add any unnecessary bulk.

TO CREATE A SKELETON
One of the most rewarding reasons for adding an interlining is to create a skeleton. This provides an anchor so that hand stitches can be sewn to the interlining, leaving no visible stitch marks such as hemming or facings on the right side of the garment. All interlining fabrics give this advantage.

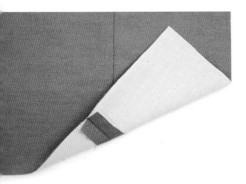

TO PREVENT RIDGES

Seams and hems lying immediately under the main fabric can cause ridges and a shine may appear through pressing or general wear. By adding a suitable interlining, the seam will be behind two (or possibly more) layers of fabric, giving a much smoother appearance from the right side.

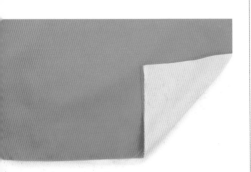

TO CHANGE THE FABRIC CHARACTERISTICS

Changing the weight or the shade of your main fabric by choosing appropriate interlining gives more potential to your creations. By adding a layer of muslin to a lightweight fabric it becomes heavier, or by using a strong-colored interlining behind a light colored, fine fabric you can alter the shade or color. For example, a dress made from a white habotai silk with a deep pink interlining becomes a subtle pink shade with more body.

Combining interlinings

In some cases, it is necessary to use more than one interlining, since one does not have enough effect on its own. For example, when using a fine fabric for a full skirt it may need density, additional body, and prevention of creasing. The answer is to back first with a cotton lawn to overcome the translucency of the fabric and then a dress net to add body and encourage creases to drop out.

Another case in which more than one interlining is required is where a fine soft fabric is used to make a dress and jacket suit. The dress may need one type of interlining to allow it to drape or not seat, while the jacket will require additional body and strength to support the structure of a jacket. Each project you tackle will be different.

Two interlinings are used when one is difficult to sew. An example of this is on a stiff corset or bodice that fits very closely to the body. Cut the bodice panels in the outer fabric (cotton lawn is a good option) and collar and cuff canvas. Cut the seam allowances off the stiff canvas and center the canvas on the cotton lawn. Sew around the outer edge of the canvas, leaving a 5/8 in. (1.5 cm) seam allowance on the cotton lawn. Place this combined layer to the wrong side of the dress fabric, stitching the layers together within the seam allowance. When the three layers are joined, you can sew just outside the stiff canvas on the sewing line through the softer fabrics.

TIP
When adding an interlining to a large panel that does not fit closely to the body—for example, a full skirt, there is no need to account for the small difference in size of the panels. In this case, just place the interlining and fabric together with wrong sides facing and smooth out any wrinkles. Pin around the outside and machine baste the layers together.

Adding an interlining to a small panel

When making a slim-fitting skirt or bodice that will shape to the body, it is important that the two layers are joined carefully so they fit well and give a smooth finish. The interlining is fractionally closer to the body than the main fabric so it will be a tiny bit smaller. If both layers were made up in exactly the same size, the under layer would crumple.

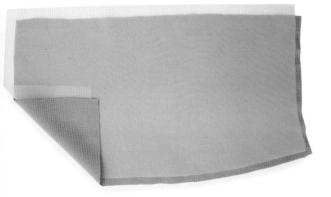

1
Cut each panel in main fabric and in an appropriate interlining fabric.

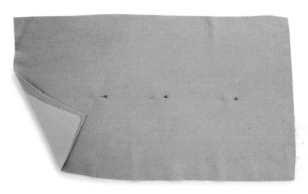

2
Lay the interlining on the work surface with the main fabric over it, right side up. Smooth the two layers out so there are no wrinkles and set a line of pins through the middle, catching both layers.

3
Drop one edge of the panel off the end of the work surface to mimic the shape of the body, which is cylindrical not flat. (You may find it easier to work at an ironing board as this is often a more comfortable height.)

4
Hand-baste the edges together within the seam allowances, making sure the two layers lie naturally. The edges may not be level, but this is correct, and the curve of the body makes the interlining layer very slightly smaller. Keep turning the panel 90 degrees to complete all four outside edges.

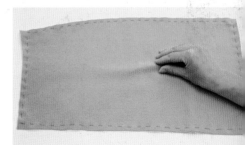

5
When the layers are sewn together, place them flat on the work surface. You will notice that there is a slight bubble demonstrating that the upper fabric is larger than the interfacing below. Treat them as one piece as you construct the garment.

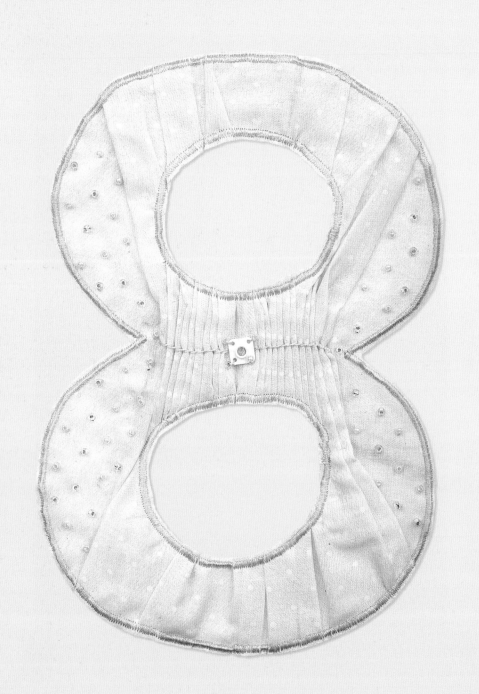

Troubleshooting

When you're creating, sewing, or adapting garments, things will occasionally go wrong. This section is an essential resource, showing you how to identify, prevent, or overcome many common problems.

Troubleshooting

Occasionally things do go wrong when dressmaking, but it needn't be a disaster. Sometimes errors can be fixed and of course, in the future, prevented. Use this guide to identify the problem, find out how to prevent it, and if necessary, how to fix it.

· ·

The best way to avoid problems in the first place is, of course, to prepare properly. To do this, make sure you read all the way through a pattern's step-by-step construction notes so that you understand what needs to be done and why. Don't skimp on fabric and always follow the pattern layouts so that the pieces are placed correctly before cutting out.

Follow grain lines on pattern pieces, making sure they are perfectly parallel to the selvage of the fabric as recommended. If placed wrongly, you will get buckling and twisting seams or the fabric may stretch out of shape.

Remember that most modern machines have excellent tension settings and rarely is the problem with stitching anything to do with the tension, so generally, leave it alone. If encountering stitch problems, start by rethreading the machine to check that it is threaded properly, making sure the presser foot is raised as you thread so that the thread goes between the tension disks easily.

ESSENTIAL TOOLS AND TIPS TO PREVENT PROBLEMS

- Make sure your equipment is in good condition. This is important for cutting tools, pins and needles, and sewing machines.

- Have a sharp seam ripper at hand. These nifty little tools, usually part of the sewing machine tool kit are a dressmaker's must-have gadget. Not only can you quickly unpick seams, you can also use them to open buttonholes neatly. Replace it if it becomes blunt.

- Clean out the fluff from your sewing machine after every project, and change your needle regularly (after every eight hours of sewing)—blunt needles can cause all sorts of stitch problems.

- Have a selection of sewing machine needles at hand – universal sharp needles ranging from U.S. 10–16 (Europe 70–100) will cope with all the different woven fabrics from chiffon and silk to fleece and fur. Ball-point needles are needed for stretchy fabric, and specialized needles such as metallic or embroidery needles are used for stitching with metallic threads and concentrated stitching.

- Regularly replace pins and hand-sewing needles—like machine needles, they blunt over time and can cause snags in fabric.

- Have a pack of soluble stabilizer at hand. Use strips along seam lines on stretchy or slippery fabrics that don't feed through the sewing machine easily, or cut a small piece to place at the start of a seam on lightweight fabric to prevent it being pulled into the feed dogs.

CUTTING OUT

Get the cutting out right and you will avoid all sorts of problems when constructing a garment.

Problem	Prevention	Fix
There are so many different layouts to follow on the pattern, I don't know which one I need.	There are different layouts depending on the width of fabric you are using and the pattern size you are cutting. Avoid accidently starting with one layout and then following another by marking the one you are using with a highlighter or asterisk.	Before cutting out the fabric, make sure you have followed the same layout throughout and all pieces are placed as recommended.
I can't tell which is the right side and wrong side of the fabric.	If it is difficult to tell it probably doesn't matter, but to make sure that there isn't a slight variation invisible in artificial light but obvious in daylight, mark one side as WS and the other as RS with pins or chalk crosses.	Use a daylight lamp to see fabrics clearly. Even if it is not clear which is the right or wrong side, do mark one as wrong so that you can ensure all pieces are cut out correctly and you get left/right sleeves, etc.
The fabric keeps slipping as I try to cut it out.	Prevent slippery fabrics shifting as you try to cut them out by laying them onto spare tissue or regular paper and pinning through all layers to hold them together. Only cut the fabric if using regular paper as backing to avoid blunting your scissors. Alternatively, cover the work surface with an old sheet before laying out your fabric to prevent it slipping.	Spray starch washable fabrics to stiffen them and provide body, which will help prevent them shifting and slipping as you cut out and sew.
The check pattern doesn't match across the seams.	When working with a distinctively patterned fabric, or stripes and checks, cut each pattern piece from a single layer of fabric so that you can place the prominent pattern/design in the same position on the pattern piece each time. Remember to turn the pattern piece over to cut a right and left where necessary.	If it is not possible to recut a matching piece so the pattern on the fabric matches up, disguise the mismatch with a surface trim or strategically placed buttons.
I can't tell which is the sleeve back and which is the sleeve front.	Keep the pattern pieces together with the fabric pieces once cut out. Remove pins and fold the pieces together so that you have the pattern to refer to. Transfer any markings such as matching points, zipper, pocket, darts, and pleats to the wrong side of the fabric. Make sure you cut out around notches that are used to match pattern pieces.	Refer to the pattern piece and check the notches. Most commercial patterns use a double notch for the back of garment and a single notch for the front so match single notch on sleeve to single notch on garment, etc.

SEAMS

Problems with seams are easy to avoid if you use the right needle and presser foot, and lots of pressing.

Problem	Prevention	Fix
Seams have stretched.	Stay stitch the seams before handling. To stay stitch, stitch just within the seam allowance, close to the seam line, using a regular stitch length to suit the fabric 1/16 in. (2.2–2.5 mm) for lightweight fabrics, and 1/8 in. (2.5–3 mm) for heavier fabrics. Alternatively, fuse some edge tape to the seam allowance butted up to the seam line.	This is difficult to fix once a garment is finished. Two possible remedies are: 1 Sew a row of gathering stitching along the seam line and pull up gently. Press with steam. 2 In a neckline, take out the excess with darts, evenly spaced between center front and armhole, to look like a design feature.
Slippery fabric layers shift as you stitch so end up different lengths.	Pin baste (using lots of pins placed at right angles to the seam) or hand baste layers together before machine stitching.	Trim the uneven lengths to an equal length. For future garments, make sure the layers do not shift as you stitch by basting seams prior to stitching.
Bulky fabric layers feed unevenly so they end up different lengths.	Use a walking foot or roller foot if available as these will help feed the fabric evenly. A walking foot has feed teeth on it that work in conjunction with the feed dogs on the machine. Alternatively, use a wider seam allowance and increase stitch length to 1/8 in. (3 mm).	If the difference in length is too much, the seam does need to be unpicked and started again (this time with a walking foot or increased seam allowance and stitch length). If it is only a small difference, trim the uneven lengths to an equal length.
Stretchy fabrics don't feed properly and I get skipped stitches.	Always use a ball-point needle when sewing stretchy fabrics—failure to do so can result in skipped stitches. Also use a roller foot if available as this will literally roll over the layers, helping them to feed evenly. For two-way stretch fabrics, use a stretch needle, which is designed for very stretchy materials.	Resew the seams with a ball-point needle. If the problem persists, cut strips of soluble stabilizer and lay over the seam line, then stitch. Wash away the stabilizer once the garment is finished.
Seams have ripples in them.	Bias-cut seams can be left with ripples unless you slightly stretch the seam behind and in front of the needle as you sew. Then press the seam to embed the stitching and it will lay flat.	Resew the seam, slightly pulling on the fabric in front and behind the needle. Press the seam to embed the stitching.
My seams don't look flat.	Make sure that you press every seam before stitching over it again. This will embed the stitching and provide a flat finish. Press from the wrong side and again from the right side, covering the fabric with a press cloth to protect the fabric surface.	Using a pressing cloth, press the seams carefully. Use the tip of the iron to get into corners and curves.
Seams in fur fabrics don't look great.	Trim away excess bulky fur from the seam allowance before stitching. Sew with the pile of the fabric running in the direction you are sewing.	Use a pin to pull out the fur fibers that are caught in the seam. This will cover the seam line.
The fabric frays really quickly.	Neaten the raw edges of all cut-out pieces before you begin construction. Use a serger if possible, and make sure the fabric feeds smoothly and doesn't stretch as you sew.	Neaten all raw edges before handling too much. On finished seams, either serge the edges, or wrap them in a lightweight bias binding stitched in place to encase the raw edges.

HEMS

Hems can be difficult to sew because of excess or stretching fabric. Follow the prevention and fix tips to achieve perfect hems.

Problem	Prevention	Fix
The hem has a rippled appearance.	This can happen on circular hems where there is a lot of fabric and the hem is cut on the bias. Use a narrow hem allowance and ease stitch $1/4$ in. (6 mm) from the raw edge, before turning up the hem. Gently gather the hem allowance to take up the excess. Pin and stitch, so that the main fabric remains flat.	Try pressing with lots of steam from the wrong side to shrink the excess hem allowance. Cover the right side of the fabric with a press cloth to protect the surface and pressing carefully from the right side. If it continues to ripple, unpick and follow the tips to prevent it happening.
The hem stretched as I stitched.	When working on stretch fabrics, prevent the hem from stretching by interfacing the hem allowance prior to hemming.	Cut off the hem and make a feature of a stretchy hem by stitching a lettuce hem edge. To do this, select a small zigzag stitch, close the length to $1/32$ in. (0.5 mm–0.7 mm) and then stretch the fabric behind and in front of the machine as you sew over the raw edge. This will then crinkle prettily to create a lettuce edging (see page 212 for a serged lettuce edge).
I've shortened a T-shirt hem using a twin needle but the fabric has bunched up.	A twin needle has two needles stitching on the top of the fabric, with the bobbin thread beneath zigzagging across between them. This can cause the fabric between the needles to bunch (which you want it to do for pintucking). However, to prevent this, use a twin needle with a wide gap between the needles $1/4$ in. (4–6 mm) and loosen the tension so that the fabric doesn't bunch.	Either unpick and stitch again with a loosened tension, or make a feature of the edging by stitching a couple more parallel rows of twin-needle stitching, letting the fabric bunch slightly between the needles.
The blind hem stitching shows on the right side when it shouldn't.	Blind hemming by machine does leave a tiny ladderlike stitch visible on the right side. Use a thread color to perfectly match the fabric, or if that is not possible, select one that is slightly darker— when it comes off the reel, it will look lighter. Fuse interfacing to the reverse of the main fabric under the hem allowance and then hand blind hem, picking up fibers from the interfacing attached to the main fabric and then the hem allowance as you sew.	Adjust the needle position on the machine so that the zigzag into the hem allowance of the blind hem only just nicks the folded fabric. Remove the thread and hem again, using a better thread match. Alternatively, pick a contrast thread and make a feature of the little ladder stitching.
The hemline has dropped at the sides so is uneven.	Stabilize the bias-cut side seams as you sew them to prevent them stretching more than the rest of the garment. (Add edge tape to the seam line). Let the garment hang for at least 24 hours before hemming, allowing the side seams to drop a little, and then trim off evenly before hemming.	Unpick the hem allowance and with the garment inside out, and re-mark the hem length all the way around using pins placed horizontally. Turn up the hem allowance and trim so that it is even all the way around. Hem using your preferred method.

FACINGS

Facings are used to finish necklines and armholes. They can look bulky or roll out to the right side if not properly finished.

Problem	Prevention	Fix
The facing doesn't fit perfectly.	Make sure the facing is the right size—if you have adjusted the neckline or armhole of the garment, you need to make corresponding adjustments on the facing pieces. Use exactly the same seam allowance on both garment and facing to ensure they match.	Check the measurements of facing and garment and if necessary unpick and re-cut the facing to the right size. Alternatively, remove the facings and replace with bias binding wrapped around the raw edges of the neckline and armhole and stitched in place.
The facing doesn't lay flat against the fabric.	Clip, notch, and layer the seam allowances as appropriate. Clip curves, take wedge-shaped notches out of inner curves, and layer the seam allowance on thick fabrics to reduce the bulk at the seam. Layer one seam allowance to 1/2 in. (1 cm) and the other to 1/4 in. (6 mm). Clip into V-necklines close to but not through the stitching.	Open out the facing to expose the seam allowances and trim them, clipping and notching as noted in the Prevention column. Press the seam allowances open to embed the seam.
The facing keeps rolling out.	Make sure you understitch the facing seam allowances to the facing, which provides a crisper edge and prevents the facing rolling to the outside. To understitch, open out the facing and press the trimmed seam allowances toward the facing. Stitch close to the previous seam around the edge of the facing, catching the seam allowances in the stitching.	If you can't go back and understitch, roll the seam between the facing and the garment between your finger and thumb so that it sits just inside the garment. Press carefully with a press cloth to protect the fabric and pin in place. Topstitch around the neckline or armhole about 1/8 in. (3 mm) from the edge, stitching through all layers.
The fabric is too bulky with the facings in place.	Use a different fabric for facings when working with heavy-weight or bulky fabrics. Use lining fabric or a cotton fabric. Layer seam allowances so that there is not too much bulky fabric in the seams. Cut one to 1/2 in. (1 cm) and the other to 1/4 in. (6 mm).	Unpick and replace the facings with a lighter-weight fabric or cover the raw edges with bias binding instead. Alternatively, line the garment bodice so facings are not needed.
The hemmed lower edge of the facing is visible from the right side of the garment.	Hem facings with an overcast stitch rather than a turned hem allowance to reduce the bulk in the hem. Press well before attaching facings.	Unpick the hemmed edge of the facing and use pinking shears to neaten it as far as you can. When pressing, place a piece of brown paper between the facing and the main garment to prevent a ridge being pressed in.

POCKETS

Pockets add another dimension to a garment and can be functional or just decorative.

Problem	Prevention	Fix
My pocket fabric is lightweight and looks flimsy.	Interface the pocket fabric before making up the pocket to give it weight and stability. Then cut a self-lined pocket piece which is twice the size of the finished pocket so the fabric will be double.	Make up an additional pocket the same size as the flimsy one, position over the existing pocket, and stitch the sides and bottom, catching the previous pocket edges in the seam. Finish by stitching the top edges of both pockets together by hand.
My pocket fabric is bulky and the pocket looks too chunky.	Line the pocket fabric with a lightweight lining or cotton fabric rather than the same as the outside of the pocket. Have contrast pockets made from a coordinating color in a lighter-weight fabric. Alternatively, leave the pockets off completely.	Remove the existing pocket and unpick so that you can line it with a lightweight lining before replacing it.
The pocket top keeps coming undone and pulling away from the garment.	Securely attach the tops of pockets with a stitched triangle at the top or reverse stitching. To stitch a triangle, start stitching ½ in. (1 cm) down from the top edge, stitching at an angle to the top opening edge of the pocket. Pivot and stitch to the side edge, then pivot again and stitch down the side. Repeat at the other side of the pocket opening.	Pin the pocket back in place and machine stitch in a triangle if possible. (See Prevention for method). On a child's garment, add a little button to the top of the pocket corners and stitch firmly in place to provide additional support and decorative detail.
How do I repair a hole in the pocket?	If pockets are going to get lots of heavy wear and tear, strengthen them before sewing them in place by interfacing the outside of the pocket pieces.	Replace the torn piece of the pocket. Cut off both front and back of the pocket above the tear, cutting horizontally across in a straight line. Using the cut-off piece as a template, cut out a new pocket bottom from a spare piece of fabric. Sew the new pocket bottom and side edges. Neaten the raw edges, including the open top edges. Slip the new pocket over the existing cut piece and stitch around to secure it in place.
The side pockets in my skirt look bulky and keep poking out.	Use a lightweight lining fabric for the pockets rather than self-fabric. Press the seam allowances attaching the pocket to the garment open and then toward the pocket. Cut into the seam allowance at the top and bottom of the pocket so that the pocket can be folded toward the garment. Roll the seam toward the inside of the pocket.	Remove the pockets completely to produce a neater and slimmer silhouette. Working from the wrong side, cut them away and stitch up the seam, neatening the raw edge afterward. If you wish to keep the pockets, stab stitch by hand around the pocket opening, catching the pocket to the main fabric close to the opening to prevent it rolling out again.

COLLARS AND NECKLINES

Perfect collar points and smoothly shaped necklines are achievable if you avoid the problem areas.

Problem	Prevention	Fix
I can't get perfect points on my collar.	Make sure you stitch the corners carefully—reduce the stitch length to about ¾ in. (2 cm) on either side of the point, and then take a stitch diagonally across the point. Trim seam allowances close to the stitching and trim the point at an angle to reduce all the excess allowance.	Make sure you have trimmed the seam allowances to a minimum. Press the seam allowances open and then turn through and use a point turner to push out the corners. Roll the seam line between your finger and thumb so it is on the very edge.
My collar feels too bulky and doesn't sit flat.	If working with a bulky fabric, cut the underside of the collar in a lighter-weight fabric or lining to reduce the bulk.	Make sure you layer seam allowances to reduce the bulk in the seams by cutting one to ½ in. (1 cm) and the other to ¼ in. (6 mm). When attaching the collar to the garment, understitch where possible to help keep the seam allowances in place and prevent the edge rolling over.
The V of my neckline doesn't sit flat.	First, stay stitch the bias-cut edges by stitching with a regular stitch length in the seam allowance close to the seam line. Stitch the facing or lining in place, taking care to keep an even seam allowance. At the point of the V, take one stitch across the end before pivoting and stitching up the other side. Trim seam allowances.	Turn the garment wrong side out to access the seam allowances attaching the facing or lining to garment. Trim down to a scant ⅛ in. (3 mm) cutting down toward the V, close to but not through the stitching. Turn back through and roll the seam line to the edge before pressing.
My shaped neckline doesn't look symmetrical.	Make sure that you cut out the relevant shaped piece very carefully with the pattern placed on the fold as directed. Take care to stitch with an even seam allowance.	Check that the seam allowance used is even through the seam. If not, resew to rectify. Trim the seam allowance to a scant ⅛ in. (3 mm) and clip into any curves before turning through to the right side. Roll the seam between your finger and thumb to ensure it is turned through completely and the seam is on the very edge.
My neckline has stretched out of shape.	Stay stitch the cut edges before handling them again by stitching in the seam allowance with a straight stitch close to the seam line. This will prevent the fabric from stretching out of shape as you construct the garment.	Try shrinking the fabric back with steam if it is only slightly stretched. Stitch with a long gathering stitch and pull up slightly to ease in the fullness. If all else fails, add small darts or tucks and make it a design feature.

Sewing machine troubleshooting

No matter how careful you are when using your sewing machine, it is inevitable that there will be occasional problems. The troubleshooting guide below should help in most circumstances, but don't forget the value of the sewing machine manual for the specifics of your own model.

SEWING MACHINE

Problem	Possible cause	Fix
Will not sew	Power not reaching machine.	Check power is on and all plugs and flexes are connected fully.
	Some machines have safety mechanisms which prevent them from operating if doors or flaps are left open.	Ensure all doors and flaps are shut.
Breaking needles	Needle not inserted fully; it is bent so hits presser foot; too fine for the fabric being sewn, or is not clamped tightly enough.	Refit or replace with a suitable needle and clamp securely.
	Stitch and presser foot not suited and needle hits foot when sewing—for example, zigzag stitch with a straight stitch foot attached.	Change stitch or foot as necessary.
	Build-up of threads under the fabric in the machine breaks the needle as it tries to sew.	Remove bobbin and threads, defluff, then reinsert bobbin in race.
	Wrong bobbin or spool (possibly from a different make or model) has been inserted into the race or bobbin holder.	Ensure correct bobbin is used.
	Upper thread is too tight and is pulling on the eye of the needle.	Cut and rethread the machine, ensuring it runs smoothly before continuing to sew.

STITCHES

Problem	Possible cause	Fix
Uneven stitches	Presser foot and/or feed dogs not feeding fabric evenly.	Make sure the feed dogs are operating (switch on if necessary) or increase the pressure of the presser foot so that the fabric progresses steadily and consistently.
	Sewing over a bulky seam—for example, hem of jeans.	Use a humper jumper—this sewing notion is placed under the back of the presser foot, keeping it horizontal over the bulky seam to ensure an even stitch feed.
	Decorative stitches unevenly spaced can be caused by using the wrong presser foot—for example, one with a smooth base.	Use a suitable presser foot with a deep groove in the base to slide over the build-up of stitches (open toe, zigzag, appliqué, or candlewicking).
Skipped/missing stitches	Needle is bent or blunt.	Replace the needle.
	Upper threading may be incorrect.	Cut and rethread ensuring it runs smoothly.
	Thread and needle combination may be wrong.	Select a more suitable needle for the thread choice or type of fabric.
	Needle incorrectly threaded.	Rethread correctly—from front to back in most cases, and occasionally left to right.
Puckered stitches/ fabric	Disappointing decorative stitches or machine embroidery pulling on the backing fabric can be caused by lack of support beneath the fabric.	Place a suitable weight of stabilizer on the wrong side of the fabric or add another layer if using one already.
Loose needle stitches	Loose upper stitches may be caused by incorrect threading, different top and bottom thread, or poor tension.	Check that the thread in the reel and bobbin are the same, then rethread the sewing machine (upper thread and bobbin). Only increase needle tension slightly if nothing else helps.
Loose bobbin stitches	Loopy threads below are likely to be due to poor threading, different top and bottom thread, or poor tension.	Check that the thread in the reel and bobbin are the same, then rethread the sewing machine (upper thread and bobbin). If the tension has not improved, loosen the needle tension slightly. Do not adjust the bobbin tension, but seek advice from an engineer.

FABRICS

Problem	Possible cause	Fix
Stretching seams and hems	If the wrong foot is fitted, fabrics can be permanently stretched making hems and seams ripple.	Fit a walking foot or roller foot to feed the fabric evenly and prevent it from stretching too much.
Stitches too visible on a blind hem	When blind hemming, choosing an appropriate color of thread is important so the stitches are hidden.	Select an appropriate thread color (a shade darker is best). Increase the stitch length so that stitches are farther apart.
	Too much stitch is seen on the right side.	Carefully adjust the blind hem foot to ensure the needle just catches the fold as it swings to the left. The chosen fabric might be too thin for a successful blind hem as it works best on medium- and thicker-weight cloth.
Fabric puckers or pulls	If fabric pulls tight, it could be the result of poor tension or pulled threads from the needle or bobbin.	Rethread the sewing machine and remove and replace the bobbin in the bobbin holder. If the puckering is minimal, or on a lightweight fabric, apply slight pressure to the fabric behind the presser foot to ease its progress while sewing. If this does not help, adjust the needle tension slightly.
Disappearing fabric	The fabric may be pushed down into the machine below the feed dogs, jamming the mechanism. This can damage the machine as well as the fabric. This can be caused by using too thick a needle for the weight of fabric.	Fit a size 10/70 needle. Place some tear-away stabilizer under the seam at the start to support the fabric and stop it being pushed down into the mechanism.
	Very fine lightweight fabrics get pulled into the feed dog gaps.	For straight stitching, fit a straight stitch foot and needle plate to give more support around the needle. For other stitching, choose a foot with more support closer to the needle.
Fabric not progressing	Feed dogs may be lowered or pressure on the foot may not be sufficient.	Check feed dogs are raised, or increase the pressure of the presser foot.
Fabric layers not being fed evenly	The pile on the fabrics rub and feed unevenly.	Sew seams with a walking foot or roller foot. Alternatively, reduce the pressure of the presser foot.

The sewing community

People who sew are the kindest and friendliest of people. They are always happy to share their knowledge and offer their help to friends. It is most unusual to find one who doesn't enjoy the company of other sewers, quilters, knitters, and crafters. But if you are new to sewing and want to find others who do, how do you go about it?

In the past it was normal for women to pass on sewing skills to their daughters and granddaughters but sadly, in recent years, this has become less common as manufactured clothes are now often cheaper to buy than fabric, pattern, and notions so fewer people have felt the need to learn to sew. With this missed generation, people are now looking for ways to rediscover dressmaking.

Local groups

Check the library, local newspaper, and fabric or notions stores in your area for groups that meet weekly or monthly. People often get together in school halls or in craft stores for a chance to chat and sew and are always eager to welcome new members. These meetings are generally inexpensive and are a chance to learn new skills from others as well as being a good social opportunity.

Classes and courses

If you want to acquire the basics or learn new techniques it is a good idea to attend a class. This may be a course run over a few months or one-off workshops where you can pick and choose the topics or projects you want to cover. Long courses are a good way for a beginner to get to know the essentials, but if you sew already,

short sessions covering particular techniques might suit you better. Opportunities to attend sewing courses and workshops are springing up all over the place and the best way to find them is to do an Internet search for your area.

Attending classes with qualified tutors are more expensive than joining a local leisure group, but you are likely to have better instruction. Check the qualifications and experience of the teacher before you commit to a class or ask other students for their recommendations.

Shows and exhibitions

Large exhibitions are an opportunity for traders to show off new products. These shows often exhibit work, providing inspiration for your own future projects and offer tuition in the form of short workshops. Attending one of these large shows is a great chance to see what is available and pick up fabrics and equipment that your local dealer may not be able to offer. Going along with a group of friends to watch runway shows and join make-and-take sessions can be a great day out.

Selling your own work

If you are an accomplished sewer and want to sell your work, finding a suitable outlet can be difficult. While craft fairs are appropriate for some items, this might not be right for your products. The most popular way to sell handmade items today is online. If you prefer not to set up your own website (this can be time consuming) sites like Etsy can be a great alternative. Sites like these charge a listing fee and take a percentage of the sale. Take a look at the various online marketplace options and see where your garments or products fit best before choosing where to sell.

Spreading the word

If you enjoy sewing and making clothes, share your enthusiasm with people you know and encourage them to take up the hobby or improve their existing skills. When you spot interesting programs on television relating to sewing tell people, and if you find useful resources let them know. Give them handmade gifts as presents or buy books or equipment to encourage them to start. If you know of someone who is eager to learn, offer to spend an afternoon with them to teach them the basics. This not only helps the new hobbyist, it will support the sewing community as a whole, sustaining notions and fabric stores or sewing machine dealers offering all of us more choice when we go looking for materials and tools. Let's get everyone sewing!

Resources

ESTIMATING FABRIC REQUIREMENTS

CLOTHING TYPE		FABRIC WIDTH		CLOTHING TYPE		FABRIC WIDTH	
		45 inch (115 cm) wide	60 inch (150 cm) wide			45 inch (115 cm) wide	60 inch (150 cm) wide
Straight skirt (above knee)	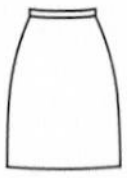	1⅛ yd (1 m)	⅞ yd (0.75 m)	Bodice (waist length)		½–1¼ yd (0.5–1 m)	½–1¼ yd (0.5–1 m)
Straight skirt (knee length)		1⅛–1⅗ yd (1–1.5 m)	⅞–1 yd (0.75–1 m)	Bodice (hip length)	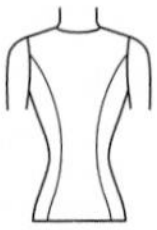	¾–1¼ yd (0.75–1 m)	¾–1¼ yd (0.75–1 m)
Straight skirt (calf length)	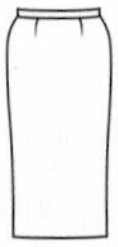	1–2 yd (0.9–1.75 m)	1–1½ yd (0.75–1.5 m)	Sleeve (short)	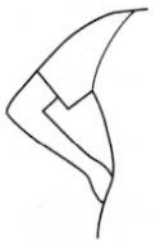	½ yd (0.4 m)	½ yd (0.4 m)
Straight skirt (full length)		1⅝–2⅛ yd (1.5–2 m)	1⅝–2⅛ yd (1.5–2 m)	Sleeve (¾ length)		½–¾ yd (0.5 m)	½–¾ yd (0.5 m)
Bias skirt (calf length)	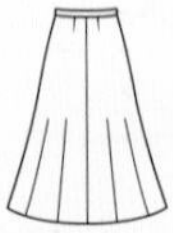	2⅛ yd (2 m)	1⅕–2⅛ yd (1.4–2 m)	Sleeve (long)	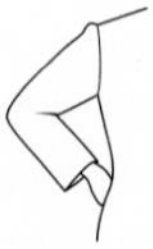	¾ yd (0.7 m)	¾ yd (0.7 m)
Shift dress (above knee)	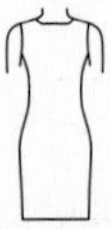	2¾ yd (2.5 m)	1⅝–2⅛ yd (1.5–2 m)	Sleeve with cuff		1 yd (0.8 m)	1 yd (0.8 m)
Shift dress (calf length)	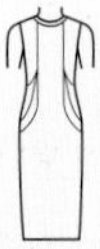	3⅞–4½ yd (3.5–4 m)	3¼–3¾ yd (3–3.5 m)	Sleeve (two piece)	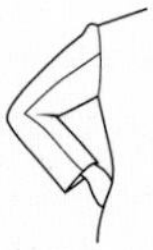	1 yd (0.8 m)	1 yd (0.8 m)
Pants	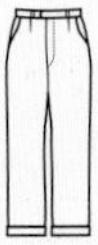	1¾–2¼ yd (1.5–2 m)	1¾–2 yd (1.5–1.75 m)				

Note: Use this rough guide to help when estimating how much fabric to buy for a particular type of garment. Combine the length (e.g., dress or skirt) with the sleeve type to estimate the yardage/meterage needed.

PRESSING GUIDE

FABRIC	TEMPERATURE	SPECIAL NOTES
Acrylic	Cool to medium	Apply light pressure
Arctic fleece	Do not iron	
Beaded/sequined	Cool	Cover with a thick cotton pressing cloth and treat gently with little pressure
Corduroy	Hot	Iron from the wrong side
Cotton lawn	Hot	Consider using spray starch to stiffen
Denim	Hot	Iron damp or use plenty of steam
Dressweight cotton	Hot	Protect with a pressing cloth if necessary
Faux fur	Cool	Dry iron with light pressure
Lace	Cool to medium, depending on fiber content	Iron over a towel or padded surface and use steam hovering the iron above without applying pressure on the lace
Leather/suede	Medium	Dry iron only
Linen	Hot	Iron damp or use plenty of steam
Microfiber	Medium	Dry iron
Muslin/calico	Hot	
Organdy	Hot	Use a pressing cloth to protect the surface
Polyester	Medium	
Silk chiffon	Hot	Use a silk organza pressing cloth
Silk dupion	Hot	Use a pressing cloth and dry iron
Silk organza	Hot	
Silk tweed	Hot	Use steam and a pressing cloth with light pressure
Stretch polyester with Lycra (spandex)	Cool to medium	Iron only when necessary
Sweat shirting	Hot	Use steam and apply light pressure
T-shirt cotton	Hot	Use steam and apply light pressure
Toweling	Hot	Use steam and light pressure so as not to flatten the pile
Upholstery	Hot	Use steam and a clapper/basher on stubborn seams
Velvet	Medium for cotton, cool for synthetic velvet	Iron with light pressure from the wrong side and use a velvet board or spare length of velvet
Wool crepe	Medium	Use a length of the wool crepe as a pressing cloth
Wool tweed	Medium	Use steam and light pressure
Worsted wool	Medium	Use a pressing cloth to prevent shining seam ridges

Glossary

Apex
Bust point.

Armscye
This is the armhole measurement.

Bagged lining
A bagged lining is one where the lining is made up and sewn to a garment leaving only a small opening to allow it to be pulled through to the right side. This does away with the need for hand stitching making a stronger finish.

Balance points
Dots and marks printed on the pattern to match and join when constructing a garment.

Basic block pattern
This is a basic pattern produced from standard measurements before any style has been incorporated. Designs are made from these basic blocks.

Bias/cross grain of fabric
The diagonal direction of fabric between the warp and the weft threads.

Break point
The turning point where the lapel twists at the center front of a jacket.

Buttonhole twist
Buttonhole twist is a strong, lustrous thread, and is used for hand-worked buttonholes and for sewing on buttons.

CB
Abbreviation used for center back.

CF
Abbreviation used for center front.

Cutting layout
The manufacturer's guide to laying pattern pieces on fabric in the most economical way and keeping pieces "on grain" or on fold lines, and so on. A number of layouts are provided for different fabric widths and pattern sizes.

Dart
A dart is a wedge of fabric that is pinched out of a garment to allow shaping or to remove excess fabric.

Dress form
A mannequin is a replica body shape and is used to assist in the fitting of garments.

Ease
Ease refers to the amount of space built into a sewing pattern—in addition to body measurements—to allow movement and to achieve the required garment silhouette.

Feed dogs
Teeth that lie under the presser foot and move the fabric to allow the needle to make each stitch.

Finger pressing
Some fabrics (for example those with natural fibers) respond to handling better than others (for example those from synthetic fibers) and some small areas or seams are better pressed into place using your finger, as an iron would flatten a whole area or create too sharp a finish.

Fold line
Used to describe the position of pattern pieces to be placed on folded fabric. The fabric is folded (usually lengthwise) so that the selvages are together. A directional arrow on the pattern tissue indicates the edge to place to the folded fabric.

French tack
Thread strands wound with thread, often used to join a lining to a coat hem.

Grain line
The fabric grain is the direction of the woven fibers. Straight or lengthwise grain runs along the warp thread, parallel to the selvages. Crosswise grain runs along the weft, perpendicular to straight grain. Most dressmaking pattern pieces are cut on the lengthwise grain, which has minimal stretch.

Grading
When seam allowances are trimmed to different amounts to reduce bulk. Also known as layering.

High hip
The high hip is approximately 2 in–4 in (5 cm–10 cm) below the waist and just above the hip bones.

Hip
The hip is the fullest part of the figure and is approximately 7 in–9 in (17.5 cm–23 cm) below the waist.

Interfacing
A stabilizing fabric used on the wrong side to support a piece of a garment, for example a collar or behind a pocket.

Lining
A separate fabric sewn on the inside of a garment to conceal all raw edges and help it to hang well.

Mercerized cotton
A treatment applied to give strength and luster.

Natural fiber
Fiber from a non-synthetic source for example, cotton or flax plant, silk moth, or wool.

Patchwork
Where small pieces of fabric are joined together to form larger designs. Used for quilts, clothing, and home décor projects.

Pressing cloth
A fine, smooth fabric piece used to protect the surface of a fabric when ironing or pressing.

Princess line
A dress with curved seaming running from the shoulder or the armhole to the hem on the front and back, giving six panels (not including the center back seam).

Quarter pinning
A technique used to arrange tucks (created with elastic) evenly. The elastic and fabric are divided into quarters and pinned at these points. Pull the elastic to match the fabric length and stitch the layers together.

Quilting
Stitches sewn to hold fabric layers together and made either by hand or machine.

Rouleau turner
A tool made of a length of wire, with a hook and latch at one end for turning narrow tubes of fabric.

Seam allowance
The area between the sewing line and the edge of the cloth normally ⅝ in. (1.5 cm) but 1 in. (2.5 cm) in couture sewing.

Serger
A machine designed to sew and finish edges in one step, although it can produce many other effects too. Also known as an overlocker.

Sleeve head
Sometimes referred to as a sleeve cap— the upper part of the sleeve that fits into the shoulder. Not to be confused with a cap sleeve, which is a small sleeve covering the very top of the shoulder.

Slip baste
Similar to ladder stitch, where two edges are joined from the right side, taking alternate stitches from each edge but used as a temporary join.

Sloper
This is a template from which patterns are made and also known as a basic pattern block.

Slub
An uneven thread woven into fabric resulting in an interesting textured surface.

Smocking
Embroidery stitches sewn over the folds of gathered fabric.

Spi
"Stitches per inch" is used to indicate the stitch length. This measurement is often shown in millimeters.

Stabilizer(s)
A material used to support fabric. Often associated with machine embroidery and normally placed under the work.

Stay stitching
Stitching used to hold fabric stable and prevent it from stretching.

Stitch in the ditch
Also called "sink stitch," this is where pieces are held together by stitching through an existing seam. Used on waistbands and on Hong Kong finishes.

Stretch stitch
A machine stitch suitable for sewing stretch fabric—either a narrow zigzag or one which includes back stitches in its construction.

Swing needle sewing machine
A machine where the needle moves to the left and right to make stitches, and not simply straight stitches.

Synthetic fiber
Fibers from a non-natural source. Examples are nylon, polyester, and acrylic.

Tailor's dummy
Also known as a dress form. A mannequin used to assist in the making up of garments.

Tailor's ham
A small hard cushion traditionally filled with sawdust and used as a pressing aid.

Truing a line
This is where a line on a pattern is slightly altered to make it smooth and adjust the fit. Often used when transferring adjustments from a toile to a pattern.

Underlining
This is a separate layer of fabric cut the same as the panels of dress fabric and placed to the wrong side. The panels are placed together then sewn up as one. Using an interlining or underlining changes the characteristics of the original fabric either to make it heavier, crisper, or less transparent.

Understitch
When the seam allowances are stitched to one edge to hold it down, for example, on armhole facing.

Underwrap
The extension on a waistband for the fastening.

Walking foot
This replaces the standard machine foot and walks over the fabric while sewing avoiding the fabric "creep" that sometimes occurs.

Zipper foot
An alternative machine foot. It allows the needle to get closer to the teeth of a zipper than a standard machine foot.

Index

Index

Credits

Quarto would like to thank and acknowledge the following for their contribution to this book:

Wendy Gardiner, Lee Hollahan, Lynda Maynard, and Margaret Rowan.

Jessica Kinnersley for the stitched numerals on the chapter openers, www.jkinnersleydesigns.co.uk.

Bernina, www.bernina.com, p.20–21; Bikeriderlondon, Shutterstock, p.246tl; CandyBox Images, Shutterstock, p.2; Elisa Locci, Shutterstock, p.247tr/br; Janome, www.janome.com, p.22–23; Monkey Business Images, Shutterstock, p.246br; Racorn, Shutterstock, p.246bl; Wachararwish, Shutterstock, p.247cr

We would also like to thank Burda for contributing images to pp.168tr, 169tr, 170
Verlag Aenne Burda GmbH & Co. KG
Fashion Factory
Hubert-Burda-Platz 2
77652 Offenburg
Germany

www.burdastyle.co.uk

Our appreciation also goes to Makower UK for providing the fabric in the book.
Makower UK
118 Greys Road
Henley on Thames
Oxon
RG9 1QW
United Kingdom

www.makoweruk.com